SALVATION

Disclosing God's provision
for man's protection
from disaster
and
salvation
to life everlasting
in complete happiness

A text book for the Jonadabs

By
J. F. RUTHERFORD

Author of

ENEMIES   RICHES   CREATION

PROPHECY   GOVERNMENT

and other books

1,500,000 Edition

Publishers
WATCHTOWER
BIBLE AND TRACT SOCIETY, INC.

International Bible Students Association

Brooklyn, N. Y., U. S. A.

Also

London, Toronto, Strathfield, Cape Town,
Berne, Copenhagen, and in other countries.

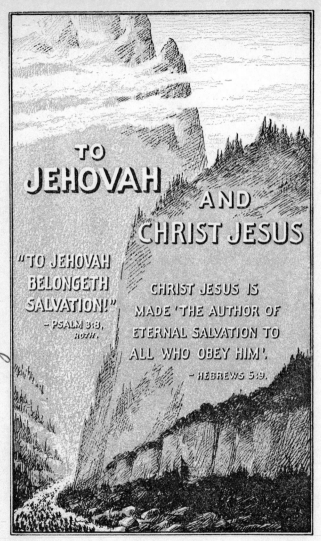

SALVATION

SALVATION

CHAPTER I

EMERGENCY

 THE streamline express, crowded with passengers, was speeding at one hundred miles per hour. It must cross the river on a bridge which made an almost fifty-percent curve, so that the persons on the rear platform of the train could see the engine. Immediately upon emerging from the tunnel the train was entering upon the bridge. Two men riding on the rear platform of the observation car were seriously discussing the troublesome world conditions and expressing hope that some means would be found to avert another world war. The alarming scream of the engine whistle and the sudden application of the emergency brakes caused the men to look, and to their great astonishment they beheld that a span of the bridge at the far end was on fire and falling into the river. They realized that they were facing great danger. That was a real emergency. Could the train be stopped in time to save the lives of the many passengers aboard?

Today every nation is in the grip of fear. In many nations there is internal distress and disturbance. This is seized upon by the ruling factors as an excuse for unprecedented taxation and an orgy of spending of public funds. The break-up of the seventh world power is threatened and greatly feared by those who rule. Dictators imperil all nations, and even now the liberties of the people are about all gone. In these modern days wars begin without a formal declaration and truly it is now said that uneasy lie the heads of those who rule. Fearing an attack from some source, each nation is making enormous preparation for war, and this furnishes further excuse to deprive the people of their liberties. It is believed by many that armed conflict involving all nations of the earth is just at the threshold, and hence all nations are attempting to fortify themselves against such an emergency. Is there any way to escape to a place of safety? Only those who believe, understand and confidently rely upon God and His Word know what is soon to come to pass. Sincere persons are anxious to know. Unbiased consideration of what follows will enable each person of good will to see and fully appreciate the only way of escape.

GREATEST TRIBULATION

"Salvation" means deliverance from impending disaster, and the finding of refuge in a place of complete safety. Because the greatest tribulation that will ever befall the world is just at the door an unprecedented emergency confronts all the peoples of the earth. There are certain universal rules which are unchangeable and which disclose the cause of the impending disaster and which point to the only means of escape and safety. To become acquainted with those rules will result beneficially to those who give heed thereto. Both profane and sacred history furnish an abundance of proof that approximately 4,000 years ago the world fell under the overwhelming disaster of the flood and a few were saved. Since then from time to time other emergencies have arisen; but the greatest of all is yet to come, and concerning that emergency the evidence is indisputable. Those who will now examine and weigh such evidence with unbiased mind will see that action must be taken immediately by those who may hope to escape to the place of safety.

All persons of good will and who desire to see righteousness prevail readily recognize that the great Creator is the Almighty God, who alone is named Jehovah, and that the Bible is a sacred record of the truth, which the Almighty God has caused to be kept for the aid of those who love that which is right. The citations herein are from the sacred record, and the reader may examine the Scripture texts for confirmation of what is here set down. Jesus of Nazareth, the Son of the Almighty God, came into the world for the express purpose of telling the truth. (John 18: 37) He bore testimony to God's universal and unchangeable rules above mentioned, which all men should learn for their own good. He made known the cause of disasters that befall men and nations, and plainly set forth the only means of escape to safety and complete salvation. He told of the flood of Noah's day and said that the wicked conditions that immediately preceded that deluge of waters would again exist throughout the earth, and which will be proof that the greatest of all disasters is quickly to follow.

Jesus is the greatest of all prophets. (Acts 3: 22, 23) His prophecies must all come true, because he is the spokesman of Almighty God who tells of the purpose of Jehovah, whose purposes never fail to be carried out. (Isaiah 46: 11; 55: 11) When we observe conditions that have come to pass about which Jesus prophesied, and see that the physical facts well known to us exactly fit the prophecy, then we are sure that it is the time for the fulfillment of the prophecy and that these events have come to pass for that very purpose. Jesus prophesied concerning the conditions now existing in the world, and which conditions immediately precede and lead up to the greatest of all disasters that the world can ever have. He foretold the World War, which began in 1914 and was suddenly stopped in 1918. He stated that such war would be accompanied or quickly followed by famine, pestilence, and great disturbances in the earth, and that such would be the beginning of sorrows immediately preceding the great disaster soon to befall the world. (Matthew 24: 7) He prophesied that following the "war in heaven" many woes would come upon the nations of the earth (Revelation 12: 7-12); and the facts show a fulfillment of that prophecy. He foretold that following the World War his true followers, who are witnesses for Jehovah, must go amongst the people and tell them the cause of these disturbances and inform them emphatically that the kingdom of heaven is at hand. That prophecy is in course of fulfillment.

He prophesied that "the abomination of desolation" would appear in the earth, and the Scriptures make it clear that such abomination is the combination or combined effort of the religious, political and commercial elements to arbitrarily rule the peoples of the earth and take away all their liberties and make them serfs. That prophecy is now being fulfilled; and in this connection Jesus added for the benefit of all persons of good will that, 'when you see the abomination of desolation standing where it ought not to stand, then flee to the mountains,' that is, to God's organization, the only place of safety. (Mark 13:14) And why flee then? Jesus answers: "For then shall be great tribulation, such as was not since the beginning of the world to this time, no, nor ever shall be." (Matthew 24:21) "And the slain of the Lord shall be at that day from one end of the earth even unto the other end of the earth; they shall not be lamented, neither gathered, nor buried; they shall be dung upon the ground." (Jeremiah 25:33) These prophecies now in course of fulfillment show that there is impending an emergency such as never before confronted the world.

With these revelations of truth from the Lord's Word the people of good will, like the passengers on the railway train aforementioned suddenly emerging from the darkness of the tunnel, are now just coming out of the darkness

of which the prophet of God wrote, to wit:
"Darkness shall cover the earth, and gross darkness the people." (Isaiah 60:2) There never was
a time in the history of the world when there
was such great ignorance generally concerning
God's purpose as set forth in the Bible, and that
particularly amongst religionists. The people of
good will toward God are just now coming into
the light of a new day and, being enlightened,
they see before them the great emergency. They
see the mad waters of the river (symbolically
representing the people) rushing on to be swal-
lowed up in the sea, that is, the turbulent and
uncontrollable conditions just ahead. They have
a vision of the greatest catastrophe ever known,
while all the other people, who are not of good
will, are totally ignorant of what is just ahead.
The flood of waters or deluge in the days of
Noah was a prophetic picture foretelling this
very time and concerning which Jesus said:
"And as it was in the days of No'e, so shall it be
also in the days of the Son of man. They did eat,
they drank, they married wives, they were given
in marriage, until the day that No'e entered into
the ark, and the flood came, and destroyed them
all."—Luke 17:26, 27.

What will be the result to those not of good
will? and what is the possible means of escape?
With the emergency aforementioned the whole
world is now faced. What is done must be done
quickly, and only those persons of good will
toward Jehovah God will give heed to the warning and act quickly and find the place of safety.

CAUSE

Jehovah is the God of love; which means he is entirely unselfish and does nothing merely to gratify self. He is the God of justice, and his every act is just and right. (1 John 4:8; Psalms 19:7-9; 89:14) He is of unlimited power, hence the Almighty God. To be sure, he has the power to stop the threatened destruction. Why should the God of justice and love permit such a terrible disaster to befall the peoples and nations of the earth? A knowledge of the facts it is necessary to have that one may appreciate the true answer, and for that reason a brief statement of the undeniable facts as set forth in the sacred history is here given. The prophecies long ago recorded in the Bible, and the facts in connection therewith, and particularly the physical facts that have come to pass in these days, are recorded for the very purpose of furnishing information to persons of good will that they may avail themselves of the opportunity to find the place of safety. Therefore the statement is made following:

God created the earth for man, and then created perfect man and woman and put them on the earth to inhabit it. (Isaiah 45:12, 18) To the perfect human pair God issued his mandate to "be fruitful and multiply and fill the earth". (Genesis 1:28, *Rotherham*) God made Lucifer a spirit creature or overlord of the world, including perfect man. (Ezekiel 28:14, 15) All creation in heaven and earth gave honor to Jehovah God, and that properly so, because every creature owes the privilege of life to the Almighty God. The exception to this rule was

Lucifer, who began to covet what he was not entitled to, namely, the honor and praise that was rightfully bestowed upon the Almighty God. Lucifer rebelled against God and attempted to set himself up as God's equal, and in this rebellion he led away from the path of righteousness both angels and men, and Adam found himself involved in that rebellion. The name Lucifer God then changed to that of Satan, which means "adversary"; Dragon, which means "devourer"; Serpent, which means "deceiver"; and Devil, which means "slanderer". Since then that great rebel has been known by the four names, Dragon, Satan, Old Serpent, and the Devil. (Revelation 20:2) The Devil then defied God and challenged him to put on the earth men who would prove faithful and loyal to God, and at the same time Satan declared he could cause all men to curse God to His face. (Job 2:4-6) That wicked challenge of the Devil raised the question as to who is supreme. If Satan could cause all men to curse God, that would prove Satan at least the equal of Jehovah God, if not his superior. God would have all creation to hear and see the proof, that there could never be a real doubt as to who is the supreme one. God had entered the judgment of death against Satan, but, instead of destroying him immediately, God deferred the execution of that judgment and accepted the challenge of Satan in order to give him full opportunity to make proof of his boastful challenge. Therefore God said to the wicked one: "But for this cause have I allowed thee to remain, in order to show thee my power." (Exodus 9:16, *Leeser*) Thus it is seen that God announced his purpose to give Satan the rebel a full and free opportunity to prove his challenge and that in due time the day of final reckoning must come, and that when that day arrives, God would cause his name to be declared in all the earth and then he would exhibit his supreme power against his adversary the Devil.

Adam and Eve, because of the sin of rebellion, were also sentenced to death, but God permitted them to live for a season that they might bring forth children. They could never fulfill the divine mandate to fill the earth with a righteous race of people, because they were sinners; but they could exercise the function of producing their own species, even though they were imperfect. All of their children were hence born in sin and shapen in lawlessness, and for that reason all such in due time must die. (Psalm 51:5; Romans 5:12) Emphasizing the issue of supremacy God gave his word of promise that in his due time he would send to the world a Savior who would purchase the human race or offspring of Adam and that he would provide a means whereby those so purchased might be saved and receive life everlasting. That would mean that all of the offspring of Adam who escape and are saved must comply with Jehovah's rules and must maintain their integrity toward God, and all so doing would be a vindication of Jehovah's name; and that of itself would prove Satan a liar.

In God's due time he sent his beloved Son to earth. Jesus was born, that is, made flesh, and lived amongst men on the earth. "And the Word was made flesh, and dwelt among us, (and we

beheld his glory, the glory as of the only begotten of the Father,) full of grace and truth."
(John 1:14) In this text Jesus is called "The
Word", because in his prehuman existence he
was the spokesman of Jehovah God. When the
man Jesus reached the age of thirty years God
anointed him to be the King of His promised
kingdom. Satan immediately attempted to bring
about the destruction of Jesus; but in that he
failed. (Matthew 4:3-10) Jesus then began to
declare the purpose of his coming to earth and
to tell the people of and concerning the kingdom,
which God would set up. At his first public appearing Jesus said to the people: "Repent; for
the kingdom of heaven is at hand." (Matthew
4:17) He was then anointed to be the King;
and truly "the kingdom", or the One who should
rule, was "at hand". For three and one-half
years thereafter, he continued to tell the people
of God's kingdom as the hope of humankind,
and during all that time he was bitterly and
wickedly opposed by Satan and the religious
men of that time, the leaders of whom were
called "Pharisees". Jesus was charged with
sedition and treason because he continued to
declare the coming of God's kingdom. When he
stood before the Roman governor, charged with
treason, he was specifically asked the question:
'Are you a king?' And to that Jesus answered,
"I am. . . . To this end was I born, and for this
cause came I into the world." (John 18:37)
Thus he continued to consistently proclaim
God's purpose to establish his kingdom, even
until the time of his crucifixion.

God did not deprive Satan of overlordship of

the world, but permitted him to continue in that position in order that he might have a free hand to carry out his wicked challenge, if possible. Thereafter when Jesus was on the earth Satan was the invisible prince or overlord of the world, and Jesus spoke of Satan as "the prince of this world". (John 12: 31; 14: 30) Satan well knew that if God should set up a kingdom on earth, with Christ Jesus as the King and invisible overlord, that would mean Satan's rulership must end and his execution must take place. Satan therefore determined to exercise everything within his power to defeat God's purpose. The kingdom of heaven, with Christ Jesus as King, is the deadly foe of Satan and of his advocates. While Jesus was on the earth the Devil and his religious agents continuously attempted to kill Jesus, and finally succeeded in having him wrongfully convicted of treason and causing his crucifixion by being nailed to the tree. God suffered Jesus to thus be put to death, knowing that He would raise Jesus out of death as a spirit creature and place him at the head of His kingdom and that this would be accomplished in his own good time and to his own glory.

Jesus told his disciples that he must go away and receive the kingdom and that then he would return and take unto himself his faithful disciples who should be associated with him in his kingdom. (John 14: 1-3; Luke 22: 28-30) Within three days after his crucifixion God raised Jesus out of death, and he was clothed with full power and authority in heaven and earth; and in forty days thereafter he ascended into heaven, and he was then the King of the world, the duly anoint-

ed and commissioned Ruler, whose right it is
to rule. (Matthew 28:18; Philippians 2:9-11;
Acts 2:32-36) Thereafter the faithful apostles
of Jesus Christ continued to look for his second
coming and his kingdom, about which he had
informed them and which he stated to them
would take place at the end of Satan's world.

All the true followers of Christ Jesus for centuries have likewise looked for and hoped for
the coming of that kingdom under the Lord
Jesus Christ. So keenly interested in his coming
and his kingdom were the apostles that they
propounded to Jesus this question, shortly before his death: "What shall be the sign [evi-
dence] of thy coming, and of the end of the world
[that is, the end of Satan's uninterrupted
rule]?" (Matthew 24:3) In response to that
question Jesus said that the first evidence dis-
cernible by men would be the world war, in which
nation would rise against nation, and kingdom
against kingdom. That came to pass in A.D. 1914.
Jesus said that the war would be quickly followed by famine and pestilence and earth-
quakes; and everyone knows that these things
did quickly follow the World War. Then Jesus
said to his disciples: 'When you see the abomination that maketh desolate standing where it
ought not to stand [that is, claiming the right
and authority to rule the world], then flee to the
kingdom.' (Matthew 24:15; Mark 13:14) That
has also come to pass at the present time, in
this, that a few men, called "dictators", and the
great religious system of the world together
claim the right to rule and regiment the people
and take away their liberties and to rule the

world in the place and stead of Christ the King. Furthermore Jesus said that great woes would come upon the peoples of the earth because of the activities of the Devil to thwart God's purpose. (Revelation 12:12) All the world is now experiencing woes such as never before have afflicted the nations, and these woes have come with increasing force since the end of the World War.

As further evidence of his invisible presence and the end of Satan's uninterrupted rule, Jesus said: "There shall be . . . upon the earth distress of nations, with perplexity, the sea [meaning peoples] and the waves [the radical, disturbing elements thereof made mad by the present conditions] roaring [causing much trouble]; men's hearts failing them for fear, and for looking after those things which are coming on the earth."—Luke 21:25, 26.

Exactly those conditions now prevail upon the earth, as every observing person well knows. During all the time of the existing conditions aforementioned, evidencing His presence and the end of Satan's uninterrupted rule, Jesus declares and commands: "And this gospel of the kingdom shall be preached in all the world for a witness unto all nations; and then shall the end come."—Matthew 24:14.

It follows that those who love God and Christ must obey this commandment. In obedience thereto a little company of Christian people made up of men and women who are known as "Jehovah's witnesses" have been and are still continuing to go about the country preaching the good news of the kingdom of God. This preaching of the gospel must continue until the great threatening emergency comes to a climax; and when this preaching of the good news of the kingdom is completed, what shall follow? "For then shall be great tribulation, such as was not since the beginning of the world to this time, no, nor ever shall be."—Matthew 24:21.

That great tribulation is the battle of Armageddon, and which is also called "the battle of that great day of God Almighty". (Revelation 16:14-16) It is the battle of Almighty God because in it will be finally and for ever settled the question at issue as to who is supreme and whether or not God can carry out his announced purpose. That great battle will result in the complete destruction of every vestige of Satan's supporters and organization.

At the time of the ascension of Jesus on high he was then the King with full power and authority to rule, but it was not then God's due time for him to begin his reign as King. God purposed to permit Satan to have full opportunity to prove, if possible, his wicked challenge. Therefore concerning Christ Jesus the King it is written: "The Lord said unto my Lord, Sit thou at my right hand, until I make thine enemies thy footstool."—Psalm 110:1.

Jesus must wait until Jehovah's due time for him to take and exercise his power to destroy Satan's rule and to set up his own righteous and complete rule in the earth. (Hebrews 10:12, 13) That time of waiting came to an end in 1914, and then God sent forth Jesus Christ to rule while the enemy Satan was still exercising his power. (Psalm 110:2-6) When that period of waiting ended, in 1914, and Christ Jesus was sent forth to exercise his royal power as the great Executive Officer of Jehovah, the Scriptures say: "Thou hast taken to thee thy great power, and hast reigned. And the nations were angry [the World War began], and thy [God's] wrath is come." (Revelation 11:17, 18) God's wrath was expressed against Satan at that time, and Christ Jesus as Jehovah's Executive Officer cast Satan and his wicked angels out of heaven.—Revelation 12:1-9.

God will express his complete wrath against Satan and his organization in the battle of Armageddon. He called a halt in the expression of his wrath in 1918, which will be resumed at the battle of Armageddon. In the meantime and just preceding and up to the time of the battle of Armageddon God will have his name proclaimed throughout the earth, as he had previously declared, and which message exposes Satan and his agents on earth; and which work is called God's "strange work". That work consists in this: that God sends forth his witnesses to give warning to the people of the impending disaster about to come upon the world. He causes his witnesses to tell the people that religion is one of Satan's schemes to blind the people and turn them away from God; that God's purpose is to shortly destroy all of Satan's agencies in the greatest tribulation that has ever come upon the world, and therefore he causes the witnesses to give warning to the people of the impending disaster.

This work called God's "strange work" is now in progress. This therefore is the time of the greatest emergency, when the people are being warned as to what is about to take place. God does not act without giving fair notice of warning. He caused Noah to give a like warning just preceding the flood, and now he sends forth his witnesses, particularly to the nations called "Christendom", and tells his witnesses to "warn them from me". (Ezekiel 33:7) He sends forth his witnesses to inform the people, and particularly the religious leaders, that Satan is the great enemy of God and men, that the religious leaders are a part of Satan's organization, and that they will be destroyed unless they abandon Satan's organization and flee to the Lord. This warning appears to religionists to be a very strange thing, and hence it is called God's "strange work"; and the Lord announces that when that work is done there will immediately follow "his act, his strange act", meaning the battle of the great day of God Almighty, which will destroy Satan's organization and all those who adhere to or support the same.—Isaiah 28:21.

Again it is appropriate that we consider the scripture caused to be recorded by Jehovah and addressed to Satan, to wit: 'For this cause have I permitted thee to remain, that I might show thee my power, and that my name might be declared throughout all the earth.' (Exodus 9:16, *Leeser*) For this reason Jehovah's witnesses in obedience to God's commandments go about the land proclaiming the name of Jehovah as the Almighty Supreme One. The warning is being sounded preceding the great disaster, and that disaster is certain to fall upon

Satan and his organization and wipe them out, in order that the world may be clean and ready for the reign of Christ Jesus forever in righteousness and peace.

It would be impossible for righteousness to prevail in the earth while Satan and his cohorts continue to exercise power over the people. For that reason Jehovah God puts an end to Satan's organization. To be sure, Satan and his forces will resist to the bitter end. Hence the necessity for the great battle of Armageddon, which will be the greatest tribulation ever upon the world, because then everything in opposition to God must be and will be completely wiped out. Up to this time the great mass of the people have been blinded by Satan, and his agents have induced them to turn against God; and hence the blind guides and the blind people who continue in blindness will go down in destruction as the Lord has declared. The multitudes that will be destroyed at the battle of Armageddon will be so great that not enough people will be left on the earth to bury them. (Jeremiah 25:33) That destruction will be so complete that it will be the last, as Jesus declared, and never again will there be such a disaster, for the reason, as it is written, "affliction shall not rise up the second time."—Nahum 1:9.

All the evidence, both that of the Bible and that of the physical facts which are well known to all persons who try to observe, overwhelmingly proves that the battle of Armageddon is impending and is very near. Hence the warning must now be given, and is given. Therefore the world is confronted with the greatest emergency

that has ever existed, and so vitally necessary
is it that all who would live must be warned that
God puts the obligation upon those who know
his truth to tell it to others; and for this reason
the publication goes on amidst great opposition
from the religionists. (Ezekiel 33:4-19) The battle of Armageddon will be fought by Jesus
Christ and his heavenly host, on one side,
against the Devil and all his forces, both visible
and invisible, on the other side. That battle will
be the expression of God's wrath against all
wickedness. Upon the earth there are now billions of people, and naturally it is asked, Is there
salvation for them? Is there to be found a place
of refuge, safety and salvation from the impending and terrible wrath of Almighty God?

YOU MAY "BE HID"

In Noah's day the Devil had turned the people
to wickedness, and God declared his purpose to
destroy all flesh in the flood of waters that was
shortly to follow. (Genesis 6:1-20) For many
years Noah, at God's command, went about
amongst the people proclaiming to them the
warning of the impending disaster of the flood
of waters. Noah was one of Jehovah's witnesses,
"a preacher of righteousness." (2 Peter 2:5)
Aside from Noah's household the people did not
give heed to the warning, and when the flood
came all were destroyed and only Noah and his
immediate family, consisting of eight persons in
all, escaped and were saved. How were they
saved? At God's command Noah had builded
the ark, and when the flood came it floated upon
the waters. In that ark Noah and his family

were hid from the wrath of God expressed by
the great deluge or flood of waters. That great
disaster upon the world prophetically foretold
the battle of Armageddon. The devastation that
the flood worked is a pattern or picture of what
Armageddon will bring upon the whole world.
Note now God's provision to hide some people
from his wrath which will be expressed during
Armageddon, and which people so hidden will be
carried over to safety and to salvation.

No person who devotes himself today to Jehovah God and his kingdom is desired by the Devil
or by any of the Devil's representatives on the
earth. It is seen that all of those who earnestly
advocate the name of Jehovah God and his kingdom are the objects of the expressed wrath of
Satan and of his religious agents in particular.
To those persons who desire righteousness, and
who have a desire to escape, and who are therefore of good will toward God and His kingdom
Jehovah addresses the following words: "Gather yourselves together, yea, gather together, O
nation not desired [by the Devil and his crowd
of religionists and allies]." (Zephaniah 2:1)
Such persons of good will are warned to gather
themselves together; meaning that they must
separate themselves from the political, religious
and like systems or organizations, which honor
men and dishonor God; and that, because they
love righteousness, they must keep themselves
separated and apart from unrighteousness.
Those persons who are of good will toward God
will automatically be drawn to each other, and
all such will seek the Lord and be diligent to
learn his ways and what the Lord requires of

them in order to find the place of safety. When
shall such persons of good will separate themselves from the wicked organizations of the
world, gather themselves together, and stand
on the side of God and his King, Christ Jesus?
The Word of Jehovah answers: "Before the decree bring forth, before the day pass as the
chaff, before the fierce anger of the Lord come
upon you, before the day of the Lord's anger
come upon you."—Zephaniah 2:2.

The act of seeking the Lord and hence seeking
the place of safety cannot be delayed until Armageddon breaks upon the world, because it will
then be too late to flee to the place of safety.
The Lord Jesus speaks of such time of tribulation as the wintertime, and concerning the people he says: "Pray ye that your flight be not in
the winter [time]." (Matthew 24:20) The day
of God's wrath expressed at Armageddon is the
'wintertime', during which time will break upon
the world such tribulation as never before was
known. If you are not hid then from that terrible
and destructive catastrophe, it will be too late
to find the place of protection and salvation.

What, then, shall one do to find the place of
safety? He must flee to Jehovah God and Christ
Jesus, spoken of by Jesus as "the mountains",
the mountains representing the kingdom of God
under Christ. Jehovah's prophet above quoted
answers the question in these words: "Seek ye
the Lord, all ye meek of the earth, which have
wrought his judgment; seek righteousness, seek
meekness; it may be ye shall be hid in the day
of the Lord's anger."—Zephaniah 2:3.

For their aid and benefit the Lord now brings before those persons of good will a mental vision of the terrible impending disaster of Armageddon and advises them to follow the rule he announces in order that they might escape. Only the meek ones will give heed to the warning and act immediately. The meek are those who desire to be taught the truth and who are willing to hear and to learn the truth, regardless of who may bring the truth to their attention. At the command of Jehovah his faithful witnesses call attention to the message of truth as set forth in the Scriptures, and place before the people the means and opportunity of gaining an understanding of God's purpose. The meek ones amongst the people will avail themselves of such opportunity to learn, and God favors such who thus try to learn, as it is written: "Good and upright is the Lord; therefore will he teach sinners in the way. The meek will he guide in judgment, and the meek will he teach his way."— Psalm 25: 8, 9.

To such meek ones Jehovah says: "Seek righteousness"; which means to seek to know God's provision for man's salvation from the impending disaster; and to know His way means to know the right way. All the ways of God are right and righteousness: "The Lord is righteous in all his ways, and holy in all his works." (Psalm 145: 17) One who desires righteousness must be diligent to learn what is set forth in the Word of God, because such constitutes his certain and perfect guide: "Righteous art thou, O Lord, and upright are thy judgments. Thy testimonies that thou hast commanded are right-

eous and very faithful." (Psalm 119:137, 138)
"Thy word is a lamp unto my feet, and a light
unto my path." (Psalm 119:105) The honest,
sincere and meek persons of good will toward
God pray the prayer which is written in the
Word of God for their benefit, to wit: "Shew me
thy ways, O Lord; teach me thy paths. Lead me
in thy truth, and teach me; for thou art the God
of my salvation; on thee do I wait all the day."
—Psalm 25:4, 5.

To "seek meekness", as God has commanded,
one must always be diligent to learn what God
through Christ Jesus teaches the people. One
who is wise in his own conceit is not meek. The
meek are those who are willing and anxious to
learn what the great Almighty God would have
them to do, and this they ascertain only by being
alert to seek what is written in the Scriptures
and to readily grasp an understanding thereof.
The Lord is now making clear the meaning of
the Scriptures by bringing to pass the physical
facts in fulfillment of his prophetic Word. In
this God is showing his loving-kindness to everyone who desires righteousness. The purpose of
what follows herein is to enable the sincere
student of God's Word to gain a knowledge and
understanding of the purpose of the Most High;
and the meek will learn God's righteous way and
will joyfully obey God's Word of truth as revealed to him. Those who thus seek righteousness and meekness have this promise from Jehovah God, as it is written in the scripture above
quoted: "It may be ye shall be hid in the day of
the Lord's anger." Those who receive Jehovah's
approval will receive his blessings by being led

to the place of safety and complete refuge and will learn the way to everlasting salvation. The ones who are thus seeking the right way are the ones who desire to know the Scriptures, and these Scriptures were written for their benefit. Hence the admonition given to all such: "Study to shew thyself approved unto God."—2 Timothy 2:15.

CHAPTER II

TO LIFE

SALVATION from impending disaster is one thing; salvation to life is another thing. The great enemy of man is death. Man's chief blessing is to receive life everlasting in a state of peace, happiness and prosperity. To obtain salvation from death means to gain everlasting life. Salvation from the wrath of God expressed at Armageddon will not necessarily mean that all such will eventually be saved from death and live forever. Jehovah God has made certain and unchangeable rules which, if obeyed by man, will result in man's salvation to everlasting life. Those who escape the disaster of Armageddon will then be entering upon the way to everlasting life. To learn of God's requirements, and to have faith and to be obedient, will then be absolutely necessary on the part of all who will be saved to everlasting life.

To have God's approval the creature must please him. "But without faith it is impossible to please him: for he that cometh to God must believe that he is, and that he is a rewarder of them that diligently seek him. By faith Noah, being warned of God of things not seen as yet, moved with fear, prepared an ark to the saving of his house; by the which he condemned the world, and became heir of the righteousness which is by faith."—Hebrews 11: 6, 7.

Noah and his sons escaped the disaster of the
flood of waters, but Noah is the only one, of the
eight, mentioned as receiving God's final approval. (Hebrews 11:7,13,39) Moses and a multitude of Israelites were saved from the waters
of the Red sea, which destroyed the Egyptians
(Hebrews 11:29); but only a few of those
Israelites are later mentioned by the Lord as
having received his approval. That does not
necessarily mean that none of the others shall
receive life everlasting, but the point here made
is that all who do receive salvation unto life
must have the approval of Almighty God. It is
therefore necessary for man to learn what God
requires of men, and then the man must diligently obey God's fixed rules. "God is no respecter
of persons," and he does not show partiality to
any. (Acts 10:34; James 3:17) All men stand
equal before God, and all are required to willingly obey God's rules. All must have and continue
to exercise faith. "Faith" means to have a knowledge of God's purpose as set forth in his Word,
the Bible, and then to confidently rely upon
God's Word of truth as therein made known.

Religious organizations, and particularly the
leaders therein, induce persons to believe that
they must join some religious system or organization, which men call "a church"; and the leaders or clergymen claim that joining such religious organization is the means to salvation.
Such claim or representation by the clergymen
is entirely wrong, because such organizations
do not have God's approval. On the contrary,
such religious organizations teach chiefly the
doctrines of men, which doctrines blind the peo-

ple to the truth of God's purpose as set forth in
His Word, and such teachings of men make the
commandments of God of none effect and hence
are exceedingly harmful to men.—Matthew
15: 6-9.

There are hundreds of religious organizations on the earth, all of which differ somewhat in the doctrines they hold and teach. Many
persons will contend that 'it matters not which
religious organization you join, because all are
traveling the same way, and if a man is satisfied
in his own mind that he is on the right way, that
is all that is required in order to guarantee his
salvation'. That doctrine is very misleading, and
to follow it means destruction in the end. "The
way of a fool is right in his own eyes; but he
that hearkeneth unto counsel is wise." (Proverbs
12: 15) "There is a way which seemeth right unto a man, but the end thereof are the ways of
death." (Proverbs 14: 12) To follow the teachings or traditions of men, therefore, leads unto
destruction. The man who ignores God's Word
and follows the way of man is designated as a
fool by the Word of God. By his course of action
he shows that he does not have faith in God,
and hence it is written in the Scriptures: "The
fool hath said in his heart [that is, the motive
that directs his course of action], There is no
God." (Psalm 14: 1) The wise man is he that
diligently ascertains God's way as set forth in
the Bible and then follows faithfully and earnestly that way: "A wise man will hear, and will
increase learning; and a man of understanding
shall attain unto wise counsels." (Proverbs 1: 5)
"Give instruction to a wise man, and he will be

yet wiser; teach a just man, and he will increase in learning." (Proverbs 9:9) "The wise in heart will receive commandments; but a prating fool shall fall." (Proverbs 10:8) "He that walketh with wise men shall be wise; but a companion of fools shall be destroyed." (Proverbs 13:20) "Trust in the Lord with all thine heart; and lean not unto thine own understanding. In all thy ways acknowledge him, and he shall direct thy paths." (Proverbs 3:5, 6) God's way is the righteous way: "In the way of righteousness is life; and in the pathway thereof there is no death."—Proverbs 12:28.

"Religion" is therefore properly defined as a belief in and indulging in a form of worship of some higher power, and which belief is based on the teachings of men handed down by tradition from one generation to another, and which system of belief or teaching is induced and put forward by God's adversary the Devil in order to turn men away from God. For this reason religion is a snare of the Devil.

Christianity is exactly opposite to religion. The name "Christianity" is derived from Christ Jesus, who at all times obeys the commandments of Almighty God. Christ Jesus is therefore the beginner of Christians. "Christianity" means to know what God has set forth in his Word disclosing his purpose, and to fully obey God's commandments at all times. To follow the lead of religion means everlasting death. To follow Christ Jesus means everlasting life. (John 17:3) With a knowledge of the truth there is set before men death and life. To live, one must

avoid religion and truly follow the lead of Christ
Jesus.

AUTHOR OF SALVATION

"Salvation belongeth unto the LORD," that is,
Jehovah God. (Psalm 3:8) No man or organization of men can give salvation to others. Religious organizations, and particularly the leaders therein, claim to save souls or to bring salvation to men; but such claim is wholly false.
Jehovah God is the Creator and Giver of life,
and no creature can get life from another. God
created man and gave the perfect man life.
(Genesis 2:7) God has made provision for the
salvation of sinful men from death and unto life.
The doctrine that man has inherent life and that
the soul of man is immortal and cannot die is
as false as the Devil himself and is the result
of the Devil's first lie. The doctrine of inherent
immortality of souls was the lie told by Satan,
the Devil, to Eve for the first time, and led to
death upon Adam and Eve. (Genesis 3:4) Every
man is a soul, that is to say, a living, breathing
creature. He does not possess a soul separate
and distinct from his body; but the body of
flesh and the breath of living creatures, together, constitute the soul. When these are separated
the soul is out of existence. If a soul were immortal it could not die; but it is plainly written
in the Word of God: "The soul that sinneth, it
shall die." (Ezekiel 18:4) "What man is he that
liveth, and shall not see death? shall he deliver
his soul from the hand of the grave? Selah."
(Psalm 89:48) When a man dies he is completely dead and entirely without knowledge or

consciousness. He is not conscious anywhere, and therefore the doctrine of "purgatory" and of "eternal torment", "where men are suffering conscious punishment," is completely false, a wicked doctrine promulgated by the Devil to deceive men: "For the living know that they shall die; but the dead know not any thing, neither have they any more a reward, for the memory of them is forgotten." "Whatsoever thy hand findeth to do, do it with thy might; for there is no work, nor device, nor knowledge, nor wisdom, in the grave, whither thou goest."—Ecclesiastes 9: 5, 10.

Why do human creatures die? Because the first man Adam willfully sinned by joining the Devil in rebellion against Jehovah God. All the human race sprang from Adam; and since Adam became a sinner before he and Eve had children, it follows naturally that all men have been born imperfect and are therefore sinners by inheritance. "Behold, I was shapen in iniquity, and in sin did my mother conceive me." (Psalm 51: 5) "Wherefore, as by one man sin entered into the world, and death by sin; and so death passed upon all men, for that all have sinned." (Romans 5: 12) Unless provision is made by the Almighty God to save men from death, in time all men would perish. God alone could provide for man's salvation, and therefore it is written: "Salvation belongeth unto the Lord." (Psalm 3: 8) It is easy to be seen, therefore, why it is recorded in the Scriptures that the man who claims there is no God is a fool, and his course of action in refusing to hear and to obey God proves him to be a fool.

UNSELFISH

God is under no obligation to provide salvation for any man, because all men are by nature sinners. The salvation of sinful man could bring no profit to Jehovah God. He could well let all men die and then create a new race and by that new race prove the Devil a liar and prove Jehovah's supremacy. It pleased him to do otherwise. It is written: "God is love" (1 John 4: 16) ; which means that he is wholly unselfish. Acting entirely unselfishly, Jehovah God has provided for the salvation of man from death. Hence it is written: "For God so loved the world, that he gave his only begotten Son, that whosoever believeth in him should not perish, but have everlasting life." (John 3: 16) That Scripture text is no authority whatsoever for the doctrine of universal redemption or universal salvation. The doctrine of universal redemption and salvation is a ruse of the Devil to prevent men from learning the only means of salvation to life. Salvation is mentioned as only to those who believe on the Lord Jesus Christ, as the foregoing scripture says: 'He that believeth on him shall not perish.' It follows, then, that those who do not believe on the Lord shall perish. "For the wages of sin is death; but the gift of God is eternal life, through Jesus Christ our Lord." (Romans 6: 23) Since life is a gift from God, then it can be received from no one else.

No man can receive a gift until he first has knowledge that the gift is offered to him, and then he must willingly accept that which is offered, in order for the gift to be completed. Anything that is forced upon another against his will is not a gift. When the gift is offered to man it becomes effective only when that gift is accepted upon the terms offered. (Romans 5:18) Jesus Christ is mentioned in the Scriptures under the symbol of "the Stone", upon which rests the great organization and kingdom of Jehovah, and it ministers life to those who receive salvation to life. Therefore it is written: "This is the stone which was set at nought of you builders, which is become the head of the corner. Neither is there salvation in any other; for there is none other name under heaven given among men, whereby we must be saved."—Acts 4:11, 12.

The name Jesus means "Jehovah is salvation"; that is to say, Jesus is the means by and through which Jehovah God has provided salvation for man to life, and such salvation is granted upon the terms which God unselfishly provides. At the birth of the child Jesus the angel of Jehovah announced to witnesses this message: "Unto you is born this day, in the city of David, a Saviour, which is Christ the Lord." (Luke 2:11) How does Jesus Christ become the Savior of men?

PURCHASE

Jesus Christ becomes the owner of the human creatures by right of purchase. The purchase price is the lifeblood of the man Jesus poured out unto death according to the will of Jehovah God his Father. (Isaiah 53:10, 12) Jesus willingly submitted to being put to death that he might purchase the human race, and concerning this Jesus said: "Therefore doth my Father

love me, because I lay down my life, that I might take it again. No man taketh it from me, but I lay it down of myself. I have power to lay it down, and I have power to take it again. This commandment have I received of my Father."
—John 10:17, 18.

Jesus was "put to death in the flesh [that is to say, a perfect human creature], but quickened [(*A.R.V.*) made alive] by the spirit [that is, by the power of the Great Spirit, Jehovah God]". (1 Peter 3:18) God raised up Jesus out of death, and hence he is alive for evermore. (Acts 2:31, 32; Revelation 1:18) Jesus, as it is written, "was made flesh [that is, a human creature], and dwelt among us [men]," as stated by John the apostle of Christ Jesus. (John 1:14) Angels are spirit creatures, and men are human and therefore lower than angels. It is written concerning Jesus: "But we see Jesus, who was made a little lower than the angels, for the suffering of death, crowned with glory and honour; that he by the grace of God should taste death for every man." (Hebrews 2:9) "And being found in fashion as a man, he humbled himself, and became obedient unto death, even the death of the cross. Wherefore God also hath highly exalted him, and given him a name which is above every name: that at the name of Jesus every knee should bow, of things in heaven, and things in earth, and things under the earth; and that every tongue should confess that Jesus Christ is Lord, to the glory of God the Father."—Philippians 2:8-11.

Jesus suffered for three and one-half years the contradiction of sinners and was continuously persecuted by the religious sinners, and under these adverse conditions he maintained his integrity toward God. It is written concerning Jesus: "Though he were a Son, yet learned he obedience by the things which he suffered; and being made perfect, he became the author of eternal salvation unto all them that obey him." —Hebrews 5:8, 9.

Concerning the purchase price by which the human race is bought it is written: "Forasmuch as ye know that ye were not redeemed with corruptible things, as silver and gold, from your vain conversation received by tradition from your fathers; but with the precious blood of Christ, as of a lamb without blemish and without spot." (1 Peter 1:18, 19) The lifeblood of the man Jesus provides the ransom price for man. The philosophy of the ransom sacrifice will be more fully considered in a subsequent chapter. Here the proof is submitted that by right of purchase Jesus is the owner of mankind, clothed with full power and authority to minister salvation from death to human creatures who comply with that which God's law requires. Jehovah God is the great Savior, because 'salvation belongeth to God' and God has made Christ Jesus the "author of eternal salvation", that is to say, God's Executive Officer, who ministers the salvation of life to men according to the will of God.—Romans 5:18; 6:23.

SALVATION FOR WHOM

Is salvation for all men, whether men desire to have salvation or not? No, it is not for those who do not desire it. Note carefully the words

of the scripture: Jesus is made "the author of
eternal salvation unto all them that obey him".
(Hebrews 5:9) Salvation is granted to man according to the specific terms and conditions
which God has named in his Word, and one
specific condition is, "That whosoever believeth
in him [Christ Jesus] should not perish, but
have everlasting life." (John 3:16) God sent
Jesus into the world "that the world through
him might be saved". (John 3:17) There are
specific conditions attached to such provision
for salvation which must be met. God's provisions for man's salvation could not mean compulsory salvation, but that salvation must be
for those who believe, because the promise is to
those who believe, that they shall not perish.
To perish means to go completely out of existence. It is the love of God that provides for
man's salvation, and hence salvation to those
who desire to be saved. Since salvation is the
gift of God through Jesus Christ (Romans
6:23), it follows that no man could gain salvation to life for man. Life is a free gift from God,
and those who comply with the terms of the gift
freely receive it.

Salvation is not provided for everyone. The
intelligent creature who willfully and deliberately is the adversary of Jehovah God certainly
would not receive salvation to life as a free gift
from God. Lucifer the Devil is a willful and deliberate enemy of God, and his end is destruction. (Isaiah 14:19; Ezekiel 28:19) Adam, when
created, was a perfect man. All the creation of
God is perfect. (Deuteronomy 32:4) Adam,
being perfect, was intelligent, and he was fully

advised of God's law and the penalty for violating it.

Satan the adversary of God deceived Eve and led her into sin, but "Adam was not deceived". He voluntarily joined the Devil in rebellion, and hence he was an intelligent, willful and deliberate sinner. (1 Timothy 2:14) Adam had the privilege of obtaining life everlasting upon condition of his obedience unto God. Adam, being duly informed that willful wrongdoing would mean death and the end of life, deliberately walked into death. There is therefore no reason to conclude that he could ever thereafter find redemption and salvation to life. God sentenced Adam to death; and God does not change. (Malachi 3:6) To Adam God pronounced in these words: "For out of [the dust] wast thou taken; for dust thou art, and unto dust shalt thou return." (Genesis 2:7; 3:19) That judgment is final and is not subject to be reversed. It must stand forever. God sentenced Adam to death while in Eden, but He deferred the complete execution of that judgment for a time, and that for his own wise purpose. In God's due time Adam died. (Genesis 5:5) There is no promise found in the Scriptures that Adam's redemption and resurrection and salvation will take place at any time. Adam had a fair trial for life and completely failed. If God should provide the second trial or second chance for Adam, that would be a denial of the justice of his own judgment entered against Adam. That is an impossibility with God; as it is written: "He cannot deny himself." (2 Timothy 2:13) "God is not a man, that he should lie; neither the son of man, that he should repent; hath he said, and shall he not do it? or hath he spoken, and shall he not make it good?"—Numbers 23:19.

But with Adam's offspring the situation or condition is entirely different. Before Adam sinned he and his wife Eve had not exercised the power and function to bring forth children. It seems that God deferred the complete execution of the judgment of death against man in order that Adam and Eve might bring forth children; which they did. (Genesis 4:1, 2, 25; 5:3-8) At the time of the judgment entered against Adam his children, not having been born, were not on trial for life, and hence they were not sentenced to death. However, when born, they were under condemnation because of inherited imperfection. The imperfect Adam and Eve under condemnation could not bring forth perfect children. Every one of Adam's children was therefore conceived in sin and brought forth in iniquity, for the very reason that Adam and Eve were sinners under the judgment of death when their children were conceived. Those children had done nothing before or at the time of birth to make them sinners, as indeed they could not do anything to that end. Their conception and birth was without their knowledge or consent. They became sinners by inheritance; and that is true with reference to every child that has been born on the earth, except Jesus alone. Upon this point of inherited sin the scripture is clear, positive and indisputable. "Wherefore, as by one man sin entered into the world, and death by sin; and so death passed upon all men, for that all have sinned." "Nevertheless, death reigned

from Adam to Moses, even over them that had
not sinned after the similitude of [manner like or
similar to] Adam's transgression, who is the figure of him that was to come."—Romans 5:12, 14.

Moses was a type of Christ Jesus, the great
Savior of man from death. The children of
Adam being sentenced by inheritance and being
therefore under condemnation, they must in the
course of time suffer death and return unto the
dust, because God could not approve imperfect
ones and permit such to live. (Habakkuk 1:13)
God could consistently have mercy upon all who
were not willful and deliberate sinners or opposers of Jehovah God. This fixed rule of Jehovah he emphasized in the declaration of his law
to the Israelites through Moses, wherein it is
written: "He that despised Moses' law died without mercy under two or three witnesses." (Hebrews 10:28; Deuteronomy 17:2-7) All of humankind, having been born as sinners and under
condemnation, must die unless some provision
is made for them to live; and God, the giver of
life, is under no obligation to provide salvation.
On the other hand, "God is love," and in the exercise of his unselfishness he could show and has
consistently shown mercy to mankind by providing salvation through Christ. Mercy is loving-
kindness extended by Jehovah to those under
condemnation (and justly so) and subject to destruction. God has shown mercy to mankind in
what manner? By providing redemption and
salvation through Jesus Christ.—John 3:16, 17.

In order to be just must God extend mercy to
every creature? No. Those who are willing and
deliberate opposers of God would not accept

his mercy if extended to them; and certainly God would not extend mercy to such opposers, and he does not. Furthermore, mercy is not the result of the exercise of justice, but is the exercise of loving-kindness when such attribute may be exercised consistently with justice. "As it is written, Jacob have I loved, but Esau have I hated."—Romans 9:13.

Jacob was faithful and obedient to God. His brother Esau spurned the goodness of God and died without mercy. (Hebrews 12:16, 17) God foreknew that Jacob would remain faithful; and hence Jacob was used to picture that class of persons who receive the mercy of God and continue faithful and obedient unto God. God also foreknew that Esau, because of his selfishness, would prove to be the enemy of God; and which he did, and therefore with Esau God made a prophetic picture of a class of persons who refuse to continue in faith and obedience unto God. Was there any unrighteousness on the part of Jehovah God in so doing? Certainly not. Concerning this it is written in the Scriptures: "What shall we say then? Is there unrighteousness with God? God forbid. For he saith to Moses, I will have mercy on whom I will have mercy, and I will have compassion on whom I will have compassion. So then it is not of him that willeth, nor of him that runneth, but of God that sheweth mercy."—Romans 9:14-16.

Jehovah's rule of action, or law, is unchangeable. (Malachi 3:6) His mercy is extended to all who comply with his fixed rules. The result to the wicked and unfaithful is stated in these words: "The Lord preserveth all them that love him; but all the wicked will he destroy."—Psalm 145: 20.

The man who begins to fear God is gaining some wisdom. The fear of Jehovah God means to hate evil and to love that which is right. (Proverbs 8: 13) The fear of the Lord is the beginning of wisdom and knowledge. (Psalm 111: 10; Proverbs 1: 7) Therefore the man who fears God, within the meaning of the Scriptures, begins to have some knowledge and to go in the right way, which is the way of wisdom. "Behold, the eye of the Lord is upon them that fear him, upon them that hope in his mercy." (Psalm 33: 18) What rule of God, then, must be followed by the creature who would receive God's mercy? The rule laid down by the Scriptures is, Faith in God and in Christ Jesus and obedience to the commandments of the Lord. Such is the way that leads to life, because that is the right way and because God's commandments are right and righteous: "Thy righteousness is an everlasting righteousness, and thy law is the truth." (Psalm 119: 142) Therefore it is written in the Scriptures: "Without faith it is impossible to please [God]." (Hebrews 11: 6) The mercy of Jehovah God to the creature who is a sinner by inheritance is granted only to those who believe on God and on Christ Jesus; as it is written: "The Father loveth the Son, and hath given all things into his hand. He that believeth on the Son hath everlasting life; and he that believeth not the Son shall not see life; but the wrath of God abideth on him."–John 3: 35, 36.

The purchase price of the human race is the precious blood of Christ Jesus, poured out unto

death for as many as believe and obey the commandments of the Lord. To that divine rule
there is no exception. Those who receive the
benefit of that rule and who continue in faith
and obedience receive salvation unto life everlasting.

WHO HAS SHOWN FAITH

Can God put on the earth men who, when subjected to the severest test put upon them at the
hand of Satan, will under such test maintain
their integrity by remaining true and faithful
to Jehovah God? That is the question raised by
the wicked challenge of Satan. (Job 2: 1-6)
Failure to maintain one's integrity toward God
means death, "everlasting destruction." Maintaining one's integrity toward God means life.
To understand and appreciate salvation to life,
that question raised by the challenge of the Devil
must always be kept in mind. If salvation were
granted to man in the absence of the test, no
opportunity would be afforded to adequately
prove the matter and settle the question at issue.

It necessarily follows that Satan must have a
free hand to put the test upon men. Since imperfect men cannot successfully cope with Satan, it follows that such men must have some
help. God has provided that needed help to be
administered to men by and through Christ Jesus; but the man or men who receive the same
must do something in order to receive the provided help. God's requirement is that man must
believe in the existence of the Almighty God,
whose name is Jehovah; and such is the first
step toward receiving help. He must believe that

Jehovah God is supreme, and that God is "the rewarder of them that diligently seek him", and that he is the One who has provided salvation for man by and through Jesus Christ. If a man says, 'I do not believe there is any Almighty God, who is the rewarder of them that diligently seek him,' that man has no faith and cannot please God and will not receive the provided help by and through Christ Jesus. (Hebrews 11:6) Or if that man says, 'When I do what appears in my own eyes to be right, and I continue in that way, I think I shall be saved,' that means that the man is without faith and cannot receive the provided help, and he puts himself in the class of the fool. (Proverbs 12:15) Likewise one who relies upon sentiment or feeling is void of understanding. Faith is the first essential to please God, and it is written in the Scriptures: "Faith cometh by hearing, and hearing by the word of God." (Romans 10:17) That means that one must be guided by the Word of God, and not by sentiment or by what some other creature may tell him. (Psalm 119:105) Then the question arises, In the many centuries that have come and gone, who have believed? "Who hath believed our report? and to whom is the arm of the Lord revealed?"—Isaiah 53:1.

In pronouncing sentence upon the rebellious at Eden God announced His purpose to raise up a Seed through his universal organization, which Seed in time would destroy "that old serpent", Satan the Devil, and all his cohorts. Later he made promise that in that Seed so raised up all blessings should come to the human race. (Genesis 3:15; 12:3) The Scriptures set forth the overwhelming proof that such Seed of promise is Christ Jesus, the Lord or Savior, and the King of the world, who shall rule the world in righteousness at the command of the Almighty, Jehovah God. (Galatians 3:16; Philippians 2:9-11; Isaiah 32:1) Some persons have had full faith and confidence in the promise thus made by the Almighty God, as the facts and the Scriptures clearly show.

Individual persons are of small importance, and classes of persons are made more prominent by the Word of Jehovah God, and it is important for one to get into one of such classes. Jehovah has laid down his rules that relate to each class, and in His due time those who comply with his rules find a place in one of his provided classes.

Abel is the first one named in the Scriptures as exercising faith in God. (Genesis 4:4; Hebrews 11:4) Then, in the eleventh chapter of Hebrews, follows a list of men among whom are named Enoch, Noah, Abraham, (Sarah,) Isaac, Jacob, Moses and others, all of whom were in a class known as faithful men, which men were counted righteous by reason of their faith in God and obedience unto his commandments. It is written of those persons that they "looked for a city [city being a symbol of a government or kingdom] which hath foundations, whose builder and maker is God". Those men lived in the world of wickedness, surrounded by the servants of the Devil, but under those adverse conditions they had faith in Jehovah God and in his promise to set up a government of righteousness that would administer life and all attending blessings to them that serve and obey God. They believed God's promise that he would send the Messiah or Christ to save, to rule, and to bless, but just how He would accomplish that great work they did not know, because God did not reveal it to them. Those persons were put to the most crucial tests, but none of such tests shook their faith in God. The Devil saw to it that those persons were caused to suffer all manner of indignities, and the record in God's Word concerning those faithful ones is that 'they had trials of cruel mockings and scourgings, bonds and imprisonment; they were stoned, and sawn asunder; of whom the world was not worthy'. (Hebrews 11th chapter) Those men, because of their faith, faithfulness and obedience, form or constitute a class of faithful men, "just men," who shall be perfected in God's due time. From Abel to John the Baptist that class of men were tested and proved their integrity toward God and received God's approval; and of them it is written: "And these all, having obtained a good report through faith, received not the promise; God having provided some better thing for us, that they without us should not be made perfect."–Hebrews 11:39, 40.

Why did that class of men end with John the Baptist? and why were not these men made perfect and given everlasting life at the time of receiving God's approval? John the Baptist lived at the time when Jesus was on the earth, there being only six months' difference between the birth of Jesus and that of John. He was the last of the prophets preceding the coming of the great Prophet of God, Jesus Christ. He died before the ransom price was paid. He was the fore-

runner and, by the grace of God, was made the
announcer of Jesus when he saw Jesus coming,
and said, "Behold the Lamb of God, which taketh
away the sin of the world."—John 1: 29.

With the coming of Jesus came another class
in Jehovah God's arrangement. As of first importance Jesus came as the spokesman of Almighty God, the Vindicator of His holy name.
The day of the other prophets had been filled,
and concerning Jesus and the prophets, including John, the latter said: "He must increase,
but I must decrease." (John 3: 30) Jesus selected twelve men from amongst the Israelites, the
covenant people of God, and whom he specially
taught, and all of those disciples, except one,
remained true and faithful to the Lord Jesus.
Later Paul was made a disciple and apostle of
Jesus Christ. Christ Jesus is the beginner, the
head and the chief one of God's capital organization called Zion. The faithful apostles and all
who are made members of the capital organization of God are the others of the "elect" class.
The apostle Paul is one of the elect class; and
learning from the Lord that Christ Jesus and
the members of his royal house must first be
selected and perfected by Jehovah in carrying
out His purposes, Paul wrote of and concerning
the faithful men mentioned in Hebrews the
eleventh chapter these words: "God having provided some better thing for us, that they without
us should not be made perfect"; that is to say,
the elect company or class must first be perfected and gathered unto Christ Jesus before
those faithful men of old shall be made perfect

and granted life everlasting. Such is the purpose of God, and such he is carrying out.

FOR JEHOVAH'S NAME

The "elect" class of Jehovah God is Christ Jesus, the Head thereof, and the members of "his body", which constitute the church of God. (Ephesians 1: 22, 23) Because Christ Jesus is the Chief One and is the Vindicator of Jehovah's name and of His Word, he must be put to the test and maintain his integrity. Likewise all the members of his body must be put to the test and maintain their integrity toward God. All careful students of the Bible are familiar with the record of the cruel persecution of Jesus that came upon him at the hand and instance of the religionists, who were the agents of the Devil. (Matthew twenty-third chapter; John 8: 42-44) From the hour of his anointing until his body hung limp upon the tree Jesus suffered all manner of contradiction of sinners and cruel persecution inflicted upon him by the enemies of God. All this was done at the instance of the Devil, and the religious leaders were the Devil's chief instruments used. Because of his faithfulness unto death and because he fully and completely maintained his integrity toward Jehovah God to the end, the Almighty God raised Jesus out of death and made him the King of the world and "the Author of eternal salvation" and exalted him to the highest place in the universe. (Hebrews 5: 9; Philippians 2: 9-11) Every one of the true followers of Christ Jesus has in like manner suffered persecution and indignities heaped upon them by the enemies of God, which

visible enemies are the religionists who carry on
the persecution of true Christians. Recognizing
the necessity for such crucial test upon the followers of Christ Jesus, the apostle wrote: "For
even hereunto were ye called; because Christ
also suffered for us, leaving us an example, that
ye should follow his steps." (1 Peter 2:21) In
support of that the apostle Paul adds his testimony: "Who now rejoice in my sufferings for
you, and fill up that which is behind of the afflictions of Christ in my flesh for his body's sake,
which is the church."—Colossians 1:24.

Concerning the necessity of all of this class'
being put to the test, it is written: "It is a faithful saying: For if we be dead with him, we shall
also live with him; if we suffer, we shall also
reign with him; if we deny him, he also will deny
us." (2 Timothy 2:11, 12) Every member of the
body of Christ must, under the test, maintain
his integrity toward God; and to such, while
undergoing the test, Jesus says: "Fear none of
those things which thou shalt suffer: behold, the
devil shall cast some of you into prison, that ye
may be tried; and ye shall have tribulation ten
days: be thou faithful unto death, and I will give
thee a crown of life." (Revelation 2:10) Christ
Jesus is "the faithful and true witness" of Jehovah. (Revelation 3:14) As Jesus declared, he
came into the world specifically to bear testimony to the truth; and every member of his
body, that is, the elect class, must bear witness
to the truth concerning the name and the kingdom of Jehovah God.—John 18:37; Isaiah
43:10-12.

The chief doctrine set forth in the Bible is that concerning the vindication of Jehovah's name. The kingdom of God under Christ is the instrument Jehovah uses to accomplish the vindication of his name; hence the importance of the kingdom. Christ Jesus is the King, and he is 'Head over the body, which is his church', and all the members thereof are kings and priests unto Christ. (Ephesians 1:17-23) John, to whom the Lord gave The Revelation and the commission to record the book of Revelation, wrote: "And from Jesus Christ, who is the faithful witness, and the firstbegotten of the dead, and the prince of the kings of the earth. Unto him that loved us, and washed us from our sins in his own blood, and hath made us kings and priests unto God and his Father; to him be glory and dominion for ever and ever. Amen."–Revelation 1:5, 6.

Jehovah God made a covenant with Christ Jesus that Jesus should be the King and rule the world; and concerning this matter Jesus said to his faithful disciples: "Ye are they which have continued with me in my temptations. And I appoint unto you a kingdom, as my Father hath appointed unto me; that ye may eat and drink at my table in my kingdom, and sit on thrones, judging the twelve tribes of Israel."–Luke 22:28-30.

The Devil at all times has attempted to destroy every one of those persons who have been called and selected to a place in the kingdom. This the Devil has done in his attempt to support his wicked challenge, and Jehovah has permitted the Devil to have a free hand in putting such tribulation upon his called ones in order that they might be tested and that under the test they might prove their integrity. Such is the real reason why God permits the Devil's agents, the religionists, to persecute Jehovah's witnesses, the faithful followers of Christ Jesus. Their persecution is because they bear testimony to God's name and to his kingdom.

"SHEEP"

Christ Jesus is also called "the Good Shepherd", and he refers to his faithful followers who are made members of "his body" or official family as "sheep", whom he leads, teaches, protects and sustains. His relationship to the members of his body is pictured by the relationship of the shepherd to his flock of sheep. The sheep know the shepherd's voice, and they obey him. Concerning those creatures that are called "sheep" and that are called to the "high calling" that they may be made members of the kingdom, Jesus said: "I am the door; by me if any man enter in, he shall be saved, and shall go in and out, and find pasture. The thief cometh not, but for to steal, and to kill, and to destroy: I am come that they might have life, and that they might have it more abundantly. I am the good shepherd: the good shepherd giveth his life for the sheep." "I am the good shepherd, and know my sheep, and am known of mine. As the Father knoweth me, even so know I the Father: and I lay down my life for the sheep."—John 10: 9-11, 14, 15.

Those who are selected and who are ultimately made members of the kingdom class must willingly and joyfully devote themselves exclusively to God and to his kingdom under Christ. To them the kingdom is of paramount importance, even greater than life itself; and therefore Jesus says to them: "Take no thought for your life," but rather devote yourselves exclusively to the interests of the kingdom and the Lord will take care of all your interests. Then Jesus adds: "And seek not ye what ye shall eat, or what ye shall drink, neither be ye of doubtful mind. For all these things do the nations of the world seek after; and your Father knoweth that

The Good Shepherd

ye have need of these things. But rather seek ye the kingdom of God; and all these things shall be added unto you."—Luke 12: 29-31.

These faithful followers of Christ Jesus do not recognize anything as of importance when compared to the kingdom. They joyfully acknowledge Jehovah God and Christ Jesus as "the Higher Powers", to whom they must "be subject". (Romans 13:1) Therefore when the law of the nations conflicts with the law of God, those faithful followers of Christ Jesus, acting as did the apostles, "obey God rather than men." (Acts 5:29) They have complete faith in God and in Christ Jesus, his King and Vindicator. Note now that such faithful ones are not to fear what men or devils might do to them, because they trust exclusively in the supremacy of the Almighty God. The members of that kingdom class are limited to 144,000 (Revelation 7:4-8; 14:1-3), and that is a small number compared with the billions in existence. Jesus speaks of them as a small number, and therefore says to them: "Fear not, little flock; for it is your Father's good pleasure to give you the kingdom."—Luke 12:32.

Comparatively, a long period of time has been employed in the selection of the little flock or kingdom class. While the selection began with the faithful apostles under Christ Jesus, others at Pentecost began to be called to that class. All such must first seek the Lord and voluntarily devote themselves to God and Christ. Later the Lord revealed to the apostles that the purpose of Jehovah is to select or take out from the nations "a people for his name". (Acts 15:14)

Those so selected or taken out, and who faithfully serve God and maintain their integrity, are truly Christians, because they follow closely in the footsteps of Christ Jesus in obedience to the commandments of Jehovah. God's purpose of taking out a "people for his name" is that such might be witnesses; that is, Jehovah's witnesses bear testimony before others, telling them of God's name and his kingdom. During the past 1900 years many persons have professed to be Christians, but only a very small proportion have proved faithful under the test. Now the time has come when Christ Jesus, the King, is enthroned and is present conducting in the earth God's "strange work", which consists of proclamation being made before the nations and the people that religion is of the Devil and is a fraud and a snare and a racket, and that Christians are those who are wholly devoted to God and Christ and who must obey him; that it is God's purpose to soon destroy Satan's entire organization, and that this will be done at the battle of the great day of God Almighty called "Armageddon"; and that the only place of safety and salvation is in God's organization under Christ Jesus.

Note again that Jehovah said to the Devil, in substance: 'I have permitted thee to remain that my name might be declared throughout the earth and that I might show thee my power.' (Exodus 9:16) The day of Armageddon is very near, when God will express his wrath and exhibit his great power against Satan and all his forces. Therefore just preceding the great battle Jehovah's witnesses, or faithful followers of

Christ Jesus now on the earth, must go about
the land and bear testimony before the people
of and concerning Jehovah's name and his King
and kingdom. These persons who are thus faithfully performing the commandments of God are
designated in the Scriptures as "the remnant of
her seed", meaning the last ones on earth of the
children of God's elect organization. (Isaiah
54: 13) They are the last ones of the called-out
class that must bear testimony to the name of
Jehovah God, and this they must do up until the
time of Armageddon. Because those persons of
that faithful class called "the remnant" do bear
testimony as commanded, the Devil, who is
called that old "Dragon", tries to destroy them;
and hence it is written: "And the dragon was
wroth with the woman [God's organization],
and went to make war with the remnant of her
seed, which keep the commandments of God, and
have the testimony of Jesus Christ."—Revelation 12: 17.

Such is the reason why Jehovah's witnesses
are so sorely persecuted in every part of the
earth, and also the reason why the chief persecutors of these faithful servants of God are the
religionists, led by the Roman Catholic Hierarchy. The religionists do the persecuting because they are the Devil's chief instrument on
the earth. The Devil and his agents expect to destroy the remnant of the little flock of the Lord
called "Jehovah's witnesses"; and Jehovah and
the King, Christ Jesus, will fully protect them,
and therefore these faithful Christians, known
as "the remnant" or "little flock" of sheep, continue to carry on their work faithfully amidst a

time of great persecution, and in so doing they maintain their integrity toward God under the test.

But now in these latter days the Lord says to those of the remnant that there is another class, who are their "companions". Immediately following his words concerning his sheep as hearing and obeying his voice, and which sheep compose the "little flock", Jesus then adds these words: "And other sheep I have, which are not of this fold; them also I must bring, and they shall hear my voice; and there shall be one fold, and one shepherd."—John 10:16.

The Lord is now gathering unto himself his "other sheep", because it is due time so to do. These are also called "sheep" because they are persons of good will toward God and toward his King and kingdom. They desire to know and to do what is right, and hence they seek the Lord, because his ways are always right. Those who will compose the Lord's "other sheep" are not limited as to the number, but are called the "great multitude" without number, and they come "of all nations and kindreds, and people, and tongues", and they rejoice and joyfully acknowledge that salvation belongeth to Jehovah God and is ministered through Christ Jesus, the King. (Revelation 7:9, 10) In a marvelous manner the Lord has manifested his lovingkindness to those of the "great multitude", as will be seen by what follows.

CHAPTER III

GREAT MULTITUDE

THE "great multitude" constitutes another class of Jehovah's favored little ones who receive rewards because of faithfulness and obedience. As the Scriptures unfold, disclosing the great multitude, one's appreciation of God's loving-kindness increases. The fact that Jesus speaks of the great multitude as his "other sheep" is evidence of the Lord's love for them and the care with which he has made provision for them. He then adds: "And they shall hear my voice"; meaning that they will give heed to what he says. No individual is predestinated to be of the great multitude, but the Lord opens the way, and those who diligently seek him find that way.

A person of good will toward God has a sincere desire to be taught and guided in the right way. Therefore, as expressed by the psalmist, he prays to Jehovah in these words: "Shew me thy ways, O Lord; teach me thy paths. Lead me in thy truth, and teach me; for thou art the God of my salvation; on thee do I wait all the day." —Psalm 25:4, 5.

Jehovah, in his loving-kindness, makes all necessary provision to answer such prayer, and hence it is written: "Good and upright is the Lord; therefore will he teach sinners in the way." (Psalm 25:8) To be meek means to be teachable, that is, willing to learn from others. One who recognizes God as supreme is anxious to learn His way, and to such the Lord says: "The meek will he guide in judgment, and the meek will he teach his way. All the paths of the Lord are mercy and truth unto such as keep his covenant and his testimonies." (Psalm 25:9, 10) The Bible is the Word of God, which he has provided for the instruction of the meek in the way of righteousness; and this he does that the man of God may be fully equipped for His service. (2 Timothy 3:16, 17) Hence the man of good will recognizes the Bible as the Word of Almighty God, and which he accepts as his true and proper guide: "Thy word is a lamp unto my feet, and a light unto my path."—Psalm 119:105.

PATTERNS

God used men and inanimate things to make patterns, types, models and pictures by which he teaches the meek and guides him in the way he should go. The Scriptures set out such patterns specifically for the aid of those who desire to learn. For more than eighteen centuries God dealt with the Israelites, and with that people he caused things to come to pass by which he made types or patterns for the guidance of the people now on the earth; as it is written: "Now all these things happened unto them for ensamples; and they are written for our admonition, upon whom the ends of the world are come."—1 Corinthians 10:11.

It is therefore seen that such "ensamples", otherwise called "types" (*margin*), are to be understood by those people on the earth at the end of the world; and now we have come to that time, and those who seek to know will learn. There would have been no purpose in making these types unless they were to be understood at some time; and now is the proper time. A type is an image or representation of something that comes to pass in some future time. An antitype is the reality of the thing of which the type is a representation. The type may properly be called a "shadow"; the antitype, the "reality". The type is also a pattern that serves as a guide by which others work. For instance, it is recorded concerning the men who served in the priests' office of the Israelites: "Who serve unto the example and shadow of heavenly things, as Moses was admonished of God when he was about to make the tabernacle; for, See, saith he, that thou make all things according to the pattern shewed to thee in the mount." (Hebrews 8:5; Exodus 25:40) Another instance is that wherein Jesus is called "the Lamb of God which taketh away the sin of the world"; and the passover lamb offered as a sacrifice by the priests of Israel was a type of the Lord Jesus.—Exodus 12:1-29; 2 Chronicles 30:15-17.

The word *pattern* may be properly applied to anything designed to serve as a guide by which men are taught to walk in the right way. The tabernacle was built in the wilderness, according to the pattern which God revealed to Moses when he was in the mountain: "And let them make me a sanctuary; that I may dwell among them. According to all that I shew thee, after the pattern of the tabernacle, and the pattern of all the instruments thereof, even so shall ye make it."—Exodus 25:8, 9.

In times past God used animate and inanimate things by which he made prophetic pictures or dramas and thereby in symbol disclosed his means to gather the great multitude, who constitute the "other sheep" and who shall receive the salvation that gives them life everlasting to serve God and his King. Many persons regard that part of the Bible which has long been called "The Old Testament" as merely historical statements of the events that came to pass long ago. In this they greatly err. Whatsoever things have been recorded in the Holy Scriptures are for the aid of those who are devoted to Jehovah God, that they may learn the right way and thereby be comforted and receive a full assurance of God's purpose to grant them salvation, with his attending blessings in abundance. (Romans 15:4) The Bible is a great treasure house of truth, and happy is the man who gains a knowledge and understanding thereof. To aid persons of good will toward God attention is now directed to some of the patterns, dramas or prophetic pictures recorded in the Bible long ago.

JONADABS

God created the earth for man, and he created men to live upon the earth and to enjoy the earth and the fullness thereof, and by the permission of the Almighty God perfect man shall, in due time, enjoy that great favor and blessing. (Isaiah 45:12, 18; Psalm 24:1) Those who shall escape the terrible tribulation and destruction of Armageddon, and who thereafter have the blessings from the Lord on the earth, will constitute the "great multitude", that is to say, the "other sheep", which the Lord gathers into his fold. There are many prophetic or symbolic pictures appearing in the Bible foretelling the great multitude, which symbols or dramas are here considered in what follows.

The Bible makes mention of a man whose name was Jehonadab, sometimes called Jonadab; and those who may form the great multitude are mentioned at times under the symbol of "Jonadab". The Israelites, or Jews, were God's covenant people, and he dealt with them as such to the exclusion of other people, and that over a period of eighteen centuries. (Amos 3:2) Jonadab was a son of Rechab, the Kenite, the descendant of Abraham through his wife Keturah. (1 Chronicles 1:32, 33; 2:55) The name Jonadab means "Jehovah is bounteous", evidently referring to the fact that Jehovah showed great favor towards Jonadab because he believed on God and refused to be drawn into the Devil's religious trap. While the many nations of the earth practiced the Devil religion the descendants of Rechab and Jonadab refused to have anything whatsoever to do with religion. (Exodus 3:1; Judges 1:16; 4:11; 5:24) They were positively and unalterably against Baalism, the religion practiced by many nations, and into which great trap or snare the Israelites fell.

The descendants of Jonadab were known as "the house of the Rechabites". They were an honest and sincere people who stood always for what is right and refused to compromise with wrongdoers. When they made an agreement they faithfully performed it. They kept their word. God spoke to his prophet Jeremiah, highly commending "the house of the Rechabites" because of their sincerity, honesty and faithfulness in keeping an agreement which they had made: "And Jeremiah said unto the house of the Rechabites, Thus saith the Lord of hosts, the God of Israel, Because ye have obeyed the commandment of Jonadab your father, and kept all his precepts, and done according unto all that he hath commanded you; therefore thus saith the Lord of hosts, the God of Israel, Jonadab the son of Rechab shall not want a man to stand before me for ever."—Jeremiah 35: 18, 19.

They were men of good will toward God, and they loved righteousness, and therefore God used them as a pattern or picture of the people of good will who now learn of Jehovah's provision for mankind, and who love righteousness, and who show their love for God when they come to know him.

God commanded Elisha to anoint Jehu to perform specifically a work amongst the Israelites for the vindication of Jehovah's name. Jehu was a captain in the army during the reign of the wicked king Ahab and his wicked wife Jezebel, who practiced the Devil religion known as Baalism, and which religion pictured the modern-day religion and religious systems commonly called "Christendom" or "the Christian religion". Jehu in the performance of his duty and commission pictured Jesus Christ, the great Executioner and Vindicator of Jehovah's name, and also the faithful followers of Christ Jesus,

and particularly "the remnant" from and after
the year 1919. The meeting of Jehu and Jonadab, and what took place at that meeting, forms
a picture or prophetic drama, pattern or type of
the relationship that the people of good will now
on earth bear towards Christ Jesus and the
members of his body; and therefore that prophetic picture was made and recorded for the
special benefit of those who are now on the earth.
(See *The Watchtower,* issues of July and August
1932, under title of "Jehovah's Executioner".)
Jehu in the performance of his commission had
just executed a number of the Devil religionists
who supported King Ahab and who were against
God and Jehu, and was then on his way to execute more of the same unfaithful class. He saw
Jonadab, who was not an Israelite, coming to
meet him. This part of the picture shows the
people of good will, but who are not of the remnant of the "little flock", seeking the Lord that
they might find the place of refuge and salvation. Jehu halted his chariot and spoke to Jonadab; concerning which the Scriptures record the
following: "And when he was departed thence,
he lighted on Jehonadab the son of Rechab, coming to meet him: and he saluted him, and said
to him, Is thine heart right, as my heart is with
thy heart? And Jehonadab answered, It is. If
it be, give me thine hand. And he gave him his
hand: and he took him up to him into the chariot.
And he said, Come with me, and see my zeal for
the LORD. So they made him ride in his chariot."
—2 Kings 10: 15, 16.

The heart is the seat of affection and motive
directing a person's course of action. If a man

has a good heart, set upon doing right, then his course of action will be in harmony with that heart or motive. If a man believes in God and Christ Jesus and desires to know what is right, then he is properly said to be a person of good will toward God. When Jehu spoke to Jonadab saying: 'Is thy heart as my heart?' clearly his meaning was: "Do you approve of my course, which is against the Devil and his deceptive religious schemes, and is your heart devoted to Jehovah God?" When Jonadab answered that he was of the same heart or motive as moved Jehu to take righteous action against the religionists, Jehu gave Jonadab his hand and took him up into his chariot, and thereby pictured that the Lord Jesus offers protection to the Jonadabs and invites them to seek that protection in or under his organization, the chariot being a picture of the Lord's organization. Jonadab was taken up into the chariot with Jehu and rode with him,

Jonadab enters Jehu's chariot

and this shows that Jonadab becomes a companion of and walks with the anointed followers of Christ Jesus, the remnant, Jehovah's witnesses now on the earth. In inviting Jonadab to go with him Jehu said to Jonadab: "Come . . . and see my zeal for the LORD." That meant that Jehu was energetic and enthusiastic in rendering service at the command of the Lord, and he invited Jonadab to show a like zeal; and this shows that the Jonadabs must have and exhibit energy and enthusiasm in their devotion and service to God and his King and kingdom. Concerning the Lord Jesus it is written: "For the zeal of thine house hath eaten me up; and the reproaches of them that reproached thee are fallen upon me."—Psalm 69:9.

As Jehu in his zeal pictured the Lord, so we observe that the Lord Jesus was at all times zealous in the performance of his commission handed to him by Jehovah. The Devil, and particularly his religious agents, have at all times brought great reproach upon the name of Jehovah God; and when Christ Jesus came to earth the reproaches that reproached Jehovah fell upon Jesus, and therefore Jesus suffered great reproach at the hands of the religious agents of the Devil. All the true followers of Christ Jesus have suffered like reproaches.—Romans 15:3.

Those who associate thus with the elect class must also suffer reproach. That means that those who form the great multitude are reproached now by the religionists, and this opposition affords the Jonadabs the opportunity to prove their devotion to the Lord and to maintain their integrity toward Jehovah. They must be subjected to the test and must devote themselves and all they have to God and his kingdom, and not to any man or man-made organization. The Jonadabs must have and exercise the same faith and obedience as that required and exhibited by the "elect" "servant" class, the "little flock". (Isaiah 42:1) For this reason it is now seen that the anointed remnant, that is, the little flock on the earth who are Jehovah's witnesses, and those who form the company known as the Jonadabs must become and have become companions in service, and they go on together in peace and in harmony, serving God and his kingdom. (Psalm 122) Wherever the name Jonadab appears in the Scriptures it may now be read as referring to those men and women on the earth who are of good will toward God and who are seeking the way to serve God and his King and kingdom.

FLOOD SURVIVORS

Another prophetic picture, which is of peculiar interest to the Jonadabs at this time, is that concerning those who survived the flood and were brought through alive. The flood or great deluge of Noah's time was typical, that is to say, a pattern or symbol of greater things to come. "The world that then was" God destroyed by a deluge of waters, and that flood pictured Armageddon, by which the present wicked world will shortly be destroyed. (2 Peter 3:5-7) The only survivors of the flood were Noah and those creatures in the ark with him. (Genesis 7:22, 23) In that picture Noah foreshadowed or represented Christ Jesus, the beloved Son of God.

Noah was "a preacher of righteousness" and was therefore a witness to the name and majesty of Jehovah God. (2 Peter 2:5) Noah's sons and their wives believed what Noah told them, and they showed their belief by entering into the ark with Noah and remaining there until the flood came to an end, and thus they found protection and safety in the ark, which pictured God's organization. Finding refuge in the ark the sons of Noah and their wives pictured those who find refuge in God's organization at the present time. Noah's sons and their wives' being carried over the flood constituted a prophetic picture foretelling the class of persons of good will, otherwise called "Jonadabs", or "other sheep" of the Lord, who seek righteousness and meekness and who because of their faith and obedience will be carried over the great fiery tribulation of Armageddon and, being faithful, will form the "great multitude". The higher critics, which call themselves preachers or clergymen or doctors of divinity, taboo the Bible account of the flood; and thus they show that they have no faith whatsoever in God, but are God's enemies. Jesus emphatically approved the existence of the flood and showed that it was a type of the coming destruction of the world.

LOT'S ESCAPE

Another prophetic picture relating to the people of good will that find refuge in the Lord, and which picture was made long ago, is that concerning Lot and his escape from Sodom. The inhabitants of Sodom were practitioners of the Devil religion and were exceedingly wicked.

(Genesis 13:13) Lot was a nephew of Abraham and dwelt in the plain near Sodom. Because of the great wickedness that existed in Sodom God sent his representatives to Sodom to destroy it. On the way those representatives of Jehovah informed Abraham of God's purpose. Abraham, having in mind his nephew Lot, who would be subject to destruction unless protected, made an earnest plea before the Lord God that Sodom might be spared from destruction if a certain number of persons there were found to be righteous. God informed Abraham that if as many as ten righteous persons could be found in Sodom he would not destroy it. (Genesis 18:20-33) But that number could not be found. Only Lot and his family were found to be the ones who had faith in God, and his family consisted of his wife and two daughters. The Lord showed his mercy toward Lot, his wife and two daughters, and caused them to be led out and away from the place of destruction: "Then the Lord rained upon Sodom and upon Gomorrah, brimstone and fire from the Lord out of heaven; and he overthrew those cities, and all the plain, and all the inhabitants of the cities, and that which grew upon the ground."—Genesis 19:24, 25.

The angels of the Lord appearing as men and as the Lord's representatives had led Lot and his family out of Sodom before the destructive fire was sent down upon the city. The angels warned them as to what they should do: "And it came to pass, when they had brought them forth abroad, that he said, Escape for thy life; look not behind thee, neither stay thou in all the plain; escape to

the mountain, lest thou be consumed."—Genesis
19:17.

In this prophetic picture Lot and his family
represented or foreshadowed those persons who
are of good will and who hear the warning concerning the great destruction that will come upon the world at Armageddon, which warning is
now being sounded throughout the earth by
Jehovah's witnesses. It is certain that the destruction of Sodom pictured Armageddon, and
that Sodom particularly foreshadowed that part
of Satan's organization called "Christendom";
and that is made certain by what is written concerning the religious systems called "Christendom", to wit: 'That great city [organization]
called Sodom, where Christ was crucified.' (Revelation 11:8) The nations which are known as
"Christendom" have in these latter days become
exceedingly wicked, and such religious practitioners are the ones that wickedly persecute
Jehovah's witnesses because they stand for God
and his kingdom and insist on obeying God and
Christ Jesus in proclaiming the message of the
kingdom. Christ Jesus counts the persecution
and punishment inflicted upon his faithful followers as though it were done unto himself.
(Matthew 25:32-46) The conditions obtaining
in and about Sodom exactly fit the conditions
that now exist in "Christendom". Jesus, speaking of the conditions that would prevail upon
earth at the time of his second coming, which is
the present time, likens them unto Sodom, thus
further proving that the destruction of Sodom
was a type or foreshadowed what shall come to
pass upon "Christendom" at Armageddon. "Like-

wise also as it was in the days of Lot; they did eat, they drank, they bought, they sold, they planted, they builded; but the same day that Lot went out of Sodom, it rained fire and brimstone from heaven, and destroyed them all. Even thus shall it be in the day when the Son of man is revealed."—Luke 17: 28-30.

The facts now conclusively prove that throughout the land of "Christendom" the men who operate the religious systems do so for selfish reasons and by these religious systems carry on a racket and are entirely oblivious to the warning God is causing to be sounded in their presence concerning the approaching time of Armageddon. Thus it is clearly seen that the prophecy of the Lord Jesus is now being fulfilled.

Not only faith, but also obedience, is emphasized in the picture of Lot fleeing from Sodom. The angels of the Lord, having led Lot and his family away from Sodom before destruction began, then warned them in these words: "Escape for thy life; look not behind thee." "Then the Lord rained upon Sodom and upon Gomorrah, brimstone and fire from the Lord out of heaven; and he overthrew those cities, and all the plain, and all the inhabitants of the cities, and that which grew upon the ground. But his wife looked back from behind him, and she became a pillar of salt." (Genesis 19: 24-26) Lot's wife utterly disregarded the warning from the representatives of the Lord, and her looking back was an act of disobedience, and the result was that a pillar of salt there stood forth as a monument of her disobedience and clearly appears to say, in substance: "When one under-

takes to obey the Lord, he must then continue
in faith and faithfully obey God's commandments. Obedience to the Lord must be continu-
ous and unconditional." "And Jesus said unto
him, No man, having put his hand to the plough,
and looking back, is fit for the kingdom of God."
—Luke 9: 62.

Jesus describing conditions that prevail on
earth at the time of Armageddon said: "In that
day, he which shall be upon the housetop, and
his stuff in the house, let him not come down to
take it away; and he that is in the field, let him
likewise not return back. Remember Lot's wife."
—Luke 17: 31, 32.

And thus Jesus emphasized the importance of
full obedience. Lot and his family received the
warning to flee, and they fled before destruction fell upon Sodom and Gomorrah; and likewise those who form the great multitude receive
the warning to flee, and they must flee to the
Lord's kingdom before Armageddon begins and
they must abide under the Lord's protection until the fire of Armageddon has completely burned
out. These things are recorded as a pattern or
guide for those who now undertake to serve
the Lord.

CITIES OF REFUGE

Moses was in command of the Israelites on
their trek from Egypt to the land of promise.
While on the plains of Moab, and before reach-
ing Palestine, God announced through Moses
his provision for the temporary protection for
the Israelites, strangers and sojourners among
them who should kill another accidentally, un-

awares and without malice. (See Numbers, chapter 35; considered at length in *The Watchtower* August 1 and 15, 1934.) Moses was a type of Christ Jesus. (Acts 3: 22, 23) By that is meant, the prophetic utterances of Moses find fulfillment in what the Lord Jesus does. Jehovah God instructed Moses to announce to the Israelites that he had made provision for three cities of refuge on the east side of Jordan and three cities of refuge on the west side of Jordan. This was made known by Moses to the Israelites just before they reached Canaan, or Palestine, and this clearly shows that the fulfillment of the picture relates particularly to the second coming of the Lord Jesus Christ and his kingdom, and what occurs shortly before Armageddon. A city is a symbol of an organization, and therefore the cities of refuge symbolized or pictured God's organization under the Greater Moses, Christ Jesus. The antitype of the cities of refuge is the organization under the Lord Jesus Christ, who is the Head of God's capital organization.

The provision of God's law was this: If a man slew another out of hatred or malice, he was a murderer and must suffer death. If the slaying was done without malice or enmity, by accident, or unwittingly or unawares, then the slayer, for his own protection, might flee to one of the cities of refuge and there find protection and safety as long as he remained within the city: "But if the slayer shall at any time come without the border of the city of his refuge, whither he was fled; and the revenger of blood find him without the borders of the city of his refuge, and the revenger of blood kill the slayer; he shall not be

guilty of blood; because he should have remained in the city of his refuge until the death
of the high priest; but after the death of the
high priest the slayer shall return into the land
of his possession."—Numbers 35: 26-28.

The six cities were established for the conven-
ience of the people of Israel who were on both
sides of the Jordan. Those cities of refuge symbolically pictured the protection which men of
good will receive by fleeing from Satan's organization to Christ Jesus and his organization, and
who remain there until Armageddon has ended.
If the killer used a deadly weapon and willfully
and deliberately killed another because of
hatred, enmity or malice, he could not have the
benefit of the city of refuge, but the revenger
of blood could kill him as soon as he met him.
One who acts maliciously exhibits a bad condition of heart, that is, a wrong motive, and the
fact that such persons did not receive the benefit of the city of refuge, and the further fact that
if a person killed another unawares or suddenly, without enmity, he might have the benefit of
the city of refuge, shows that the cities of refuge
antitypically apply only to those persons of
good will toward God, and who have a sincere
desire to do right, and who have been drawn into
an undesirable position because of circumstances over which they had no control. Such persons
are the ones that are of good will and that,
proving faithful, go to make up the "great multitude".

Human life cannot be taken at will of any
person, but can be taken only in accordance with
God's law. The one who assumes authority to

kill another is a murderer. God's everlasting covenant, which he stated to Noah, emphasized the sanctity of life. (Genesis 9:1-6) The provision is made for the execution of murderers under certain conditions; and no one can take life with impunity when the same is done contrary to God's law. In this day, as the facts conclusively show, all the nations of earth have broken that everlasting covenant by wantonly and maliciously causing the death of many human creatures. This has been done by the nations' engaging in wars of conquest and by other means of oppression and killing, in which many human creatures have been willfully slain. Selfish political and commercial men have fomented and carried on wars, and the clergy of the religious organizations have sanctified such wars and pretended to bless those who indulge in the killing of others. Particularly in the World War, every regiment had its clergymen who, while they were sober, attempted to bless men as they went to battle. The religious systems likewise approve war when it seems popular to do so. The war of Italy against Abyssinia and the war in Spain carried on by rebels against the government had the full approval, co-operation and support of the Roman Catholic Hierarchy religious organization.

It requires no proof, because the information is general, that the leaders of the religious organizations approve, support and co-operate in bloody wars, resulting in the killing of many human creatures, and thus those religious leaders are parties to the crime of breaking the everlasting covenant. All nations are included in this condemnation of the Lord; which is made certain by the following: "Behold, the Lord maketh the earth empty; and maketh it waste, and turneth it upside down, and scattereth abroad the inhabitants thereof. The land shall be utterly emptied, and utterly spoiled; for the Lord hath spoken this word. The earth mourneth, and fadeth away; the world languisheth, and fadeth away; the haughty people of the earth do languish. The earth also is defiled under the inhabitants thereof, because they have transgressed the laws, changed the ordinance, broken the everlasting covenant. Therefore hath the curse devoured the earth, and they that dwell therein are desolate; therefore the inhabitants of the earth are burned, and few men left." (Isaiah 24: 1, 3-6) Armageddon is near, and God declares that all willful and deliberate killers shall perish at Armageddon.

On the other hand there are many men who have been forced into the wars and who have been misled by the religious leaders' informing them that it is their God-given duty to kill. These young men, being drafted and pushed into the war by the ruling powers, and having no knowledge of God's law and his provision for salvation, have indulged in wars and killings without knowing all the responsibility; and these may, by the grace of God, have the benefit of the antitypical city of refuge. These men thereafter learning what God requires and who then believe in God and Christ Jesus, who seek forgiveness through the merit of his blood, and who flee to God's organization under Christ, may find refuge and protection until Armaged-

don is past. There are many others who are under the influence of religious organizations and
their leaders, which religious leaders have informed them that it is right to kill certain persons, and, believing the religious leaders, they
have indulged in the persecution of the true followers of Christ Jesus and even consented to
the killing of them. Saul of Tarsus was a striking example of this. He was an ardent religionist, a Pharisee amongst the Pharisees, and when
that faithful follower of Christ Jesus, Stephen,
was wrongfully convicted and stoned to death,
Saul of Tarsus stood by and consented to the
killing. (Acts 7:58, 59) Afterwards the Lord
revealed to Saul the truth and Saul became a
Christian, and then the Lord changed his name,
and thereafter he was known as Paul and made
an apostle of Jesus Christ and a special witness
for the kingdom. His own testimony shows the
marked difference between a religionist and a
Christian.—Galatians 1:13-16; Acts 26:5, 9-17.

During the World War many young men
were compelled to join the army and fight. They
saw daily the religious clergymen swaggering
about, sometimes sober and sometimes not.
They observed the duplicity of those clergymen,
who always mingled with the soldiers in the
rear; and when the war ended, some of those
men who returned learned that religion is a
snare of the Devil and that God's Word is the
truth, and then they understood what they had
seen the religionists do during the war. Those
young men of good will and kind heart wanted
to know and to do what was the right thing, and
so when they came in contact with the truth as

set forth in God's publications, they began seeking the Lord that they might find him and learn his provision for protection and salvation. Such persons are of good will toward the Lord.

Since the coming of the Lord Jesus and the proclamation of his kingdom by his faithful followers the religious leaders have caused great persecution to come upon Jehovah's witnesses. They have secretly and wrongfully induced political officials, police officers, and others of the "strong-arm squad" to arrest, persecute and imprison many faithful Christians because they were telling the truth which exposes the Devil's religious system. Many of these faithful Christian men and women have been cruelly beaten, and some of them killed, and the religious leaders, particularly the clergymen, have been the chief instruments and instigators of such persecution and killing. Other persons connected with the religious institutions have been misled and ill advised by the clergymen and have participated in such wrongful treatment of Jehovah's witnesses, but, afterwards learning that Jehovah's witnesses are the faithful servants of the Lord, those men who had been misled and who are of good will toward God have turned to the Lord, shown their kind treatment to Jehovah's witnesses, fled to the Lord's antitypical city and there found refuge. Continuing in this condition and obeying the Lord, they will find protection and safety until Armageddon and, proving their integrity to God, they shall be made members of the great multitude.

"The revenger of blood" mentioned in the Scriptures (Numbers 35:19) pictured the Lord

Jesus Christ, the Executioner of Jehovah, who carries out Jehovah's commandments and who at Armageddon will slay all God's enemies. If those persons of good will show their faith in God and in Christ Jesus and their obedience by fleeing to the Lord before Armageddon and then continuing to seek righteousness and meekness and to serve the Lord as commanded, such may be spared in the great devastation that shall be wrought at Armageddon. Therefore the cities of refuge, and those who found protection thereunder, prophetically picture and foretell the place of refuge for the people of good will who continue in faith and faithfulness and who afterwards may form the great multitude. When a person of the right condition of heart sees that the Lord God long centuries ago had in mind such persons of good will above described, his heart responds to the Lord in love and devotion.

RAHAB

Rahab of Jericho, and the members of her family, played a part in one of the Lord's prophetic dramas, foreshadowing and foretelling the great multitude; and therefore the Bible account of Rahab is of peculiar interest to the Jonadabs or people of good will at this time. The part played by Rahab also emphasized the importance of faith and obedience. The fact that it was a prophetic drama directed by Jehovah God is proof that sometime in the future the same must have complete fulfillment. Rahab conducted a harlot's house, but the fact that Jehovah used her to make this prophetic picture shows that one of mean reputation may seek the

Lord and find him and gain a place of safety and protection during the impending tribulation of Armageddon, which is near at hand.

Moses was dead, and God had put Joshua in command of the Israelites. The march of the Israelites through the wilderness was about done and the time had arrived when they must enter the land of promise, then known as Canaan. The name Joshua means "Jehovah will save". He was a type of Jesus Christ, whose name means the same, *Joshua* being the Hebrew and *Jesus* the Greek way of pronouncing the name. (Acts 7:45; Hebrews 4:8, *margin*) The time of the beginning of the fulfillment of this prophetic drama, as now fully appears from the indisputable facts known to true Christians, is about the year 1918 (A.D.), at which time Christ Jesus, the greater Joshua, came to the temple of Jehovah. (See *The Watchtower,* February 1, 1939.)

Jehovah commanded Joshua to lead the host of Israel across the Jordan river. Before beginning the march to the Jordan Joshua sent two trusted men to spy out Jericho, which city pictured the religious organizations which the Lord has declared his purpose to destroy. These two men went to Jericho to get information and report to Joshua. "And they went, and came into an harlot's house, named Rahab, and lodged there." (Joshua 2:1) God could have acted against Jericho, to be sure, without first sending the spies; but the people of that city had heard of the Israelites and of the great things God had wrought for them, and now the opportunity would be offered for the people of Jericho to display their attitude toward God and his covenant people Israel. Also, Jehovah discerned a woman at Jericho who had faith and hope in God based upon what she had heard God had done for the Israelites, and the opportunity was given to her to demonstrate her faith. Her faith and obedience led to her salvation when others of Jericho were destroyed. The city of Jericho and its surroundings showed that it pictured the present-day nations that compose "Christendom" and that practice religion, and who are against Christianity. The two men who went there as spies pictured Jehovah's witnesses, who are commissioned to investigate "Christendom" and there declare the name and kingdom of God, and to do this just preceding the battle of the great day of God Almighty.

Regardless of what religious leaders have said or may say concerning those two spies' going to the house of a harlot and lodging there, we may be absolutely sure that Jehovah sent them there to carry out his purposes. There is no occasion to find fault with those two men. As to Rahab, it appears she was used in the picture to show that persons who are of less reputation than others, that is to say, those who are of the common people, are in a better condition of mind and heart and have a greater desire for righteousness than many of the higher-up, self-satisfied and sanctimonious persons who practice religion. Jesus did not have a good reputation amongst the religionists of the Jews, but "the common people heard him gladly". (Mark 12: 37) Many young women have been deceived by high religious leaders and forced into a

course of conduct that is extremely humiliating
to them. Some young women have found themselves in that unfortunate position while having
a great desire for righteousness, and such are
much more susceptible to hearing the message
of God's kingdom than the men and women of
high reputation among others. Today the religionists, and particularly the leaders of the
Roman Catholic system, the Hierarchy, deliberately attempt to besmirch the name and reputation of true Christians. They do this in utter
disregard of the message of the King and kingdom and the warning that that message sounds
to them. Their action, however, in no wise hin-
ders or reduces the force and power of that kingdom message. Honest and sincere people will
give heed to the message of truth when brought
to them, regardless of the instrument that
brings it.

Rahab's house was situated on the wall of the
city of Jericho, which appears to suggest that
she was quite out of touch with the *élite* class
of that city. When the city should fall, her house
would be in a very dangerous position and only
the Lord God could save her and her household.
Her condition is much like that of many of good
will, otherwise called "Jonadabs", at the present
time. Only God's provision can save them at
Armageddon. The police officers of the city of
Jericho, at the instance of the big religious leaders, went to the house of Rahab for the purpose
of taking into custody the two men or strangers
who had entered there. Likewise today the religious leaders induce the official element of the
land, the police or strong-arm squad, to take

into custody Jehovah's witnesses, who go about bringing into the houses the testimony of God's kingdom in obedience to God's commandment. Rahab showed her faith in God by hiding the men or spies and in later aiding them to escape. Had those two men been found in her house, no doubt she would have been put to death for shielding a spy. But she believed that her salvation depended entirely upon the Almighty God, and she acted accordingly. She refused to lend herself to the enemies of God; and in this she well pictured the people of good will of the present time who shield the Lord's faithful witnesses, and refuse to lend themselves and their power to the police. Today the Jonadabs or persons of good will, who make up the great multitude, see the righteous course of Jehovah's witnesses and they put forth their best endeavors to aid such witnesses of the Lord, instead of yielding to the demand of the clergy to do them injury.

After the officers had left Rahab's house and gone in search of the two men, Rahab went to the roof of her house, where she had hid the men, to confer with them: "And before they were laid down, she came up unto them upon the roof; and she said unto the men, I know that the Lord hath given you the land, and that your terror is fallen upon us, and that all the inhabitants of the land faint because of you. For we have heard how the Lord dried up the water of the Red sea for you, when ye came out of Egypt; and what ye did unto the two kings of the Amorites, that were on the other side Jordan, Sihon and Og, whom ye utterly destroyed. And as soon as we had heard these things, our hearts did melt,

neither did there remain any more courage in
any man, because of you: for the Lord your God,
he is God in heaven above, and in earth beneath."
—Joshua 2: 8-11.

Note this fact: that Rahab there acknowledged
Jehovah God as the Supreme Being. She believed that Jericho would fall, and she desired
to be spared from that disaster and desired to
be saved. Then Rahab and the two men entered
into a solemn agreement. She promised to keep
secret their mission and their presence, and to
co-operate with them in their work; and the men,
in the name of God, promised to protect Rahab
and the members of her household when the city
fell. Those two men there represented the Lord
in making this agreement, and the Lord God had
respect for that agreement and saw that it was
carried out. Then Rahab let the men down the
wall by a scarlet line or rope, and their agreement was that, after the Israelites should "come
into the land, thou shalt bind this line of scarlet
thread in the window which thou didst let us
down by; and thou shalt bring thy father, and
thy mother, and thy brethren, . . . [into thy]
home unto thee. And it shall be, that whosoever
shall go out of the doors of thy house into the
street, his blood shall be upon his head, and we
will be guiltless; and whosoever shall be with
thee in the house, his blood shall be on our head,
if any hand be upon him." (Joshua 2: 12-20)
This prophetic picture shows that those who will
form the great multitude must fear God and
have faith in him, make a covenant to do God's
will, and then faithfully obey God's commandments.

The line of scarlet thread by which the men escaped, and which Rahab afterwards hung out of her window as a signal, symbolically represented the shed blood of Christ Jesus, in which all persons must trust who are saved. Those who are of the heavenly class must rely upon the precious blood of Christ Jesus as their means of gaining life. Likewise the great multitude must have faith and reliance upon the shed blood of Christ Jesus, and

Spies escape from Jericho

in which they 'wash their robes', thereby identifying themselves as the servants of God; and then they must take their place on the side of God and his kingdom and faithfully remain there. Rahab was required, under the terms of their agreement, to bring the members of her household into her home, and which part of the picture shows that the Jonadabs, who form the great multitude, must be active in taking the message of the kingdom to others, that such others may find the place of safety and refuge in God's organization before Armageddon. Every member of the household of Rahab was required to remain in the house during the siege of Jericho, and anyone who went into the street during that siege would have no protection. This is exactly in harmony with the requirements put upon those who fled to the city of refuge. All such must remain under the protection of the Lord and his organization prior to and continuously up to and through the final tribulation upon the world at Armageddon. If Rahab and those of her household obeyed and were faithful to the requirements put upon her, their salvation was guaranteed when the city of Jericho fell. This part of the picture marks the way for those who will form the great multitude, showing that they must flee to the Lord's organization and then continually seek righteousness and meekness and faithfully participate with the witnesses of Jehovah, giving testimony to the name and kingdom of Almighty God. The agreement made, and which was faithfully carried out by the two men towards Rahab and her household, shows that the relationship between the remnant of Jehovah's witnesses and the "other sheep" of the Lord, the Jonadabs, must be mutually helpful and that they at all times must look well to the protection of each other and to safeguarding each other's interests as servants of the Lord. They must be real companions, dwell together and work together in peace.—Psalm 122.

Within a short time after the two spies returned to the Israelites across the Jordan the siege of Jericho began. On the seventh day of that siege, and at a given signal, Jericho's walls fell down flat, and the only part of those walls that remained standing was where Rahab's house was located. Joshua, as the representative of Jehovah, saw to it that the agreement made by his two men with Rahab was faithfully kept and performed. He sent those same two men in and brought out Rahab and all the members of her household alive. (Joshua 6:20-25) Rahab had faithfully kept her part of the agreement with the representatives of Joshua and the Lord. She had gathered the members of her family into her house, where they remained as commanded. She had kept the scarlet line hanging out of the window. She had demonstrated her faith in God and her obedience, and the Lord rewarded her. (James 2:25) The Lord caused her faith and obedience to be honorably mentioned long years thereafter, to wit: "By faith the walls of Jericho fell down, after they were compassed about seven days. By faith the harlot Rahab perished not with them that believed not, when she had received the spies with peace." —Hebrews 11:30, 31.

This prophetic drama was made many centuries ago and the record preserved, and the meaning thereof is now made known for the purpose of aiding and benefiting those on earth who love and serve God and his King, and particularly now for the guidance of those who will form the great multitude.

GIBEONITES

The land of Canaan was inhabited by the enemies of God, and most of them entered into a conspiracy to fight against Joshua. The exception was those people of Gibeon, who showed they had faith in the God of Israel. The combined enemies in Canaan pictured the religionists and allies of the land now called "Christendom", who conspire to destroy the faithful followers of Christ Jesus and to prevent them from becoming a nation, God's chosen nation. (Psalm 83:4) The Gibeonites were a people of good will and pictured the people of good will who today are among the peoples of "Christendom", but which people of good will desire righteousness and salvation. The Gibeonites had heard what Joshua and his army had done to Jericho and to Ai, and they feared Joshua and the God whom he worshiped. This shows that "the fear of the Lord is the beginning of wisdom". The Gibeonites sent ambassadors to Joshua that they might find with Joshua protection and salvation. (See Joshua nine; considered in detail in *The Watchtower*, August 15, September 1 and 15, 1936.)

The battle which Joshua fought at Gibeon is, without a doubt, a picture of the great day of God Almighty, called "Armageddon"; because it is written, in Isaiah 28:21: "For the Lord shall rise up as in mount Perazim, he shall be wroth as in the valley of Gibeon, that he may do his work, his strange work; and bring to pass his act, his strange act."

The act, "the strange act" of Jehovah in this text mentioned, is the battle of Armageddon. The Gibeonites did not stand aloof and wait for that battle to begin before taking any steps for self-preservation. This shows that today those who are of good will toward God cannot wait till Armageddon begins, to seek the Lord, but must act quickly upon hearing of the truth as set forth in the Scriptures, and must take such steps as the Lord directs for them, that they may find protection and salvation. The ambassadors of the Gibeonites, addressing themselves to Joshua, told Joshua that they had come to him because of the name of the Lord God, whom he served: "And they said unto him, From a very far country thy servants are come, because of the name of the Lord thy God; for we have heard the fame of him, and all that he did in Egypt." "And they answered Joshua and said, Because it was certainly told thy servants, how that the Lord thy God commanded his servant Moses to give you all the land, and to destroy all the inhabitants of the land from before you, therefore we were sore afraid of our lives because of you, and have done this thing. And now, behold, we are in thine hand; as it seemeth good and right unto thee to do unto us, do." "And Joshua made them that day hewers of wood and drawers of water for the congregation, and for the altar of the Lord, even unto this day, in the place which he should choose."—Joshua 9: 9, 24, 25, 27.

Those Gibeonites who joined with the Israelites in their service under Joshua's command prophetically foretell the people of good will today who join themselves to Jehovah's witnesses and serve Jehovah God under the command of the Greater Joshua, Christ Jesus.

The kings of the various provinces of Canaan
heard that the Gibeonites had associated themselves with Joshua; so those Canaanites formed
a combination that all their forces might go up
and fight against the Gibeonites. (Joshua
10:2-5) This part of the prophetic drama pictures how the religionists combine to destroy
the Jonadabs of the present time because they
have sought the Lord and associated themselves
with Jehovah's remnant. So, learning that the
combined forces of the Canaanites were march-
ing against them, the men of Gibeon sent unto
Joshua and said: "Come up . . . quickly, and
save us." Thus is foretold that persons of good
will today, in this time of great distress, appeal
to Christ Jesus, the Greater Joshua, to save
them from the abominations committed in
"Christendom" and from the assaults made upon them by the religionists, because all the religious systems are against such persons of good
will. Joshua quickly responded, and by night
he marched his army to the city of Gibeon. This
shows that the work in behalf of the great multitude must now be done quickly, when the night-
time covers the peoples of the earth who are
against God. The confederated enemy had laid
siege to the city of Gibeon, when Joshua arrived
on the scene. The refusal of the Gibeonites to
surrender to the enemy shows that those who
declare themselves for the Lord must stand firmly on his side regardless of all opposition. The
Jonadabs are today learning that they have
much opposition, and this really strengthens
them to follow as the Lord directs.

Arriving at Gibeon with his army, Joshua immediately assaulted the enemy: "And the Lord said unto Joshua, Fear them not; for I have delivered them into thine hand: there shall not a man of them stand before thee. Joshua therefore came unto them suddenly, and went up from Gilgal all night. And the Lord discomfited them before Israel, and slew them with a great slaughter at Gibeon, and chased them along the way that goeth up to Beth-horon, and smote them to Azekah, and unto Makkedah."—Joshua 10: 8-10.

This is further evidence that the battle of Gibeon was a picture of the battle of Armageddon. Jehovah fought the battle of his covenant people and gained for them a victory to the praise of Jehovah God. "And it came to pass, as they fled from before Israel, and were in the going down to Beth-horon, that the Lord cast down great stones from heaven upon them unto Azekah, and they died; they were more which died with hailstones than they whom the children of Israel slew with the sword. Then spake Joshua to the Lord in the day when the Lord delivered up the Amorites before the children of Israel, and he said in the sight of Israel, Sun, stand thou still upon Gibeon; and thou, Moon, in the valley of Ajalon. And the sun stood still, and the moon stayed, until the people had avenged themselves upon their enemies. Is not this written in the book of Jasher? So the sun stood still in the midst of heaven, and hasted not to go down about a whole day. And there was no day like that before it, or after it, that the Lord hearkened unto the voice of a man; for the Lord fought for Israel."—Joshua 10: 11-14.

The Gibeonites were delivered and saved from the destruction purposed upon them by the combined enemy, and this pictures that the persons of good will, the Jonadabs, who will form the great multitude who put themselves under the command of the Lord Jesus, the Greater Joshua, shall be saved at the battle of Armageddon and enter into the great multitude that survives.

JOSEPH AND HIS BRETHREN

Every child that has attended Sunday School has heard something about Joseph and his brethren. The religious teachers have had much to say about that "Bible story", as they call it; but they have understood nothing about it. They have looked upon it merely as a historical fact. But no one could understand it until God's due time for those devoted to him to understand it. Now the time has come for the people of good will toward God to see and to understand that God used Joseph and his ten half brothers to make a wonderful picture prophetically showing the relationship of the great multitude to the Lord Jesus Christ, whom Joseph pictured. That great prophetic drama is further corroborative evidence showing that "known unto God are all his works, from the beginning of the world". —Acts 15: 18.

These prophetic facts and the Scripture, together, should cause all sincere persons to have strong faith in the Almighty God. It should be particularly helpful, and will be, to those of good will today. Space here permits giving only a

Salvation by the Lamb of God foreshadowed   Page 64

Joseph sees nine half brothers return with Benjamin   Page 100

brief statement of that great prophetic drama. In *The Watchtower* of 1937, pages 35-88, is a detailed consideration of the matter. The Bible account appears at Genesis, chapters 37-49 inclusive. In that prophetic drama Jacob played the part representing Jehovah God; Rachel his wife, the part picturing God's organization; Joseph, the part picturing Christ Jesus; and Joseph, together with Benjamin, picturing the royal house of Jehovah God, otherwise known as Zion; while Joseph's ten half brothers played the part that pictures those persons in the religious organizations who at first envy and ill-treat the faithful followers of Christ Jesus, and in the latter part of the drama those same half brothers picture persons of good will who, upon learning the truth, gladly devote themselves to the Lord; and, hence, from that time forward picture the great multitude, the Lord's "other sheep".

The Bible record, in brief, is this: Joseph was a shepherd boy, dutifully giving attention to his father's flocks. Jacob, his father, sent Joseph to a distant town to ascertain the condition of the flocks which Joseph's half brethren were attending. Here Joseph pictured Christ Jesus, the Son of Jehovah God, whom Jehovah sent to the earth to look after the interest of the flock that had strayed away from the Lord. Joseph's half brothers hated him because his father favored him; and when they saw him coming they conspired together to kill Joseph. Likewise when Jesus came to the earth and began his ministry, the Devil put it into the minds of the religious leaders of the Jews to get rid of Jesus, and

therefore they conspired together to kill him.
Joseph's half brethren then conspired amongst
themselves to make disposition of Joseph, and
they sold him as a slave, and he was carried
away to Egypt, where he became the slave of
Potiphar, an officer of the king. In Egypt Joseph
played parts in the great prophetic drama recorded, picturing Christ Jesus, which includes
the faithful members of "the body of Christ",
and particularly the remnant thereof now upon
the earth. The wife of Potiphar attempted to
seduce Joseph, and, failing in this, she charged
him with an attempt of criminal assault. She
pictured Satan's religious organization that attempts to seduce the faithful followers of Christ
Jesus and to induce them to join in illicit relationship with the Devil's organization, which is
spiritual fornication or idolatry, within the
meaning of the Scriptures.—James 4:4.

When Joseph was charged with this crime he
was imprisoned. After his being imprisoned for
about two years Pharaoh the king had a dream,
and it was represented to the king that the prisoner Joseph could interpret his dream. Joseph
was brought before Pharaoh and interpreted his
dreams. Pharaoh then made Joseph ruler over
all Egypt, and he held the position of authority
next to the king. Pharaoh and Joseph were then
the earthly "higher powers", and at this point
in the drama pictured Jehovah God and Christ
Jesus, the "higher powers" of the world.

A great famine came upon the world: "And
the famine was over all the face of the earth."
"But in all the land of Egypt there was bread,"
which supply of bread was due to Joseph's hav-

ing made provision beforehand by buying and storing up the corn for a period of seven years. This part of the prophetic picture began to have fulfillment particularly following the World War, when the religious institutions abandoned the Lord and openly took the side of Satan's organization, and hence there was no truth amongst them; and this is foretold by Jehovah's prophet in these words: "Behold, the days come, saith the Lord God, that I will send a famine in the land; not a famine of bread, nor a thirst for water, but of hearing the words of the Lord." —Amos 8:11.

That famine for want of the understanding of God's Word, due to the unfaithfulness of the religious organizations, has now spread over all the world, but within God's organization, namely, his faithful people on the earth, there is an abundance of spiritual food and the Lord continually supplies this "meat in due season". This is absolute proof from the Scriptures that the fulfillment of the prophecy concerning Joseph and his brethren is now taking place, and the understanding thereof is made clear now for the benefit of the Jonadabs who shall compose the great multitude. The Lord Jesus Christ is the Greater Joseph, who feeds those persons in the world who seek him. His faithful servants carry the food to the hungry people who constitute the Lord's "other sheep". Now the people of good will toward God find no spiritual food whatsoever in the religious organizations, and they, being hungry and thirsty for righteousness, seek Christ Jesus, the Greater Joseph, and are fed by him. He sends them the truth from his Father's table by the hand of Jehovah's faithful witnesses in the earth today. People from all over the world came to Joseph to be fed, because that was the only place to find food. The impartiality of the Lord toward the great multitude is shown in this picture, because the Scriptures declare in other places that these come 'of all nations, kindreds, peoples and tongues' and stand before the throne of the Lord and cry, "Salvation to our God which sitteth upon the throne, and unto the Lamb [Christ Jesus]." Concerning those who diligently seek and serve the Lord it is further written: "They shall hunger no more, neither thirst any more; . . . For the Lamb [Christ Jesus], which is in the midst of the throne, shall feed them, and shall lead them unto living fountains of waters; and God shall wipe away all tears from their eyes."—Revelation 7:9-17.

Because of the famine Jacob sent his sons, the half brothers of Joseph, down into Egypt to buy food. (Genesis 42:1-5) They were brought before Joseph, but they did not recognize him, for the reason that years had elapsed since they had sold him into Egypt and they believed that Joseph was dead. Again they went to Egypt for food, at the instance of their father. Joseph had held Simeon as hostage until they returned. On this occasion the nine half brothers brought Benjamin, the younger and the full brother of Joseph, with them; and when they arrived with Benjamin, Simeon was released and they stood before Joseph, but none of those discovered his identity. At the command of Joseph they were again laden with food and started away for

Canaan. Joseph's silver cup had been concealed in the sack of one, and he sent his officer after them and intercepted them, charging them with stealing the cup; and upon search the cup was found in Benjamin's sack. That was a test upon all of Joseph's brethren. Benjamin here pictured Jehovah's witnesses, a part of the remnant who in recent years have been charged with crimes of which they were entirely innocent, God having permitted such to come upon them as a test that they might prove their integrity. The arrest of these witnesses of the Lord has also been a test upon the Jonadabs, or "other sheep", who, seeing Jehovah's witnesses wrongfully charged, willingly become the companions of Jehovah's witnesses and suffer with them.–Hebrews 10: 33.

The placing of the cup in Benjamin's sack, and the subsequent arrest, was a part of the prophetic picture God purposed to have fulfilled in his due time, which is being fulfilled in order to carry out his purposes and to teach the meek who seek the way to righteousness. Joseph then rendered decision in the case, holding that Benjamin should become his slave and therefore must remain with him in Egypt. This decision of Joseph brought great grief upon the ten half brothers, and Judah, acting as their spokesman, made an impassioned speech, pleading in behalf of his young brother Benjamin, and for his old father Jacob, who would greatly suffer in the absence of Benjamin. Here the ten half brothers show they had received a change of heart towards Joseph and towards their father.

Judah had been the one who had proposed the selling of Joseph into Egypt, whose sale and deportation pictured the enmity of the religionists toward the Lord and toward his true followers. Judah then asked for permission to speak, and here doubtless he acted as spokesman for all. He recounted the facts before Joseph. He told that a son had been taken away from their father and was supposed to be dead, and that the father had bestowed his love upon the younger son Benjamin, and that if Benjamin did not return his father would die of grief. He made an eloquent and touching plea that Benjamin should be returned and that he, Judah, might become a slave in Egypt in the place and stead of Benjamin. The fervor with which Judah presented the case before Joseph proved that those ten men were of good will towards Jacob and also towards Benjamin, and, not yet recognizing that they stood before Joseph, doubtless supposing he was dead, they had great sorrow for the wrong that they had done him. This great test upon them disclosed a complete change of heart; and while, no doubt, they inwardly suffered great remorse because of their treatment of Joseph years before, they were willing to make any possible amends. In this test they bravely met it and demonstrated their good will. (Genesis 44: 14-34) And what did this test in the prophetic drama foretell? It plainly identified and foretold a class of persons who at one time were antagonistic to the consecrated spiritual children of God, the brethren of Christ Jesus; but who, upon becoming acquainted with the conditions of their own situation, showed a deep contrition of heart and a sincere desire to do good toward all who love the Lord. Looking now to the facts: The persecution came upon the brethren of Christ, particularly in 1918, and this persecution was at the instance and instigation of the religionists. That stirred the hearts of many to enmity against the Lord's people, that is, those of the original faithful remnant. But later on, when these came to more clearly understand their own situation and the purpose of God towards them, they had a change of heart and showed themselves in a proper heart condition to be gathered by the Lord as his "other sheep" into the fold of Jehovah. Thus the Lord shows that all of the "other sheep" class must be of good will toward Jehovah, pictured by Jacob, toward Christ Jesus, pictured by Joseph, and toward the remnant, pictured by Joseph and Benjamin, before they can be gathered into the Lord's organization.

The faithful remnant of Jehovah's witnesses have suffered much persecution at the hands of the religious leaders, and continue thus to suffer, and God has permitted this suffering as a test upon his people. He also permits those "other sheep" to see Jehovah's witnesses suffer and to share with them therein in order that their good will toward God may be demonstrated. Such is necessary in order to test the faith and obedience of all who love Jehovah and Christ Jesus. As the severity of the persecution upon Jehovah's witnesses has increased in these days the Lord's "other sheep" have shown their willingness to become companions of those who suffer for righteousness' sake. By this means they have shown their faith in God and in Christ Jesus and a willingness to faithfully obey the Lord regardless of opposition.

The time had come for Joseph to make himself known to his brethren, and then he caused everyone to withdraw from his presence, except his brethren: "And there stood no man with him, while Joseph made himself known unto his brethren." (Genesis 45:1) Does not this strongly suggest that only those of good will toward God, and who give a hearing ear to the message of the kingdom and recognize and accept Christ Jesus as the Savior of the world and turn to him, will be saved, and that all others will go down in the cataclysm of Armageddon? No doubt Joseph's brethren exhibited great fear when they recognized the brother whom they had sold into Egypt; and Joseph, seeing this, said to them: "Now therefore be not grieved, nor angry with yourselves, that ye sold me hither; for God did send me before you, to preserve life."— Genesis 45:5.

In so doing Joseph showed no resentment; no priding himself by reason of the humiliation of his brethren; no shame for calling them his brethren; no hatred or ill will because of what they had done to him; but, on the contrary, he showed a loving consideration for their welfare, and he acknowledged God's goodness and all-powerful hand for good in all that had come to pass. He acknowledged that he had suffered at the hands of his misguided brethren, but it was for their good. At the time Joseph disclosed his identity the young brother Benjamin stood with him, and Joseph revealed himself to all of them at the same time; and thus it is shown that all who are on the Lord's side, whether of the heavenly or of the earthly class, stand together.

Joseph then disclosed the fact that this entire prophetic drama was directed by Jehovah that people might in due time be enlightened concerning his provision made for them to obtain life everlasting. "So now it was not you that sent me hither, but God: and he hath made me a father to Pharaoh, and lord of all his house, and a ruler throughout all the land of Egypt. Haste ye, and go up to my father, and say unto him, Thus saith thy son Joseph, God hath made me lord of all Egypt; come down unto me, tarry not."—Genesis 45: 8, 9.

In the fulfillment of this prophetic picture Jehovah sent Christ Jesus to the world to save the world. He sent him to the temple "to preserve life". He has made Christ Jesus "the Everlasting Father" in behalf of all subjects of the kingdom, and has made him Lord and Head over his royal house, and rightful Ruler of the world. (Isaiah 9: 6, 7) His kingdom is the hope of the world, and in Christ Jesus' name and in his kingdom shall the nations hope. (Matthew 12: 21) There is no other hope, because such is God's provision, and that provision is entirely adequate and complete. Since the Lord has revealed the above-mentioned truths to the remnant and those of the "other sheep" class, they all the more clearly discern the application of the prophetic words of Joseph, which are fulfilled upon the Greater Joseph, to wit: "Tell . . . of all my glory in Egypt, and of all that ye have seen; and ye shall haste, and bring down my father hith-

er." To all such now appears the glory of Christ
Jesus in all the world. The language of the
prophecy at this point shows clearly that the
obligation is laid upon the remnant, and upon
the "other sheep" who hear, to 'make haste' and
tell all, as opportunity presents, that they may
learn of God's gracious provision for the salvation of obedient men.—Verse 13.

Joseph then told his brethren that there were
yet five years of famine and that they should
haste and tell their father, and that all of them,
his father and his household, should come to
Egypt and be near Joseph, the governor, "lest
thou, and thy household, and all that thou hast,
come to poverty." (Genesis 45:8-11) This shows
that at the time of the identification of the
Greater-than-Joseph, who is pictured by Joseph, there is still much more work to be done
by the Lord Jesus through his earthly remnant
in behalf of those who shall live on the earth.

It was in 1931 that there was disclosed to the
faithful remnant a class to which food must be
ministered. But at that time the "great multitude", as such, was not discerned. Joseph's sending for the entire household of Jacob, including
the families of his own half brothers, showed
that after 1931, when the earthly class was disclosed to whom the remnant must now minister,
they must continue to minister to that class, the
famine-stricken ones. This is exactly what has
come to pass and is now in progress. From and
after 1931 the remnant have appreciated that
they must go throughout the land of "Christendom" and give information to those who desire
righteousness; but it is interesting here to note

that it was not until May 31, 1935, at the Washington (D.C.) convention, that the "great multitude", as such, was identified and made known to the anointed class. From that time onward a specially organized effort has been made, and continues with increased zeal, in behalf of the great multitude, to bring to their attention the truths of God's Word; and this they do while the Lord himself gathers the great multitude into the fold, where they shall receive fullness of bread.

INVITATION

The news soon spread throughout the land of Egypt that "Joseph's brethren are come", and this good news reached Pharaoh, and it pleased him. Pharaoh now appears upon the stage, and in this particular part he represents Jehovah God: "And Pharaoh said unto Joseph, Say unto thy brethren, This do ye: lade your beasts, and go, get you unto the land of Canaan; and take your father, and your households, and come unto me: and I will give you the good of the land of Egypt, and ye shall eat the fat of the land. Now thou art commanded, this do ye; take you wagons out of the land of Egypt for your little ones, and for your wives, and bring your father, and come. Also regard not your stuff; for the good of all the land of Egypt is yours."—Genesis 45:17-20.

Likewise Jehovah God was pleased with the work of Christ Jesus, the Greater-than-Joseph, who had disclosed at the temple his identity and his true relationship to the remnant and to the "other sheep"; and the Lord confirms the gracious invitation to the people of good will by saying to them: 'Come, and drink of the water of life freely.'—Revelation 22:17.

Joseph, picturing Christ Jesus, then instructed Benjamin and his ten half brothers to extend the gracious invitation to others of the family relationship, and these were all invited to journey to Egypt. It is Christ Jesus, the Greater-than-Joseph, who causes the truth to be held forth and who is gathering unto the Lord's fold the great multitude; and therefore Jesus says: "And other sheep I have, which are not of this fold; them also I must bring, and they shall hear my voice; and there shall be one fold, and one shepherd."—John 10:16.

The Benjamin class, the remnant, share in this work, in this, that they bear the message of the gracious invitation to the "other sheep", and when these latter ones hear the message it is also the privilege and duty of those "other sheep" to say, as Joseph said: "Come . . . tarry not." This is further proof that the "other sheep", who make up the great multitude, must participate in the work of bearing testimony concerning the kingdom before others of the world, that the latter may flee to the place of safety, where they may be fed by the Greater-than-Joseph.—Revelation 7:16.

The subsequent dealings of Joseph with the Egyptians disclose the great responsibilities and requirements that are now laid upon those who are of the "other sheep" of the present time, that is, who will form the great multitude. They must be fully and wholly consecrated to the Lord and must render themselves in full obedience to his commandments and joyfully engage in his service. Those who are now of the "other sheep" of the Lord must, together with the remnant, joyfully take up the message of life, which God has provided, and bear that message before the people of the famine-stricken world, to the end that those who are now in the world and who so desire may learn the way of life and flee to the place of refuge. There are others that the Lord will yet gather into the great multitude before Armageddon.

As the famine continued sore upon Egypt and the countries round about, so now the spiritual famine continues sore upon the world: "And there was no bread in all the land; for the famine was very sore, so that the land of Egypt, and all the land of Canaan, fainted by reason of the famine." (Genesis 47:13) The famine had been upon Egypt for two years when Jacob and his household reached Egypt. Assuming that some of the Egyptians had given heed to Joseph's interpretation of the dream of Pharaoh, and to his advice to conserve food, and that they had conserved food, such provided stock of grain would at the end of the two years doubtless be used up and the Egyptians would then have to apply to the government for food. This they were compelled to do in order to live. Likewise now those of the "other sheep", who are in the world, will have to come to Jehovah's visible organization, represented by the remnant of God's people on earth, and learn the way to life by obtaining and feeding upon the food which the Lord has prepared and stored up for such. This they must do before Armageddon.

Mark now the striking contrast in the action of Joseph and in the action of the "Democratic New Deal schemers" of the present day. These modern worldly-wise men, instead of conserving the food supply when there was plenty, curtailed the food supply by restricting crops that should have been planted and harvested and by ruthlessly destroying animals, and this they did in order to increase the price of food. The fallacy of their conduct is now being experienced by the American people. Joseph was not interested in pegging up higher and higher the price of food, but was interested in taking care of the people. When the famine increased upon the land Joseph did not raise the price of food and permit anyone to profiteer at the expense of the people.

The modern "new dealers", headed by one whom the Press has designated as "Franklin Deficit", make no provision for food storage and food supplies for the people of America, but they all together participate in speculation and continuously juggle with the food supply and continue to raise the price thereof at the cost and to the distress of the people. It seems strange that the masses of the people are so very listless and foolish as to refuse to hear or give heed to what the Word of God says and, on the contrary, continue to listen to the world-schemes brought forth by selfish men, which schemes can never bring them any relief. In this distress upon the people the commercial religionists harangue those who will listen to them and tell them that their food scarcity and the dust storms that devastate their lands, and the burning heat that destroys their crops, and the pests that participate in such destruction, all these things, have come upon the people as a judgment from God because the people have been negligent in the support of the religious organizations. The charging of Jehovah God with responsibility for these calamities that have befallen the people is a malicious lie and defamation of his holy name. The Scriptures plainly declare that it is the Devil who brings these present-day woes upon the people, and he is doing so for the very purpose of defaming God's name and turning the people away from him. (Revelation 12:12) This is further and strong proof that the clergy who resort to such schemes of haranguing the people and charging God with bringing the calamities upon them represent the Devil, and do not represent God. Great therefore is the privilege and the responsibility laid upon those who have received the truth, to make known that life-giving and life-sustaining spiritual food to other hungry souls who desire to know of the way to life. The truth is the only thing that will bring consolation and help to the people.

The Egyptians had many cattle, money and lands, and they enjoyed personal freedom. Joseph did not set up a starvation-dole system that would bring all to poverty, but he sold the life-sustaining corn to the Egyptians, first for their money; which money Joseph brought into Pharaoh's treasury. He did not permit private and greedy money-changers to profit by the distress of the people. When their money was gone, then he sold corn to the Egyptians for their cat-

tle and herds; and then Joseph bought all their
lands and paid for them in corn or food; and
then the people said to him: "Buy us and our
land for bread"; and this Joseph did. (Genesis
47:14-20) Pharaoh the king thereby became the
rightful owner of everything in Egypt, and the
people became the "servants unto Pharaoh";
and this was according to the wish of the people,
"that we may live and not die." Life is the gift
of God through Jesus Christ; and this does not
mean that man can buy his life from God. It
does mean that in order for the great multitude
to survive Armageddon and to get life from God
through Christ Jesus these must fully comply
with God's terms, which terms are that men shall
fully, unreservedly and completely consecrate
themselves to God and his faithful service, and
acknowledge and serve his King, Christ Jesus.
There is nothing that they may withhold. Nothing that they can give can compensate for the
free gift of life and all its attending blessings,
because all that men have, to begin with, belongs
to the Lord. "The earth is the Lord's, and the
fulness thereof." (Psalm 24:1) They must show
their full willingness to become the servants of
God and Christ Jesus, and must serve day and
night, that is, all the time. (Revelation 7:15)
Christ Jesus, as the great official Agent of the
"King of Eternity", has bought the entire human race, and life will be given to those only
who comply with the terms Jehovah has provided, and to such life is a free gift through
Christ Jesus.

For their welfare the people were brought together in the cities: "And as for the people, he

removed them to cities from one end of the borders of Egypt even to the other end thereof." (Genesis 47:21) In a similar way Christ Jesus now brings his "other sheep" together or under the organization of Jehovah, pictured by a city, and in those "cities" they find refuge, and nowhere else. This corresponds exactly with the cities of refuge which Jehovah provided for the people in the day of Moses. (Deuteronomy 19:1-6) The land of the priests was not sold: "Only the land of the priests bought he not; for the priests had a portion assigned them of Pharaoh, and did eat their portion which Pharaoh gave them; wherefore they sold not their lands."—Genesis 47:22.

That was not an act of discrimination against the people and in favor of the clergy, as some would try to make it appear. Even before the famine the priests of Egypt received government support, and this provision continued unaltered during the period of the famine. The priests were under no necessity to sell their land. It was a previous arrangement that they should receive their food from the king. Those priests or princes of Egypt, together with Joseph, were servants of the king, and, in the drama, here appear to picture the great "elect" "servant", of which Christ Jesus is Head, together with the earthly remnant, who are "the feet of him". (Isaiah 52:7) These today are "joint heirs with Christ" Jesus and belong to "the meek" which "inherit the earth" with Christ Jesus. (Matthew 5:5; Romans 8:16, 17) They are therefore in a different position from that of those of his "other sheep", the great multitude, although all

must and do receive life from Jehovah by Christ
Jesus.

It has always been and always will be that men
must work. "If [a man] would not work, neither
should he eat." (2 Thessalonians 3:10) The idler
is an abomination in the sight of God and is
classed as a waster. (Proverbs 19:15; 31:27;
Ezekiel 16:49) In behalf of the great multitude
and their future life, the Lord provides that
they must not be idle, but must serve him continuously. (Revelation 7:15) "Ye are not your
own; for ye are bought with a price; therefore
glorify God." (1 Corinthians 6:19, 20) Joseph
did not arrange for a dole to be set up and that
the people receive a dole from the government
and continue idle. (Genesis 47:23) On the contrary, the people must be diligent and work, and
not become a public charge in idleness. They
were commanded and must sow the seed given
to them, and sow it upon the land and trust to
God for the increase.

A liberal arrangement was made for the people: "And it shall come to pass, in the increase,
that ye shall give the fifth part unto Pharaoh;
and four parts shall be your own, for seed of the
field, and for your food, and for them of your
households, and for food for your little ones."
(Genesis 47:24) Since the land was not then
their own, that was a very generous arrangement for them. A like requirement is laid upon
the great multitude, as prophetically shown at
Zechariah 14:16-18. The requirement of the
great multitude is just and reasonable, and "not
grievous". (1 John 5:3) Christ Jesus, according to the will of God, puts them all on an equal

footing before Jehovah and requires all of them to render faithful service unto God, and that not beyond measure. This arrangement the people of Egypt appreciated, even as the great multitude will recognize and be glad with the arrangement which the Lord has made for them: "And they said, Thou hast saved our lives; let us find grace in the sight of my lord, and we will be Pharaoh's servants."—Genesis 47: 25.

God, foreknowing from the beginning what would come to pass, made this and other prophetic pictures to aid his "other sheep", who at this time of great stress are being gathered to the Good Shepherd, Christ Jesus. These pictures set before those of good will patterns showing them what course they must take in order to receive the protection and salvation that Jehovah has provided for those that love and serve him.

LOVER OF DAVID

Jehovah in his loving-kindness has provided many other prophetic pictures for the benefit of those who love him, and amongst which is the following one concerning the lover of David. King David received God's approval, and of him God said: "David [is] a man after mine own heart." (Acts 13: 22; Psalm 89: 20) David was diligent to obey God's commandments. He was a type of Christ Jesus, the beloved Son of God. The Bible contains a beautiful prophetic drama involving David, wherein are pictured the faithful royal members of the house of Jehovah, together with the Lord's "other sheep", which will compose the great multitude. It is the record of the close relationship that existed between David and Jonathan. (See 1 Samuel, chapters 17 and 18; *The Watchtower,* September 1 and 15, 1938.)

The Israelites were Jehovah's covenant people and under God's command. But the Israelites selfishly asked for a king. In this they were wrong; but God permitted them to have a king. Saul was chosen and anointed as king. Saul did not give heed to the commandments of Jehovah God, and for this reason God rejected him. Saul's debasement was due to his lack of faith and his failure to obey. Jehovah God, through his prophet Samuel, said to him: "Hath the Lord as great delight in burnt offerings and sacrifices, as in obeying the voice of the Lord? Behold, to obey is better than sacrifice, and to hearken than the fat of rams. For rebellion is as the sin of witchcraft, and stubbornness is as iniquity and idolatry. Because thou hast rejected the word of the Lord, he hath also rejected thee from being king." (1 Samuel 15:22, 23) Thus the divine rule is made clear that a rebellion against God's commandments is the sin of witchcraft, that is to say, serving devils; stubbornness is iniquity and idolatry. This emphasizes the fact that all religions are of the Devil, because they are in opposition to God's commandments.

At the beginning of Saul's reign he had a son who commanded a division of the army; and that son was Jonathan. David, the youngest son of Jesse, was a shepherd boy residing at Bethlehem with his father. After rejecting Saul God anointed David to be king over Israel. David was then a mere lad and, although anointed at that time, did not begin his reign for some time thereafter. In the prophetic drama here described the players and the things pictured by them follow:

Saul, because of his unfaithfulness, played the part picturing the unfaithful clergy and other religionists who have claimed to be followers of Christ Jesus but who for selfish reasons have become unfaithful and rebelled, willfully disobeying God's commandments. Also, he pictured those who have consecrated themselves to do God's will and who start to follow in the footsteps of Christ Jesus, and who become unfaithful and rebellious because of their selfishness. All of such persons, pictured by Saul, form what in the Scriptures is called "the man of sin", "the son of perdition."—2 Thessalonians 2:3.

King David in the drama pictured Christ Jesus, including the faithful members of his body, all of whom compose the royal house of Jehovah. Jonathan played the part at first picturing the faithful men of olden times, who are specifically described in Hebrews the eleventh chapter; and in the latter part of the drama he pictured the "men of good will", the "other sheep" of the Lord of the present time, and who will form the great multitude. The Philistines pictured the Devil's organization made up of the various elements which are against God and against Christ Jesus and his kingdom.

Jonathan and David were not lads of similar age, as Sunday-school teachers have tried to make it appear, but Jonathan was much older than David. The first time they met was after David had been anointed king over Israel, and Jonathan was then a man of mature years and in command of a division of the army. He was at least twenty-five or thirty years older than David. Only those parts of the prophetic drama are here described which show the meeting of Jonathan and David and which disclose their relationship to each other foretelling the relationship of the Jonadabs to the Lord Jesus and the faithful members of his body.

Jonathan was past fifty years of age when he was killed and before David began to reign as king; and this suggests that the part played by Jonathan at the beginning of the drama pictured those faithful men who lived on earth and served Jehovah God before the coming of Christ Jesus into the world.

The Philistines had come up to give battle to Saul and his army. The two armies were on the opposite sides of the valley which divided two mountains. (1 Samuel 17:1-3) A monstrous giant named Goliath was amongst the Philistine army, and he was put forward to fight against someone to be selected by Saul. Goliath was monstrous in size and vicious and extremely wicked. He pictured the dictatorial or totalitarian ruling powers which today have grabbed control of some of the nations and bluff and oppress the people and take away their liberties.

The evidence today overwhelmingly shows that the political dictators and the Roman Catholic Hierarchy, the leading religious system on earth, work together, the political side forming the outstanding rulers, while the Roman Catholic Hierarchy acts as spiritual overlord or adviser, and thus forms a part of the totalitarian government. Mussolini rules Italy with an iron hand. At the beginning of his rulership he was an atheist, and later he professed to be a Catholic and entered into a working agreement with the pope, and since then the Vatican, including, of course, all the Hierarchy, has supported Mussolini in his cruel exhibition of his power in Spain, his vicious assault and destruction of Abyssinia, and his wickedness in other places. Likewise Hitler is a cruel dictator of Germany, and he and the pope have entered into an agreement for the mutual support of each other, and they work together; and the Roman Catholic Hierarchy supports Hitler in his cruelty exercised against God-fearing people in Germany, and also in his cruel assault upon Austria, Czechoslovakia and other people. The facts show that God, by this prophetic drama, foretold that such political dictators and the religionists would work together to form the "abomination of desolation", claiming the right to rule the world instead of Christ Jesus. (Matthew 24: 15, 16; Daniel 11: 31; 12: 11) Religion being the chief instrument of the Devil to blind and defraud the people, the Papacy, that is, the pope and other members of the Hierarchy, are used by the Devil in the capacity of spiritual adviser of the political dictators, their allies. Goliath pictured the entire combine that bluff and bully and threaten to destroy other nations and people that do not submit to them.

Goliath continued to bully the Israelites, all of whom were so frightened that not one of Saul's army was willing to engage Goliath in combat. David, being sent by his father to carry food to his brethren who were in Saul's army,

appeared upon the scene just at the time that
Goliath was bellowing his challenge to the
Israelites. (1 Samuel 17:4-23) Although a mere
stripling lad compared with others of the Israelites, David was righteously indignant against
the bluffer Goliath, and he said to those who
stood by: 'Who is this uncircumcised Philistine,
that he should defy the army of Jehovah?' David
then volunteered to fight Goliath, and advanced
to the combat armed only with his sling and a
few small stones. "Then said David to the
Philistine, Thou comest to me with a sword, and
with a spear, and with a shield; but I come to
thee in the name of the Lord of hosts, the God
of the armies of Israel, whom thou hast defied.
This day will the Lord deliver thee into mine
hand; and I will smite thee, and take thine head
from thee; and I will give the carcases of the
host of the Philistines this day unto the fowls
of the air, and to the wild beasts of the earth;
that all the earth may know that there is a God
in Israel. And all this assembly shall know that
the Lord saveth not with sword and spear: for
the battle is the Lord's, and he will give you into
our hands."—1 Samuel 17:45-47.

Here David pictured the Lord Jesus, who
fights against the combined enemies of God and
destroys them to the vindication of Jehovah's
name. In that combat God gave to David the
victory, and the monster Goliath lay dead with
his skull crushed by one of David's stones.
Jonathan stood by and witnessed the fight. He
immediately recognized that David was the favored one of the Almighty God. Saul, the king,
being impressed by the combat, immediately

called David to him and engaged him in conversation. Jonathan stood by and heard the conversation, and particularly what David had said to Jonathan's father, Saul. (1 Samuel 17 : 57, 58) "And it came to pass, when he had made an end of speaking unto Saul, that the soul of Jonathan was knit with the soul of David; and Jonathan loved him as his own soul. And Saul took him that day, and would let him go no more home to his father's house. Then Jonathan and David made a covenant, because he loved him as his

Jonathan meets David

own soul. And Jonathan stripped himself of the robe that was upon him, and gave it to David, and his garments, even to his sword, and to his bow, and to his girdle."—1 Samuel 18:1-4.

This was the beginning of the heart devotion of Jonathan to David. The love of Jonathan to David was not for selfish reasons, nor was his a love such as exists between creatures of the opposite sex. Jonathan saw that David was right and was fighting a righteous cause, and he loved David for his righteous work, that is, his complete devotion to Almighty God. Jonathan here pictured that class of persons that have been associated with the religious systems, pictured by Saul, and who, upon learning that religion is a snare of the Devil, immediately turn away from it. Jonathan was a man of good will, and, desiring that which is right and righteous, his heart was immediately knit to David. Likewise when the people in the religious organizations today see that the faithful followers of Christ Jesus are valiantly fighting the cause of righteousness in proclaiming the truth against the Devil and his cohorts and are magnifying the name of Jehovah God, those persons of good will love Jehovah's witnesses as Jonathan loved David and give their support to and their full co-operation with Jehovah's witnesses. Jonathan, therefore, here clearly pictured those "other sheep" of the Lord that form the great multitude.

MUTUAL LOVE

There is a mutual love flowing from one to another where both parties love righteousness and hate iniquity. Their hearts are united in a righteous cause. Such is an unselfish devotion to what is right. Where such love exists between persons, neither one looks upon the other from the standpoint of the flesh, but looks upon the heart and his outward devotion to righteousness.

Such was the love Jonathan had for David; and David returned that love. (1 Samuel 20: 41) It was a mutual love, because both were devoted to right and they were doing the right thing as the servants of Jehovah; and thus they pictured those classes of persons, namely, the remnant and the Jonadabs, both of whom are devoted to Jehovah God and hence have and manifest mutual love for each other. Jonathan manifested his love to David by helping David, and in due time David as king expressed his love for Jonathan by his kindness to Jonathan's son. (2 Samuel 9: 1; 21: 7) Jehovah loved both Jonathan and David because they were both striving in the right way; and in harmony with this it is written in God's Word: "He loveth righteousness and justice." (Psalm 33: 5, *Am. Rev. Ver.*) The love of God for the Jonathan class, the "other sheep", is shown in Jehovah's provision made in his law for "the stranger". (Deuteronomy 10: 17-19) Christ Jesus, the Greater David, loves the Jonathan class because they are his "other sheep" and it is his Father's will that he shall gather them into the fold. (John 10: 11, 16) The anointed remnant on the earth, being the "feet of Him", Christ Jesus, must also love the Jonathan class; and they do love them, and prove it by diligence in carrying to them the message of truth and aiding them to understand God's purpose. This is further pictured by the prophet Ezekiel's vision concerning the man clothed with linen with an inkhorn by his side and who marks the seekers of righteousness in the forehead, that is, gives to them an intelligent understanding of the truth. (Ezekiel 9:1-11) True love between the remnant and the Jonathan class, therefore, shows that they must stand firmly together, being companions in service and unselfishly devoted to God and to the kingdom interest, and hence to each other's interests.

COVENANT

A covenant is a solemn agreement between two or more parties to do the things expressed within the terms of that agreement. With their hearts in tune with righteousness Jehovah God would put it into the mind of both Jonathan and David to enter into a solemn agreement for the mutual love and support of each other. Therefore it is written: "Then Jonathan and David made [(literally) cut] a covenant, because he loved him as his own soul." (1 Samuel 18:3) Evidently they first offered an animal sacrifice, thus cutting or making a solemn agreement over the body of the dead animal and which agreement was that they would mutually support each other. That covenant would not mean that those two men would love each other for some selfish purpose; but their love for each other was because they were both following a righteous course, and their covenant would compel them to deal justly one with the other and to avoid envy and criticism and family feuds. The facts show that this is exactly what they did, it being fully supported by the words of David addressed to Jonathan. (1 Samuel 20:8) Jonathan readily discerned that David was God's choice and that he must love David and support him faithfully. This recognition of the superiority of David was shown by Jonathan's bestowing upon David his garment, his sword, and his bow. "And Jonathan stripped himself of the robe that was upon him, and gave it to David, and his garments, even to his sword, and to his bow, and to his girdle."—1 Samuel 18:4.

Saul had four sons, and Jonathan was the only one who entered into a covenant with David. This clearly indicates that those who compose the "other sheep" of the Lord have, many of them, been associated with the religionists, but only those who have the spirit of Jonathan enter into a covenant to serve the Lord and therefore break away from religionists and devote themselves to the David class. Therefore Jonathan pictures the "great multitude" that serve Jehovah and his kingdom.

Likewise the Jonathan class must make a covenant with Christ Jesus, the Greater David, and who is the representative of Jehovah God. They must recognize Christ Jesus as one of the "higher powers" and Jehovah's anointed King, and that Jehovah is the Supreme Power, and hence Jehovah and Christ Jesus alone constitute the "higher powers". (Romans 13:1) Christ Jesus is Jehovah's great Foundation and Chief Corner Stone of Zion, God's royal house. (Isaiah 8:14, 15; 28:16) The Jonathan class do not "stumble" over that great Stone, but joyfully accept him as the One provided by Jehovah for the head of His capital organization. All the religionists stumble over that Stone and are crushed. The covenant between Jonathan and David did not picture the law covenant which Jehovah made with the nation of Israel (Exodus 19:1-5), nor was it any part of that covenant, and it was not any part of the "new covenant" with spiritual Israel (Jeremiah 31:31-34); but it was a solemn agreement which bound the Jonathan class to Jehovah's organization, over which Christ Jesus, the Greater David, is Head and of which the remnant on earth are a part. The covenant shows the binding relationship of companions between the two. Jonathan, by bestowing his garments and his war equipment upon David, assigns to David royal honors, recognizing him as higher than Jonathan. Likewise the "other sheep", those who make up the great multitude, now place themselves and their equipment at the disposal of Christ Jesus for the service of God and lend full co-operation to the manner of service carried on under Christ Jesus' directions. The present-day facts show that the Jonathan or "other sheep" class are doing that very thing.

David was respected by the people far more than Saul. (1 Samuel 18:6-9) Likewise today the remnant receive more real respect at the hands of honest men than the big religionists receive. All honest men know that religion and religionists are men who carry on a racket and hence they are racketeers; and they see that Jehovah's witnesses are honestly and sincerely proclaiming God's message of truth. Jonathan loved David more than he loved Saul, because he knew that David was God's favored one and that David represented the righteous cause. Today the Jonathan class love the remnant, the "feet of Him", Christ Jesus, far more than they do the religionists, because they know that the remnant represents on earth the great and righteous Ruler, Christ Jesus. The breach between the Jonathan class and the Saul class today continues to widen. All those on the side of Christ the King must now stand firmly together, showing mutual love toward one another and harmoniously serving together, and in doing this they of necessity must oppose the Saul class, and do oppose such religionists.

Saul tried to incite and induce Jonathan to kill David, but Jonathan refused to join his conspiracy. (1 Samuel 19:1) Jonathan called Saul's attention to the "strange work" of righteousness which Jehovah was doing through David, and cited this to show that Jehovah's favor was upon David. (1 Samuel 19:4, 5) Likewise the modern-day Jonathan class defend before the clergy the work of Jehovah's witnesses and vigorously protest against the acts of the clergy in persecuting Jehovah's witnesses, and they refuse to join the clergy in any of their schemes to do violence to Jehovah's witnesses. The Jonathan class, or "other sheep" of the Lord, see and appreciate God's "strange work" in which Jehovah's witnesses are permitted to participate, and they know that such is evidence that God's favor is upon the remnant or David class. Therefore the Jonathan class render assistance to Je-

hovah's witnesses, even as Jonathan rendered
assistance unto David. This is further corrob-
orated in the parable of the "sheep" and the
"goats". (Matthew 25:31-46) Jonathan never
approved of Saul's hatred of David. Today the
"other sheep", or Jonathan class, are of a like
mind, and are against those who persecute Jehovah's witnesses.

Because Jonathan showed an interest in
David Saul tried to kill Jonathan. (1 Samuel
20:33) Knowing that Saul conspired to kill
David, Jonathan warned David of the impending danger by shooting arrows as had been
agreed between them, thus shooting the arrows
as a means of communication and warning.
(1 Samuel 20:18-41) Today the Jonathan class
try to shield Jehovah's witnesses and hence warn
them of impending danger. Jonathan thus used
his arrows as the Jonathan class today use their
fighting equipment in aid of Jehovah's witnesses. Thus they show mutual love for each other
and that both are devoted to righteousness. The
antitypical David class, that is, Jehovah's witnesses, have for some time tried to interest the
Saul class, or religionists, in God's message of
his kingdom, and in this work the people of good
will have co-operated, but because of the selfish
and cruel hearts of the religionists little or no
progress is made. This shows that there is now
no possibility for the leaders among the religionists to repent and turn to God and his King,
and that there is no further need for the Jonathan and the David class to put forth their
efforts in this behalf. Those of the Saul class are
bent on destroying Jehovah's witnesses and

their work, just as Saul was bent on destroying David and chased him from place to place. The war is on now, and the remnant of God's people on the earth must, in obedience to Jehovah's commandments, go forth and participate in that war, by faithfully bearing witness to God's kingdom.

From this prophetic picture it clearly appears that Jehovah God purposed from the beginning to have a faithful class of men associated with Christ Jesus in his kingdom and a faithful class of persons on the earth who will receive life from the antitypical David, and that in these latter days of distress upon the world the remnant of the first and those of the latter class walk together, serving together, and promoting the name and kingdom of God, and that ultimately these shall all be of one fold of sheep or obedient ones under Christ Jesus.

ISRAELITES COMING TO DAVID

After the death of Saul David reigned as king of Judah for seven and one-half years, and later the other tribes of Israel came to David and anointed him as their King. "Then came all the tribes of Israel to David unto Hebron, and spake, saying, Behold, we are thy bone and thy flesh." "So all the elders of Israel came to the king to Hebron; and king David made a league with them in Hebron before the Lord; and they anointed David king over Israel." (2 Samuel 5:1, 3) (See also 1 Chronicles chapters 11 and 12.) Those Israelites who came to David, as above described, pictured those persons of good will who today come to the Greater David,

Christ Jesus, after he begins his reign, and who give their allegiance and devotion to the Lord. They pictured the "other sheep" that will form the great multitude, which the Lord today is gathering unto himself.

STRANGERS

The Israelites alone were God's covenant people. (Amos 3:2) All other people were "strangers", and were so called. They are mentioned as Gentiles, meaning non-Jews or non-Israelites. God did not turn away even strangers who sought him and who complied with his law, although they were not in a covenant with him. (Exodus 12:48; 20:10) Hobab, the Kenite, was a brother-in-law of Moses; and when Moses in command of the Israelites began the journey to the land of Canaan, he invited Hobab, the Kenite, to go with him, saying: "Come thou with us, and we will do thee good." (Numbers 10:29) Those Kenites journeyed with the Israelites and were strangers, so far as God's covenant was concerned. (Judges 1:16; 4:11) The strangers that sojourned with the Israelites, God's covenant people, were required to obey God's law. (Leviticus 16:29; 18:26; 19:33, 34) Moses, recounting to the Israelites God's goodness, said to them: "He doth execute the judgment of the fatherless and widow, and loveth the stranger, in giving him food and raiment. Love ye therefore the stranger; for ye were strangers in the land of Egypt."—Deuteronomy 10:18, 19.

When the Israelites were assembled in Moab to hear the final address of Moses, strangers were there also to receive the admonition given by Moses at the command of Jehovah. (Deuteronomy 29:10, 11) The strangers that sojourned with the covenant people of God, the Israelites, and who worshiped and obeyed God, picture those who are now of good will toward God and his people, and who will form the great multitude, if they continue faithful and obedient.

TEMPLE BUILDERS

At the command of Jehovah God Solomon built the temple at Jerusalem, "an house unto the name of the LORD my God." (1 Kings 5:5) Hiram of Tyre loved David, the father of Solomon, and he sent his servants to Solomon to learn what he might do to aid him. Solomon directed Hiram to have his servants prepare material for the temple: "So Hiram gave Solomon cedar trees and fir trees, according to all his desire."—1 Kings 5:10.

King Hiram sent his servants to work for Solomon. "And Hiram king of Tyre sent his servants unto Solomon; for he had heard that they had anointed him king in the room of his father; for Hiram was ever a lover of David." "And the Lord gave Solomon wisdom, as he promised him; and there was peace between Hiram and Solomon; and they two made a league together." "And Solomon's builders and Hiram's builders did hew [stones], and the stonesquarers; so they prepared timber and stones to build the house." (1 Kings 5:1, 12, 18; 2 Chronicles 2:3-10) Other strangers or proselytes of Israel were brought into service: "And Solomon numbered all the strangers that were in the land of Israel, after the numbering wherewith David his father had numbered them [showing that those outside of the land of Israel were unnumbered]; and they were found an hundred and fifty thousand and three thousand and six hundred. And he set threescore and ten thousand [seventy thousand] of them [strangers or proselytes] to be bearers of burdens, and fourscore thousand [eighty thousand] to be hewers in the mountains, and three thousand and six hundred [3,600] overseers to set the people a work." (2 Chronicles 2: 17, 18) This corresponds with extending to the "great multitude" or Jonadabs a part in the witness work of the present time.—Revelation 22: 17.

The building of the temple by Solomon began 1035 B.C., and seven years and six months thereafter the temple was completed and dedicated. (1 Kings 6: 1, 37, 38) Solomon was a type of Christ Jesus, the builder of the antitypical temple or real temple of God, the building of which began in 1918; and seven and one-half years thereafter, to wit, 1925, corresponds to the completion of the temple. Strangers or foreigners who assisted the building of Solomon's temple pictured the people of good will or "other sheep" of the Lord.

At the dedication of the temple King Solomon prayed and in his prayer referred to the "stranger", or foreigner, that should duly come to Jehovah's temple for mercy because of Jehovah's great name. (See 2 Chronicles 6: 32, 33; 1 Kings 8: 41-43.) Such "strangers" would foreshadow or correspond with the Lord's "other sheep", or Jonadabs, or people of good will, who go to make up the "great multitude". Note now the facts showing God's beginning to reveal to the remnant of his people the great multitude.

In the "eleventh year" after 1914, or seven years after the coming of the Lord Jesus to the temple in 1918 and his beginning to rear up the temple, to wit, in 1925, God's consecrated people were assembled in convention at Indianapolis, Indiana, and on the 29th day of August 1925 that assembly of God's people adopted a resolution entitled "Message of Hope", and which was the first and only one of the seven resolutions adopted over a period of seven years that was addressed "To All People of Good Will". In this connection note that the great multitude (Revelation 7: 9, 10), being people of good will, joined with God's anointed remnant of the temple company in celebrating the great antitypical feast of tabernacles. Interesting, therefore, it is to note that the fourteen-day celebration by King Solomon, of the feast and the dedication of the building, in the seventh Jewish month of 1028 B.C. embraces not only the Jewish atonement day (on the 10th day) but also the entire seven-day feast of tabernacles (the 15th to the 21st, inclusive) with its booths and temple gatherings, with palm branches being waved by the people.

After the feast and dedication celebration King Solomon completed the temple in the eighth Jewish month, and this corresponds with November 1925. The aforementioned resolution, "Message of Hope," addressed as it was "To All People of Good Will", began to be distributed by the millions of copies all over the earth on Saturday, October 31, 1925, and continued for some time thereafter, and thus the "Message of Hope" was taken to the "people of good will". Did the Lord direct this matter? Surely!

TEMPLE SERVANTS

Another prophetic picture of the "other sheep" of the Lord who will form the great multitude is that concerning the Nethinim who served at the temple. When the remnant of the Israelites came from Babylon to Jerusalem to rebuild the temple Nethinim were assigned to help them and serve with them. The Nethinim were not Israelites, but in serving with the Israelites they completely separated themselves from the non-Israelite nations and took their stand and their places with God's covenant people. (Ezra 2: 1-70; 8: 20; Nehemiah 10: 1, 28, 29) *Nethinim* means "given ones". They were servants who assisted at the temple service. In this they pictured the "other sheep" of the Lord who form the great multitude. The name "Nethinim" is properly applied to any helpers that come from any nation and devote themselves to the service of Almighty God. (See *The Watchtower*, 1936, pages 264, 265, ¶ 31-34.)

QUEEN OF SHEBA

King Solomon possessed much power and great riches and occupied a position of glory, and in this he was a type of Christ Jesus, the King upon his throne and who is the "Greater than Solomon". (Matthew 12:42) The queen of Sheba was from the land of South Arabia. She had heard of the glory and riches and wisdom of King Solomon, and she made a long journey with her retinue of servants to gain firsthand information concerning the same. "And when the queen of Sheba heard of the fame of Solomon, concerning the name of the Lord, she came to prove him with hard questions. And she came to Jerusalem with a very great train, with camels that bare spices, and very much gold, and precious stones: and when she was come to Solomon, she communed with him of all that was in her heart. And Solomon told her all her questions; there was not any thing hid from the king, which he told her not. And when the queen of Sheba had seen all Solomon's wisdom, and the house that he had built, and the meat of his table, and the sitting of his servants, and the attendance of his ministers, and their apparel, and his cupbearers, and his ascent by which he went up unto the house of the Lord; there was no more spirit in her. And she said to the king, It was a true report that I heard in mine own land of thy acts and of thy wisdom. Howbeit I believed not the words, until I came, and mine eyes had seen it; and, behold, the half was not told me; thy wisdom and prosperity exceedeth the fame which I heard." "Blessed be the Lord thy God, which delighted in thee, to set thee on the throne of Israel; because the Lord loved Israel for ever, therefore made he thee king, to do judgment and justice. And she gave the king an hundred and twenty talents of gold, and of spices very great store, and precious stones: there came no more such abundance of spices as these which the queen of Sheba gave to king Solomon."—1 Kings 10: 1-7, 9, 10.

That was a picture of the people of good will toward Jehovah God who receive some knowledge of God and Christ Jesus in his glory and who go themselves to seek and to serve the Lord and who give all they have, that is to say, their full substance and support, to the King Christ Jesus and his kingdom, and who have part thereafter in promoting the kingdom interests.

SAILORS WITH JONAH

Jehovah God commanded his prophet Jonah to go to Nineveh, which was a very wicked city, and to there preach, giving warning to the inhabitants of the impending destruction upon the city. Nineveh pictured the religious organizations of the earth, and particularly "Christendom". Instead of obeying God's commandments Jonah attempted to flee to Tarshish, a town of Spain, and for that purpose he went to Joppa and there went aboard a ship that was sailing for Tarshish. (See book of Jonah, considered in *The Watchtower*, issues January 15 and February 1 and 15, 1938.)

A great storm arose, and the ship in which Jonah was sailing was about to be wrecked. The sailors who manned the ship became greatly afraid. An effort was made to determine who on the ship was at fault, causing the evil of the storm to befall them; and to ascertain this, lots were cast: "And the lot fell upon Jonah." Upon being questioned Jonah told the men of the ship that God had commanded him to go to Nineveh and that he had disobeyed, and that the storm was the result; and, he being to blame, he requested to be cast into the sea. But instead of cast-

ing him into the sea, "the men rowed hard to
bring [the ship] to the land," but were defeated
in their efforts. Up to that time, it appears, the
seamen had never known of Almighty God; but
hearing from Jonah that Jehovah God had sent
him and that Jonah was his servant, and not
wishing to do anything wrong or to shed innocent blood by throwing Jonah overboard, they
began to pray unto God. "Wherefore they cried
unto the Lord, and said, We beseech thee, O
Lord, we beseech thee, let us not perish for this
man's life, and lay not upon us innocent blood;
for thou, O Lord, hast done as it pleased thee."
(Jonah 1:14) Thus the sailors began to show

Miraculous
deliverance

that they were of good will toward God and had
faith in him. Jonah was cast into the sea. "Then
the men feared the Lord exceedingly, and
offered a sacrifice unto the Lord, and made
vows." (Jonah 1:16) The sailors on that ship
were a type or picture of the men of good will
or "other sheep" of the Lord of the present time,
who, continuing faithful, will go to make up the
great multitude.

NINEVITES

Jonah would, of course, have perished in the
sea, but God performed a great miracle in his
behalf: "Now the Lord had prepared a great fish
to swallow up Jonah. And Jonah was in the
belly of the fish three days and three nights."
(Jonah 1:17) God caused that fish to land Jonah
on the coast toward Nineveh, and again Jonah
was commanded by the Lord to go to Nineveh
and preach God's message as He had commanded. Here Jonah pictured those consecrated persons who are in a covenant to do God's will and
who are commissioned and commanded to preach
"this gospel of the kingdom" to all the world as
"a witness". (Matthew 24:14) Jonah then obeyed
Jehovah and went to Nineveh and preached
as commanded by telling the people that within
a short space of time Jehovah God would destroy that city. The Ninevites gave heed to that
warning: "So the people of Nineveh believed
God, and proclaimed a fast, and put on sackcloth, from the greatest of them even to the least
of them."—Jonah 3:5.

Those repentant Ninevites pictured the people of good will toward God who are now in the

land of "Christendom", and who show faith in God and in Christ Jesus by seeking him and doing his will. The prophetic picture of Jonah and the people of Nineveh began to have fulfillment after the year 1914, and particularly after 1918. Since 1918 Jehovah's witnesses have been continuously preaching "this gospel of the kingdom" throughout the land of "Christendom" and many people of good will have given heed, while the greater number have rejected the truth. The clergy, the religious leaders, and their close allies of "Christendom" were foreshadowed by the religious leaders of the Israelites at the time when Jesus was on earth, and which religionists of the Jews refused to hear God's warning given at the mouth of Christ Jesus. In this the religionists of the Jews pictured the wicked and unrepentant of the organization of "Christendom". The Lord Jesus strongly contrasted the people of Israel, who were in a covenant to do God's will, with the repentant Ninevites, who were not in a covenant to do God's will, when he used these words: "The men of Nineveh shall rise in judgment with this generation, and shall condemn it; because they repented at the preaching of Jonas; and, behold, a greater than Jonas is here."—Matthew 12:41.

Among the religionists that are in "Christendom" at the present time, and that have been associated with religious organizations, are many persons of good will who have been kept in ignorance of God and his purpose. Those persons of good will were pictured by the repentant Ninevites. Hearing the kingdom message that is brought to them by Jehovah's witnesses, such people of good will fear the Lord and turn to him. Those repentant ones of Nineveh, therefore, picture the "other sheep" of the Lord, all of whom upon learning of the Lord and his kingdom must repent, that is to say, they must change their course of action, turn away from religious institutions and follow and obey the commands of Christ Jesus, the great Vindicator of Jehovah.

"SHIPS"

Another prophetic picture recorded in the Scriptures foretelling the Lord's "other sheep" who will form the great multitude is found in Psalm 107. When Jonah attempted to flee to Tarshish he took passage upon a ship manned by those who were not Israelites but who later learned about God and his purpose. These men were going to sea in ships. In the prophecy it is written: "They that go down to the sea in ships, that do business in great waters; these see the works of the Lord, and his wonders in the deep."—Psalm 107: 23, 24.

Those seamen here mentioned picture persons of good will who go to make up the great multitude. Symbolically the "sea" means the peoples of the earth who are alienated from God and who bear up, support and carry Satan's commercial organization. Ships are vessels that carry men upon the sea to do the commercial work. Many good persons are engaged in doing work upon the seas, and these "many waters" or seas symbolically picture the people alienated from God. (Jeremiah 51: 13; Revelation 17: 15) Jehovah's witnesses at the command of the Lord carry the message of the kingdom to the people pictured by the sea, and those "mariners", or sailors, who work upon the "sea", hear the message of the kingdom. The time has now come when "they that go down to the sea in ships" have the opportunity to hear the message of the kingdom and they, being of good will, do hear and they see God's "wonders in the deep". They begin to have an appreciation of his marvelous provisions for the salvation of men. They cry unto God, and he hears them and shows his mercy toward them (Psalm 107:28-30); and, continuing thus to seek righteousness and meekness, as the Lord commands, they will be a part of the great multitude, and thus "they that go down to the sea in ships" are a picture of that class of the Lord's people.

"ABOMINATIONS" IN "CHRISTENDOM"

At the ninth chapter of Ezekiel is recorded a prophetic picture of the "abominations" that refer to the wickedness done in "Christendom" at the present time. That symbolic or prophetic picture shows six men, each of whom is armed with a weapon of destruction called a "slaughter weapon", standing ready to destroy the city, that is, the organization called "Christendom". The city of Jerusalem is the city mentioned in the picture, and symbolically represents the organization of "Christendom", which latter organization claims to serve God but in fact serves the Devil. Among those six men is another one, "clothed with linen, with a writer's inkhorn by his side." This one pictures Jehovah's witnesses, the faithful followers of Christ Jesus who go to make up the remnant of the Lord now on the earth; while the six men with slaughter weapons picture the invisible forces of the Lord that will destroy "Christendom" at Armageddon. In the prophetic picture God's command to the man clothed with linen with the inkhorn by his side is that he go through the city and put a mark "upon the foreheads of the men that sigh, and that cry, for all the abominations that [are] done in the midst thereof"; antitypically meaning the abominations done within "Christendom".

This part of the picture shows that Jehovah's witnesses, the little flock or remnant, must go throughout "Christendom" and declare God's message concerning his name and his kingdom; and, by so doing, they put "a mark upon the foreheads" of the persons who desire to learn the truth concerning Jehovah's purpose. The forehead represents the seat of knowledge and means antitypically that the persons on earth of good will toward God receive a knowledge of God's truth and give heed thereto. There are within "Christendom" today many persons of good will who have been associated with the religious systems because they did not know anything better. They observe the many abominations committed by the religionists contrary to God's Word. For instance, they see the religious leaders or clergymen indulging in the crooked politics of the world, and in many unscrupulous and unrighteous schemes, teachings and practices. They see the clergy and hear them proclaiming false doctrines and resorting to lies and deception in order to work and carry on a racket by which the people are robbed. For instance, the Roman Catholic Hierarchy now works in full accord with the dictators in an effort to rule the world arbitrarily and take away all the liberties of the people. They foment and carry on wicked wars and all manner of cruel schemes resulting injuriously to the people and to the dishonor of God's name. The Hierarchy teaches such false doctrines as "purgatory", which, in effect, is that a person, when he dies, goes to "purgatory" and is there suffering conscious torment, and that the priests can offer prayers and relieve the dead one supposed to be the sufferer of that punishment; and this falsehood is used to extort money from the living friends of the deceased. Seeing these many abominable things committed, the honest and sincere persons in those religious institutions cry unto the Lord. Being of good will toward God they desire a knowledge of him and his righteous ways, and the Lord hears their cry and sends his message of truth to them by and through his faithful servants. When these persons of good will learn of God and his King and kingdom they readily turn to him and serve him and his King. Therefore it is made clearly to appear that those who now sigh and cry because of the abominations done in "Christendom", and who receive the truth and obey the Lord, are the "other sheep" who, thereafter continuing faithful, will form the great multitude.

FRIENDLY SLAVE

Jehovah sent his faithful prophet Jeremiah to give warning to Jerusalem of her impending

destruction, and in this Jeremiah pictured Jehovah's witnesses, who are sent to give warning
to "Christendom", the antitypical Jerusalem, of
her impending destruction at Armageddon. Because of his faithfulness in declaring the message of Jehovah Jeremiah was thrown into
prison at the instance of the religionists. In that
filthy prison a friend appeared.

Jehovah has very wonderfully and in a simple manner pictured those who put their trust
in him, and not in worldly powers. In the house
of King Zedekiah was an Ethiopian, whose name
was Ebed-melech. His name means "servant"
or "slave". He was a eunuch. (Jeremiah 38:7)
He was not an Israelite; and this is made certain
by the fact that he had been sterilized and made
a eunuch, which was contrary to the law of
Israel. He was in effect a prisoner of unfaithful
Jerusalem, being a trusty and a harmless one,
who had general access to the king's house to
serve the king. He was not at all in sympathy
with the harsh deeds of the ruling house of Jerusalem, and therefore pictured a class subjected
to "Christendom" which is not at all in sympathy
with the harsh and cruel methods employed by
"Christendom". Being a slave, this Ethiopian
could not take the advice of Jeremiah and go
away to the Chaldeans. He saw the great injustice that had been done to Jeremiah. He had
faith in Jeremiah's God. Therefore he pictured
the "other sheep" of the Lord Jesus, and hence
pictures the same class of persons as did Jonadab. (2 Kings 10:15-23) As an Ethiopian he
symbolized a natural sinner who desires to learn
of God. He had heard of God's purposes through

the preaching of Jeremiah. This is in harmony
with the words of the psalmist: "Ethiopia shall
soon stretch out her
hands unto God."—Psalm
68:31.

The king was sitting in
the Benjamin gate, prob-
ably holding court there,
and it was then that
Ebed-melech, the Ethi-
opian, had the opportu-
nity to publicly approach
the king and speak to him
in open court. In doing
this the Ethiopian pic-
tured those persons, oth-
er than the spiritual Is-
raelites, taking their
stand on the side of Je-
hovah God and speaking
in favor of Jehovah's witnesses. Correspondingly,
early in the year 1919,
and while the represent-
atives of the Lord's or-
ganization were in pris-
on, many thousands of
persons of good will to-
ward God and his people
gladly signed a petition
to the govern-
ment that the
Society's serv-
ants might be
given a hear-

Ebed-melech rescues Jeremiah

ing and released from prison. (See *The Watchtower,* 1919, page 101.) These also picture the prisoners in Babylon, other than the anointed, coming forth and showing themselves and manifesting their sympathies on the side of those who served Jehovah God.—Isaiah 49:9.

Approaching the king, Ebed-melech the Ethiopian addressed him and said: "My lord the king, these men have done evil in all that they have done to Jeremiah the prophet, whom they have cast into the dungeon; and he is like to die for hunger in the place where he is; for there is no more bread in the city." (Jeremiah 38:9) The king heard his speech and then commanded the Ethiopian to take thirty men to assist him and to draw Jeremiah out of the dungeon. (Jeremiah 38:10) This corresponds with the release of God's people who were then in prison. The Ethiopian, with the other men, proceeded to make arrangements to take Jeremiah out of the dungeon and to do so in the most comfortable manner that they could, thus preventing the least possible injury to him. (Jeremiah 38:11,12) This shows that antitypically the faithful followers of Christ Jesus were imprisoned, and were visited by persons of good will, who are commended by the Lord Jesus in these words: "I was in prison, and ye came unto me." (Matthew 25:36) The Ethiopian showed much kindness to Jeremiah in putting old clouts under his arms to lift him out of the prison. The clergy had done exactly the contrary when they shoved Jehovah's servants into prison. In taking this kind action toward Jehovah's servants the

Ethiopian probably had in mind the words of the psalmist, as set forth in The Psalms chapters 142, 102, and 69. Those of good will drew the servants of the Lord out of prison, and thus "the Lord looseth the prisoners".—Psalm 146: 7.

Neither the religionists nor the politicians lifted the Lord's servants out of the dungeon. No effort was made to do so until the people of good will filed an urgent petition with the public officials. These pictured the Jonadabs or "other sheep" class that showed sympathy for and interest in God's faithful servants, whom the Lord released from prison in 1919. This releasing refers to all of those who were faithful, some who were actually in prison, and others under restraint. "So they drew up Jeremiah with cords, and took him up out of the dungeon; and Jeremiah remained in the court of the prison." (Jeremiah 38: 13) From the time of their release until now, Jehovah's witnesses have been under surveillance by the ruling factors, and particularly at the instance of the clergy, who increasingly try to limit and circumscribe the freedom of activity of the faithful servants of Jehovah. God's witnesses go on regardless of this surveillance and restraint. Jeremiah was in the court of the prison until Jerusalem was taken, which foreshadowed the surveillance of God's people now. But did he stop testifying to the name of the Lord? Not by any means!—Jeremiah 39: 15-18.

SUPPORTERS OF MORDECAI

Another striking picture foretelling the "other sheep" of the Lord is this: Mordecai, a Jew,

together with many others, was a captive in
Babylon. He brought up his cousin Hadassah,
otherwise called Esther. Cyrus the Persian
overthrew Babylon and released the captive
Jews. Cyrus was succeeded by Ahasuerus. Mordecai and Esther resided at Shushan, that city
being the residence of the king. Ahasuerus the
king did not know that Mordecai and Esther
were Jews until after Esther had become his
queen. Haman was an Agagite, against whom
God had previously entered his adverse judgment. (1 Samuel 15: 2, 3, 8) Haman held a responsible position under the king. (Esther 3: 1)
Mordecai, being a faithful Jew and loyal to
Jehovah, refused to bow before Haman as the
other people were required to do. Mordecai in-
sisted on obeying God, and not men. He was like
those who refuse to salute flags or hail men today. Being angry, Haman formed a conspiracy
to have Mordecai put to death; and that conspiracy included all the Jews within the king's
realm, and, of course, included Esther the queen.
The king, at the instance of Haman, and without knowing his queen was included, signed a
decree to have the Jews destroyed.—Esther
3: 4-15.

The duplicity and conspiracy of Haman were
brought to the attention of the king, who ordered
Haman to be hanged; which was done. (Esther
7: 10) The law of the Persians was such
that a decree once signed by the king must remain unchangeable; therefore the decree of the
king for the slaughter of the Jews must stand.
In order, however, to offset that decree for the
slaughter of the Jews, the king issued another

decree providing for the self-defense of the Jews: "Wherein the king granted the Jews which were in every city to gather themselves together, and to stand for their life, to destroy, to slay, and to cause to perish, all the power of the people and province that would assault them, both little ones and women, and to take the spoil of them for a prey." (Esther 8:11) The day was set for the fight to take place: "And in every province, and in every city, whithersoever the king's commandment and his decree came, the Jews had joy and gladness, a feast and a good day. And many of the people of the land became Jews; for the fear of the Jews fell upon them." (Esther 8:17) "The Jews gathered themselves together in their cities throughout all the provinces of the king Ahasuerus, to lay hand on such as sought their hurt; and no man could withstand them; for the fear of them fell upon all people. And all the rulers of the provinces, and the lieutenants, and the deputies, and officers of the king, helped the Jews; because the fear of Mordecai fell upon them." (Esther 9:2, 3) Many of the people of the Persian empire, seeing that God was with the Jews, had fear of God, and therefore those Persians became Jews, and in order to do so they must show their faith in God and agree to be bound by God's law. Those Persians, therefore, who voluntarily became Jews before the battle began between the Jews and Haman's crowd pictured the people of good will of the present day who turn away from religionists and turn to God and his King, Christ Jesus, and who do so before the battle of the great day of God Almighty begins. Thus is again shown

God's loving-kindness exhibited toward those who will form the great multitude. (For further explanation see book *Preservation,* pages 9-168.)

VIRGIN COMPANIONS

In the prophecy recorded at the 45th Psalm is found a description of the assembly of Jehovah's royal family in the palace of the King Eternal. Both the "little flock" and their "companions", the "other sheep", are shown in that prophetic picture: "The king's daughter within the palace is all glorious; her clothing is inwrought with gold. She shall be led unto the king in broidered work; the virgins her companions that follow her shall be brought unto thee."—Psalm 45: 13, 14, *A.R.V.*

The beginning of the fulfillment of this prophetic picture was at the coming of the Lord Jesus to the temple of Jehovah, when he gathers unto himself his faithful followers, including the remnant.—2 Thessalonians 2: 1.

A "virgin" is one completely separated from Satan's organization and fully devoted to God, and this class is not limited to spirit-begotten ones. Having taken their stand openly and completely on the side of Jehovah and his organization, and trusting entirely in the shed blood of Christ Jesus, and devoting themselves unselfishly to the Lord, they are chaste ones, and they defile not their purity or virginity by consorting with the Devil's organization. Says the prophet: 'The virgin her companions that follow her [the bride] are brought forth.' First the bride class is gathered to the royal house; and then, by the Lord's invitation, foreshadowed by Jehu's inviting Jonadab into his chariot, others associate themselves with the Lord's royal house. That means that they go along with and are following after the bride company, which is now represented by the remnant on the earth.

This prophetic picture therefore shows the daughter of the King Eternal, who is the bride of Christ, Jehovah's anointed King, and that the companions who follow after her are the ones who go to make up the great multitude.

MOUNTAIN OF JEHOVAH

In the Scriptures the word *mountain* is used as a symbol of the kingdom of Jehovah God, with Christ Jesus as the Chief One and Head thereof. The "mountain of the Lord's house" is the exalted royal family, consisting of Christ Jesus and his bride. In the prophecy it is written: "And it shall come to pass in the last days, that the mountain of the Lord's house shall be established in the top of the mountains, and shall be exalted above the hills; and all nations shall flow unto it." (Isaiah 2:2) The people of all nations who obtain salvation must come to the house of the Lord to worship there; that is to say, they must believe on and worship Jehovah God and the Lord Jesus Christ, his chief instrument. (Philippians 2:10, 11) We are now in the "last days", and the people of good will are coming from all nations, seeking the Lord. "And many people shall go and say, Come ye, and let us go up to the mountain of the Lord, to the house of the God of Jacob; and he will teach us of his ways, and we will walk in his paths; for out of Zion shall go forth the law, and the

word of the Lord from Jerusalem." (Isaiah
2:3) This prophecy foretells the "other sheep"
of the Lord being gathered to him, and who,
continuing faithful, will form the great multitude. They now seek the Lord that they may find
protection and salvation.

THE PRISONERS AND THE ISLES

Other prophetic pictures in the Bible disclose
the great multitude that come to serve Jehovah
and his King, and amongst which are those symbolized by "prisoners", and "the isles afar off",
and as children of Zion. When the Israelites
were in Babylon as captives others who were
non-Jews, who associated with the Jews and who
were kind to them, pictured the great multitude.

The "elect" "servant" of Jehovah is Christ
Jesus. (Isaiah 42:1; Matthew 12:17, 18) Jehovah, addressing his "elect" "servant", as set
forth in the prophecy, says: "That thou mayest
say to the prisoners, Go forth; to them that are
in darkness, Shew yourselves. They shall feed
in the ways, and their pastures shall be in all
high places." (Isaiah 49:9) The word *prisoners*
used in this prophecy, being in the plural, refers
to more than one. Those prisoners are the many
persons who have been held in restraint by the
religious organization of Satan, which organization is designated under the term *Babylon*.
The "prisoners" are those persons of good will
toward God, who, because of being kept in ignorance, are "in darkness"; but in due time such
persons hear the gospel of the kingdom and they
come into the light. Concerning those who do
hear and give heed and who continue faithfully

to serve the Lord, he says: "They shall feed in the ways, and their pastures shall be in all high places"; the "high places" here meaning the kingdom heights. They no longer sit in darkness, neither are they hungry for spiritual food, but they are led and fed by God and his good Shepherd, Christ Jesus: "They shall not hunger nor thirst; neither shall the heat nor sun smite them: for he that hath mercy on them shall lead them, even by the springs of water shall he guide them."—Isaiah 49:10; Revelation 7:16, 17.

For his name's sake Jehovah saves those who honestly and diligently seek him. To them he brings salvation through his elect servant, Christ Jesus. To this class he speaks through his great Prophet. Christ Jesus, the great Prophet, is here represented as speaking to such and using the symbol of "isles" as representing them. "Listen, O isles, unto me; and hearken, ye people, from far." (Isaiah 49:1) These "isles" here picture those who seek the Lord and who desire a righteous government. There are giant commercial, maritime powers who carry on traffic selfishly. There are also legitimate-business men in the world who have unwittingly been supporters of the Devil's organization and who are out of heart harmony with the wickedness of that organization, and these are pictured as isles which "isles shall wait for his law". (Isaiah 42:4) Receiving some knowledge of God's purpose, and having faith in God and in Christ Jesus, these honest-hearted, legitimate-business men described as isles turn to the Lord, and concerning them it is written: "My righteousness is near; my salvation is gone forth, and

mine arms shall judge the people: the isles shall
wait upon me, and on mine arm shall they trust."
(Isaiah 51:5; 60:9) It is to those honest and
sincere ones that Jehovah sends his witnesses
with his message concerning his King and his
kingdom. (Isaiah 66:19) These isles ultimately
will form a part of the great multitude, and concerning which it is written: "The multitude of
isles be glad." (Psalm 97:1) This means that
the great multitude rejoice when they learn of
God's kingdom and their opportunity of receiving salvation. Those thus symbolized under the
word *isles* the prophet declares shall in due time
worship and contribute toward the service of the
Most High under his King, Christ Jesus, saying:
"And [they] shall worship him, every one from
his place, even all the isles of the nations."—
Zephaniah 2:11, *A.R.V.*

TEN MEN

In symbolic language the prophecy of God
describes ten men taking hold of the skirt of one:
"Yea, many people and strong nations shall
come to seek the Lord of hosts in Jerusalem,
and to pray before the Lord. Thus saith the Lord
of hosts, In those days it shall come to pass, that
ten men shall take hold, out of all languages of
the nations, even shall take hold of the skirt of
him that is a Jew, saying, We will go with you;
for we have heard that God is with you."—
Zechariah 8:22, 23.

The word "ten" represents completeness of
things pertaining to the earth. The word "Jew"
in this text is from the word "Judah" and means
"one who praises Jehovah", and refers specifi-

cally to Christ Jesus, "the Lion of the tribe of
Juda" and the King of all who follow him and
serve Jehovah God. His faithful followers yet
on the earth are called "the feet of him". (Isaiah
52: 7, 8) Therefore the "Jew" refers to Christ
Jesus and the faithful members of his body, the
witnesses of Jehovah on the earth. In this
prophecy two companies are shown to be closely knit together as companions; namely, the
'elect servant' class, the remnant; and their companions, the Jonadabs or "other sheep" of the
Lord, who will form the great multitude.

The prophecy above quoted discloses the people of good will coming from many parts of the
earth, saying to each other: "Let us go speedily
to pray before the Lord, and to seek the Lord
of hosts." (Zechariah 8: 21) This they do in the
day of Jehovah, that is to say, the present time
after the coming of the Lord Jesus to the temple. Then the prophet adds that "ten men",
meaning all the men on earth who are of good
will and who will compose the great multitude,
"shall take hold of the skirt of him that is a
Jew," meaning they will take hold of Christ
Jesus. Since the skirt hangs down in close prox-
imity to the feet, the "Jew" here also represents
the remnant of the faithful witnesses of Jehovah, which remnant are "the feet of him", Christ.
(Isaiah 52: 7) Coming to associate with the remnant, the Jonadab class or "other sheep" of the
Lord say: "We will go with you; for we have
heard that God is with you." They openly declare themselves on the side of God and his King
and kingdom. They bend their backs and their
knees to the Lord Jesus Christ and praise him.

They will take hold upon the Lord, and declare their heart devotion to God and Christ Jesus the King. They are not ashamed to publicly declare themselves on the side of Christ and Jehovah. They do not hesitate, but delight, to be associated with the remnant of Jehovah's witnesses. In this prophetic picture the remnant take the lead and the "other sheep", pictured by the "ten", follow with them, all together serving the Lord. All of these devote all their substance, energy and everything to Jehovah's King and kingdom, serving faithfully to his praise.

"FEAST OF INGATHERING"

The Jews were commanded by the Lord to keep the seven-day feast on the seventh month 'when they gathered their fruits of the land', and it was called the "feast of ingathering". (Exodus 23:16; Leviticus 23:39) (See *The Watchtower,* April 15, 1936.) It was called in the Scriptures "the feast of Jehovah", and foreshadowed a feast of rejoicing in vindication of Jehovah's name. It being the feast of "ingathering", its fulfillment in antitype takes place at the time the Lord Jesus gathers his elect to the temple and then begins to gather unto himself his "other sheep" that will form the great multitude. Thus the feast of ingathering pictured the gathering of the great multitude, and which feast is now in course of fulfillment.

It was at the feast of ingathering, or "feast of tabernacles", that Jesus showed the clear distinction between religionists, who are on the side of the Devil, and those of honest heart, who took the side of Jesus. (John 8:43, 44) The religious

Jews not only rejected Jesus, but sought to kill him. Many of the common people believed on him, and Jesus assured them that if they continued in the truth they should be free. (John 8: 31, 32, 36) By associating himself with the feast of ingathering (John 7: 2, 14) Jesus proves conclusively that he fulfilled the type in miniature and that its fulfillment in completeness begins while his "feet" members are on the earth and during the time that these are gathered by the Lord at the temple. As the officer of his Father, Jesus, at the last of the feast of ingathering, boldly cried out to the people, saying: "If any man thirst, let him come unto me, and drink." (John 7: 37) So now the Lord Jesus is at the temple, and to those who would be of his "other sheep" he says: "But the LORD is in his holy temple; let all the earth keep silence before him."—Habakkuk 2: 20.

At the feast of ingathering the people were required to dwell in booths, that is to say, a temporary dwelling place. In symbol this means that the people who are gathered unto the Lord, that is, the little flock and the "other sheep", are not of this wicked world over which Satan exercises power, but are for the kingdom of God under Christ and are temporarily dwelling in the present world condition, waiting for the establishment of the kingdom. They do not bow down to and worship men or man-made things, but their allegiance, worship and devotion are wholly to Jehovah God and his kingdom. They recognize Jehovah God and Christ Jesus as the "higher powers", and they refuse to compromise with any part of Satan's organization.

HAILING JESUS THE KING

Shortly before his crucifixion Jesus rode into Jerusalem on the back of an ass, presenting himself to the Jews as King, even as God had foretold by his prophet. (Zechariah 9:9; Matthew 21:5) Great multitudes of the common people hailed him, waving palm branches and saying: "Blessed is he that cometh in the name of [Jehovah]." (Matthew 21:8,9; Psalm 118:26) In this another prophetic picture was made foretelling the coming of Christ Jesus the King, at which time he gathers unto himself his "other sheep" who form the great multitude, and which multitude are shown as waving palm branches and shouting the praises of Jehovah God and Christ Jesus and attributing all protection and salvation to Jehovah and to the King Christ Jesus.—Revelation 7:9.

OTHER PICTURES

In the prophecy of Zephaniah 2:1-3 hereinbefore considered, there appears a class of persons who gather themselves together and who are not desired by the worldlings. These associate themselves with Jehovah's remnant, and they seek righteousness and meekness; and such are the "other sheep" of the Lord's flock and, continuing faithful, will constitute the great multitude. These are the ones that have the promise of Jehovah's protection at Armageddon. Jesus specifically foretells of his "other sheep" aside from the elect members of his body, and which must be gathered and which are the ones that form the great multitude:

"And other sheep I have, which are not of this fold; them also I must bring, and they shall hear my voice; and there shall be one fold, and one shepherd."—John 10:16.

The faithful men of olden times, among whom were Abraham, Isaac and Jacob, are pictured as dwelling forever with the Lord on the earth, and in this connection Jesus said: "And I say unto you, That many shall come from the east and west, and shall sit down with Abraham, and Isaac, and Jacob, in the kingdom of heaven."

The multitudes here mentioned by the Lord as coming from many parts of the earth to sit down with the faithful men above mentioned foretell the "other sheep" of the Lord who form the great multitude; and this is recorded for the consolation of those today who love God and Christ Jesus.—Matthew 8:11.

WORSHIPERS

The tabernacle built in the wilderness by men under God's command had but one court to which all the people at times had access. (Leviticus 1:1-9) The same was true with reference to the temple at Jerusalem. God's prophet Ezekiel was given a vision of the temple, or organization, where all those assemble who will worship Jehovah God during the reign of Christ. In that vision the multitudes are shown in the "outer court", which court was trod by the priests and the people in general who worship Jehovah God; and this is another prophetic picture of the great multitude assembled before the throne worshiping God and his King.—Ezekiel 40:17; 46:3, 9, 21-24.

"GOOD WILL"

By and through his faithful prophets Jehovah foretold the birth of a child who should become the Savior and King of the world and upon whose shoulder the government and peace would forever rest. (Isaiah 9:6, 7) The time came for the fulfillment of that great prophecy to begin. Relative to that part of the prophecy concerning the birth of Jesus, the record is found disclosing that humble shepherds, watching their flocks in the field, were permitted to be witnesses to Jehovah, and concerning which it is written: "And, lo, the angel of the Lord came upon them, and the glory of the Lord shone round about them; and they were sore afraid. And the angel said unto them, Fear not; for, behold, I bring you good tidings of great joy, which shall be to all people. For unto you is born this day, in the city of David, a Saviour, which is Christ the Lord."—Luke 2:9-11.

Immediately following that announcement to the shepherds there appeared a host of angels praising God and saying: "Glory in the highest unto God! and on earth peace, among men of good-will." (Luke 2:14, *Rotherham*) Here, according to *Rotherham,* the text is properly rendered. The promise is given only to "men of good-will", that these shall dwell together on earth in peace. Men of good will are otherwise spoken of in the Scriptures as forming the great multitude.

"SHEEP AND GOATS"

In the year 1914 the Lord Jesus was enthroned as king of the world. (Matthew 24:3-14)

Three and one-half years thereafter Christ Jesus the King appeared at the temple of Jehovah and gathered unto himself his faithful followers and commissioned them and sent them forth to 'preach this gospel of the kingdom'; and thus is marked the beginning of the Lord's judgment of the nations, and concerning which it is written: "And before him shall be gathered all nations; and he shall separate them one from another, as a shepherd divideth his sheep from the goats; and he shall set the sheep on his right hand, but the goats on the left."—Matthew 25: 32, 33.

This identifies specifically two classes of persons. One class, being extremely selfish and who oppress others and persecute those who serve God, are designated under the symbol of "goats". The other class, being kind to God's people, who love righteousness, are designated as "sheep". These latter ones are good and do good unto those who serve Jehovah as his witnesses. Such persons of good will are the "other sheep" of the Lord, which he gathers unto himself and who, continuing faithful, form the great multitude. The statement of Christ Jesus, the great Prophet, concerning these two classes, draws a strong contrast between the ultraselfish, cruel ones, and the persons of good will. That prophecy is now in course of fulfillment, and has been since the coming of the Lord to his temple. During that time the faithful followers of Christ Jesus, otherwise known as Jehovah's witnesses, have been going about from place to place in obedience to the Lord's command, telling the people that the kingdom of heaven is here and

that the only means of salvation and everlasting
blessings is to be found by those who turn to and
faithfully support Christ Jesus the King. At
the same time, in obedience to the Lord's commandments, these witnesses give warning of the
impending disaster that shall fall upon the
world at Armageddon. Therefore this is the time
of great emergency, because Armageddon is
very near.

All nations, and particularly the rulers thereof, see something terrible about to befall the
world and, not knowing what it is and having
no faith in God and in his Word, such rulers
rush to the Roman Catholic Hierarchy, and
particularly the pope, to seek his advice, that
they may have consolation and that their
fears may be allayed. This is particularly emphasized in recent times by the various rulers
of the nations that are dictatorial, making a
pilgrimage to Rome or Vatican City. The Roman
Catholic Hierarchy of Authority constitutes the
leading religionists on the earth, and that Hierarchy is the bitter enemy of Jehovah's witnesses
because those witnesses of the Lord announce
God's kingdom under Christ. The Hierarchy of
Authority selfishly and wrongfully claim that
the Papacy shall rule the world as the spiritual
part of the arbitrary governments. Hence that
religious organization is the Devil's chief representative on the earth. The Devil uses the Hierarchy and allies to persecute the Lord and to
abase His kingdom and all who support his kingdom. It is well known by all that the Roman
Catholic Hierarchy and allies now bitterly persecute and oppose the true followers of Christ

Jesus who are the witnesses of Jehovah and his kingdom. Those religious organizations and persecutors the Lord Jesus designates as "goats", and his words concerning the same are, to wit: "For I was an hungred, and ye gave me no meat: I was thirsty, and ye gave me no drink. Then shall he answer them, saying, Verily I say unto you, Inasmuch as ye did it not to one of the least of these, ye did it not to me." (Matthew 25:42, 45) Thus Jesus declares that whatsoever is done to his faithful followers he counts as done to himself, and he takes note thereof accordingly.

The people of good will now on earth desire to see right done, and all refuse to have anything to do with such persecution of Jehovah's witnesses. Many of such people are under the Roman Catholic Hierarchy because they have long been associated with that religious organization. Seeing the injustice heaped upon Jehovah's witnesses by the Hierarchy, those persons of good will toward the Lord turn away from that religio-political organization and seek the Lord and his service. They observe the wicked things done; and seeing Jehovah's witnesses are harmless and that they are doing good unto the people as God has commanded and carrying the message of consolation to the hungry souls, those persons of good will, whether they be Catholic, Protestant, or outside of all religious organizations, take advantage of every opportunity to do good unto the true followers of Christ Jesus, Jehovah's witnesses. When those of the faithful remnant come to them, such persons of good will will treat them kindly and minister unto their needs, and the Lord designates such persons of good will under the symbol of "sheep", and to them he says, in this prophetic parable now in course of fulfillment: "For I was an hungred, and ye gave me meat; I was thirsty, and ye gave me drink; I was a stranger, and ye took me in; naked, and ye clothed me; I was sick, and ye visited me; I was in prison, and ye came unto me. Then shall the righteous answer him, saying, Lord, when saw we thee an hungred, and fed thee? or thirsty, and gave thee drink? When saw we thee a stranger, and took thee in? or naked, and clothed thee? Or when saw we thee sick, or in prison, and came unto thee? And the King shall answer and say unto them, Verily I say unto you, Inasmuch as ye have done it unto one of the least of these my brethren, ye have done it unto me." (Matthew 25:35-40) At Armageddon the end of the "goats" will be destruction, whereas the "sheep" class will receive from the Lord protection and salvation.

IDENTIFIED

To John, the faithful servant of the Lord Jesus Christ, was granted a vision pertaining to the kingdom of God. Christ Jesus showed John what must come to pass, and John made a record thereof, which is called The Revelation, or Apocalypse. (See Revelation 1:1-3.) Here John, the faithful witness of the Lord, pictured or represented the faithful followers of Christ Jesus who are now called "the remnant" of the elect class while on the earth. That vision from the Lord disclosed to John that "the body of Christ" is made up of Christ Jesus, the Head, and 144,000 faithful and true followers. (Revelation 7:4-8; 14:1-3) Such members the Lord began to gather to himself at his coming to the temple in 1918. The vision then disclosed to John many others coming to the Lord, and, he learning that these are not of the "elect" "servant" class of the body of Christ, inquiry is made as to who they are. The information is then given that such picture the "great multitude", and thus the great multitude is identified. Note how well this vision corresponds with the pictures Jehovah long ago made and caused to be recorded in his Word concerning the great multitude as recorded by John: "After this I beheld, and, lo, a great multitude, which no man could number, of all nations, and kindreds, and people, and tongues, stood before the throne, and before the Lamb, clothed with white robes, and palms in their hands."—Revelation 7:9.

Mark this: that the great multitude comes from all nations and peoples, kindreds and tongues, and few there be as compared with the number in all the nations. They are all of good will toward God, and they see that religion is the product of the Devil, employed by him to deceive and to turn the people away from Jehovah and his kingdom. They see that salvation could not come to them by associating with any religious organization, because 'salvation belongeth to Jehovah God'. These faithful ones turn to God and his King and serve him. They are identified in symbol as being clothed with white robes, showing that they are lovers of that which is pure, and righteous. They are also pictured under the symbol of having palms in their hands, which they wave while they hail the Lord, and say: 'We hail Christ the King and Vindicator of Jehovah.' (Revelation 7: 10) All creation that loves and serves God joins in the song of praise to his name. (7: 11, 12) That symbolic vision shows that the faithful "elect" "servant" class could not identify the great multitude until after those of the remnant are gathered by the Lord to his temple and enlightened by him, that is, the time when the church comes to full unity in Christ Jesus. (Ephesians 4: 12, 13) It was in the year 1935 that God's faithful "elect" "servant" class on earth was first permitted to identify the great multitude, in fulfillment of what is stated in the Scriptures, to wit: "And one of the elders answered, saying unto me, What are these which are arrayed in white robes? and whence came they? And I said unto him, Sir, thou knowest. And he said to me, These are they which came out of great tribulation, and have washed their robes, and made them white in the blood of the Lamb. Therefore are they before the throne of God, and serve him day and night in his temple; and he that sitteth on the throne shall dwell among them. They shall hunger no more, neither thirst any more; neither shall the sun light on them, nor any heat. For the Lamb, which is in the midst of the throne, shall feed them, and shall lead them unto living fountains of waters; and God shall wipe away all tears from their eyes." (Rev. 7: 13-17) Thus the great multitude is definitely identified, and now all those who are of good will toward God and his King are appreciating the privilege of devoting themselves to Christ the King and serving him continuously to the praise of the Most High.

GRACIOUS INVITATION

Christ Jesus is the Great Spirit, the Lord and King and Head of Jehovah's capital organization. He is now at the temple of Jehovah God, which temple is made up of his faithful anointed and true followers. (1 Corinthians 3:16; 2 Corinthians 6:16) He is the Bridegroom, and his faithful body members constitute his bride. These Christ Jesus, at the command of his Father, has enlightened at the temple and he sends them forth as his servants and servants of the Most High, to promote the interest of the kingdom. His command to them is: 'This gospel of the kingdom shall be preached to all the world as a witness before the end comes.' All members of the bride class must be and now are at unity with Christ Jesus, the Bridegroom, and all are wholly and completely devoted to his kingdom. The time is here to proclaim the Lord's gracious invitation to all persons of good will, that they may hear the message of salvation; and therefore it is written: "And the Spirit and the bride say, Come. And let him that heareth say, Come. And let him that is athirst come; and whosoever will, let him take the water of life freely."— Revelation 22:17.

The "other sheep" of the Lord, the Jonadabs, the people of good will, now come prominently into view. They have fled to the 'city of refuge', the Lord Jesus and his capital organization, and hence they are the ones who are described as 'them that hear'. "And let him that heareth say,

Come." This is a specific and direct command to the "other sheep", the Jonadabs, to take up the glad message of the kingdom and join with the remnant of Jehovah's witnesses by diligently declaring to whosoever will hear the message of salvation and saying to them, "Come." Thus is seen that the remnant now on earth and those who will form the great multitude known as Jonadabs are companions in the Lord's service.

The proof found in the Bible and the well-known physical facts fully corroborating the same show beyond all doubt that 'salvation belongeth to Jehovah' and that he shows his mercy to the human race and offers protection, safety and salvation to those who comply with his fixed rules. That the faith of all should be made strong, Jehovah has exhibited his loving-kindness to all those of good will by making many prophetic pictures foretelling his purpose to gather not only the little flock, but the Lord's "other sheep", who shall be to his praise and to the vindication of his name. Now every one of the "other sheep" who has fled to the Lord for protection and salvation must be diligent in rendering obedience to His commandments, and therefore must 'seek righteousness and meekness'; which means that he must study to show himself approved unto God and must serve him. They will henceforth render all their devotion, substance and service to God and to his kingdom. The sure foundation for the protection and everlasting salvation should now be learned by every person of good will, and that opportunity is just before those who love righteousness.

CHAPTER IV

THE RANSOM

JEHOVAH GOD is the Savior of men, and he has provided and revealed to man the sure foundation for hope of salvation: "For other foundation can no man lay than that is laid, which is Jesus Christ." (1 Corinthians 3:11) "This is the stone which was set at nought of you builders, which is become the head of the corner. Neither is there salvation in any other; for there is none other name under heaven given among men, whereby we must be saved."—Acts 4:11, 12.

Why did God lay the foundation for salvation of sinful men? For the vindication of his holy name. The challenge of Satan put God's name at issue. Imperfect men, when relieved from inherited disability, and who then prove their integrity toward God, are a vindication of the name of Jehovah and a complete refutation and disproval of Satan's challenge. The judgment entered against Adam was just. It must stand forever. Adam's offspring are sinners by reason of inherited sin. God could consistently permit another to purchase the offspring of Adam; and those men who would exercise faith in God and in the purchaser and render themselves in obedience and who would then maintain their integrity toward God would be a vindication of God's name. God exercised mercy towards sinful man

by laying the foundation for man's salvation.
How is the foundation for man's salvation laid?
It was laid by permitting the man Jesus to bring
the required price for the purchase of mankind,
that is, the descendants of Adam, and pay over
that purchase price for the relief or release of
such offspring of Adam from bondage.

What price is required for the purchase of
mankind? The life of a perfect human creature.
God's law requires a life for a life. (Deuteronomy 19: 21) Adam was a perfect man when he
willfully and deliberately sinned in violation of
God's law, and the law of God required the forfeiture in death of that perfect human life.
(Genesis 2: 17) Nothing less and nothing more
could be required to purchase the offspring of
Adam, but only a perfect life. The life of an
angel could not furnish the perfect price, because an angel is greater than man. Because all
of Adam's offspring are by inheritance imperfect, no one thereof could bring the required
purchase price. (Psalm 49: 7) All men, being
imperfect, could live only a short space of time
and then die and remain dead forever, unless
God makes provision for such to have life. What
has been done for man's relief from death and
for his salvation to life?

The answer to the foregoing question is found
in the scripture, to wit: "But we see Jesus, who
was made a little lower than the angels, for the
suffering of death, crowned with glory and
honour: that he by the grace of God should taste
death for every man." (Hebrews 2: 9) Since
Jesus always does the will of God, it must have
been understood between God and his beloved

Son that Jesus should become a man, "lower than the angels," and suffer death, thereby proving his faithfulness unto God even to an ignominious death, and by his death also providing the required purchase price for man's salvation from death. The original name of the Son was Logos, and from the beginning the Logos was with God and, by God's direction, carried into operation God's purpose. He was the spokesman of Jehovah God. He was a spirit. By the miraculous power of Almighty God a virgin conceived and gave birth to the man-child Jesus. (Matthew 1:18-23) It is written that from the beginning the Son was "the Word", or Logos, "with God," and by him were all things created.—John 1:1-3, *Diaglott.*

The time came to begin laying the foundation for man's salvation and God caused the Logos to become a man. "And the Logos became flesh, and dwelt among us, and we beheld his glory, a glory as of an Only-begotten from a Father, full of favor and truth." (John 1:14, *Diaglott*) "But when the completion of the time arrived, God sent forth his son, having been produced from a woman, born under law." (Galatians 4:4, *Diaglott*) "And the child grew, and waxed strong in spirit, filled with wisdom; and the grace of God was upon him."—Luke 2:40.

When the man Jesus was thirty years of age he presented himself unto God in full and complete consecration or agreement to do the will of God, and this was symbolized by his immersion in the Jordan river. (Luke 3:21-23; Psalm 40:7,8; Matthew 3:16,17) Jesus was then a perfect man possessing all the qualifications req-

uisite to the furnishing of the purchase price
of sinful man. Was there an agreement between
Jesus and his Father, Jehovah God, that he,
Jesus, the man, should die? The answer is written: "As the Father knoweth me, even so know
I the Father; and I lay down my life for the
sheep." "Therefore doth my Father love me,
because I lay down my life, that I might take it
again. No man taketh it from me, but I lay it
down of myself. I have power to lay it down, and
I have power to take it again. This commandment have I received of my Father."—John
10: 15, 17, 18.

From the beginning, it clearly appears, it
was agreed between the Father and the Son
that Jesus should become a man, suffer contradiction and indignities and reproach upon
his name, prove his integrity toward God, die as
a sinner, and, proving his faithfulness, then
be resurrected out of death and take life again,
which would mean that by his death Jesus did
not forfeit his life or the right thereto, as Adam
had forfeited life. Jesus laid down his life and
received life again in full accord with the commandment he had received from Jehovah God,
and which commandment Jesus fully agreed to
obey. Carrying out that agreement, God raised
Jesus out of death and gave him life as a spirit.
—1 Peter 3:18; Acts 3:26; 1 Corinthians
15: 3, 4, 20.

Jesus, not having forfeited his right to human life, still possessed that right to human
life when he was raised from the dead; and
that right to human life constitutes the purchase
price for sinful man. When God raised Jesus

from the dead he clothed Jesus with all power
in heaven and in earth; that is to say, God
made Jesus Christ his Executive Officer, fully
equipped with all necessary power and authority to carry into operation the purpose of Jehovah, both in heaven and in earth. (Matthew
28: 18; Philippians 2: 9-11) When Jesus Christ
was exalted to heaven he presented to God in
heaven the value of his human life; and that
asset, which was exactly equal to what Adam
had forfeited, was received by Jehovah God as
the offering of Jesus for sin, that is to say, as
the purchase price offered and presented by
Jesus in behalf of sinful men. This God caused
to be shown in type or picture in the sacrifice
performed at the tabernacle in the wilderness.
(See Leviticus chapter 16.) On the typical atonement day the picture was made in this manner:

A bullock without spot or blemish, which represented the man Jesus, was brought into the
court of the tabernacle and slain there, which
court of the tabernacle pictured the earth. The
blood of the bullock, representing the lifeblood
of Jesus, which lifeblood was poured out as an
offering for sin (Isaiah 53: 10), was then carried
by the typical priest into the Most Holy of the
tabernacle and thereafter sprinkled upon the
mercy seat. (Leviticus 16: 14) The Most Holy
of the tabernacle pictured heaven itself, where
Jesus Christ appeared, presented and offered
the asset or valuable thing, his right to human
life, as the purchase price for the offspring of
Adam. (Hebrews 9: 3-25) The sacrifice offered
at the tabernacle in the wilderness once each year
on the typical atonement day foreshadowed or

pictured the work of Jesus in offering himself, that is, his human life, as the purchase price for man. Concerning the type, or picture, and the reality, it is written: "Now when these things were thus ordained, the priests went always into the first tabernacle, accomplishing the service of God. But into the second [the holiest of all, or Most Holy, picturing heaven] went the high priest alone once every year, not without blood, which he offered for himself, and for the errors of the people." "It was therefore necessary that the patterns of things in the heavens should be purified with these; but the heavenly things themselves with better sacrifices than these. For Christ is not entered into the holy places made with hands, which are the figures of the true; but into heaven itself, now to appear in the presence of God for us. Nor yet that he should offer himself often, as the high priest entereth into the holy place every year with blood of others; for then must he often have suffered since the foundation of the world; but now once in the end of the world hath he appeared, to put away sin by the sacrifice of himself."—Hebrews 9:6, 7, 23-26.

Thus it is seen that Christ Jesus, God's great High Priest, the spirit creature, when he appeared in heaven, presented and offered unto Jehovah the asset he possessed, to wit, his right to human life, as the purchase price for man, which offering was accepted by Jehovah, and Christ Jesus became the owner of all of Adam's offspring that willingly comply with the rules of Jehovah governing salvation. Thus God laid the foundation in Christ Jesus for the salvation of man, and there is no other possible means of salvation.

The lifeblood of the man Jesus is the ransom price for man. As God declares in his law: "The life of the flesh is in the blood: . . . the blood of it is for the life thereof." (Leviticus 17:11, 14) So the lifeblood of the man Jesus is the asset, the valuable thing, by which he ransomed sinful men. The English words *ransom, redeem, redeemed* and *redemption* are often used in the Bible, but do not always mean the same thing exactly. That part of the Bible written by the inspired followers of Christ Jesus and which for long has been commonly called "the New Testament" is translated from the Greek into the English, and in our Authorized Version of the Bible different Greek works are translated *ransom*. While comparatively few persons read the Greek, it will be profitable to here call attention to the different Greek words used in translating *ransom*, and these words appearing herein in English will enable all students to get an understanding. A well-known authority is Parkhurst. Parkhurst's Greek and English Lexicon says concerning "ransom": *"Anti'lytron* is from *anti* [meaning] *in return,* or *correspondency;* and *lytron, a ransom.—A ransom, price of redemption,* or rather *a correspondent ransom.* 'It properly signifies a *price* by which captives are *redeemed* from the enemy; and that kind of *exchange* in which the *life of one is redeemed by the life of another.'* [Hyperius] So Aristotle uses the verb *antilytro'o* for *redeeming life by life."*

The word *anti'lytron* appears only once in the Scriptures, and that in the following text, to wit: "Who gave himself a ransom in behalf of all [whom God wills to be saved (verse 4)], the testimony in its own seasons; for which I was appointed a herald and an apostle." (1 Timothy 2:4-7, *Emphatic Diaglott*) According to *Parkhurst:* "Who gave himself a correspondent ransom."

This text does not say or mean that Adam was or is ransomed, but does mean that the human perfection once possessed by the perfect man Adam (and which human perfection carried with it the right to life, which life and right thereto were forfeited by the willful disobedience of Adam) is purchased or bought back or ransomed for Adam's offspring, who were prevented from receiving that life and right thereto by reason of Adam's sin. The offspring of Adam who accept God's provision for their purchase, and who comply with God's fixed rules concerning the same, are privileged to receive the benefit of the ransom price. By his own lifeblood Jesus ransomed or purchased life and the right to human life for those of Adam's offspring that are saved. The clear meaning of the Scripture is this, to wit: That God desires all men to be saved and to come to an accurate knowledge of the truth who comply with his fixed and unchangeable provisions. "For this is good and acceptable in the sight of God our Saviour; who will have all men to be saved [by availing themselves of the ransom price, because God is impartial], and [then] to come unto [an accurate] knowledge of the truth [in order that they might continue to walk in the right way]. For there is one God, and one mediator between God and men, the man Christ Jesus; who gave himself a ransom for all [who will be saved], to be testified in due time." (1 Timothy 2:3-6, *A.V.*) It is this gracious provision that God has made for the salvation of men, concerning which the apostle then adds: "Whereunto I am ordained a preacher, and an apostle."

The man Jesus, by the will of God his Father, turned his perfection and right to life as such a man into a thing of value with sufficient purchasing power to purchase or buy back all the rights which Adam forfeited for himself and which his offspring lost by reason of Adam's sin. That does not mean that Adam was purchased, but that every right that Adam once possessed was purchased. It was not the will of God to send Jesus to the earth to give his life a ransom price and that in so doing Jesus should for ever go out of existence in the place or stead of Adam, in order that Adam and his offspring might exist forever; but that the man Jesus might lay down his life as a man and thereafter take life again, as Jesus said: "Therefore doth my Father love me, because I lay down my life, that I might take it again. . . . This commandment have I received of my Father." (John 10:17, 18) Life or existence Jesus did take again, not as a man, but as a spirit. At the same time he still held the right to life as a man because he had not forfeited that right. God raised Jesus out of death a spirit; and, Jesus still possessing that right to life as a man, that asset or thing of value he paid over to Jehovah God as the price required, and thereby became the owner of Adam's offspring who had not willfully sinned as did Adam, and who should in due time avail themselves of the value of that ransom price. Jesus then could release or deliver Adam's offspring from the bondage of sin and death which had come upon them by reason of Adam's sin, by which the right to life had been denied Adam's offspring. That means that the ransom sacrifice would inure to the benefit of the worthy ones of Adam's offspring; and by "worthy ones" meaning those who would follow God's rules.

For instance, Abel was a worthy one and had God's approval, but could not receive life or the right thereto until the ransom or purchase price was paid over and accepted by Jehovah. Being murdered a long time before the ransom price was paid, he must await God's due time to be awakened out of death and receive the full and complete benefit of the ransom price. When Jesus Christ paid over the value of his perfect human life he then by right of purchase became the owner of obedient mankind. He did not become a substitute for Adam in death, but he became the purchaser of Adam's offspring by paying over a thing exactly similar to that which Adam forfeited; therefore the life of the man Jesus, which he gave up, is a price exactly corresponding to the life of perfect Adam. Jesus purchased for Adam's worthy offspring the right to life, and it is his privilege to minister life according to the will of God; as it is written: 'Life is the gift of God through Jesus Christ our Lord.' (Romans 6:23) Who is to determine what ones of Adam's offspring are worthy? The Lord Jesus Christ, who acts with full authority from Jehovah God. Christ Jesus is "the Everlasting Father", or "Life-giver". (Isaiah 9:6) As a father he has power and authority to bring creatures into life who have died and to give life to as many as he will according to the pleasure of Jehovah God. Such rescued life Jesus Christ could rightfully bestow on those only, and no others than the ones for whom Adam had lost the right to life; and since Adam lost the right to life for all mankind, He can bestow life on only such of Adam's race as meet the required rules made by Jehovah.

"FOR ALL"

Does not the ransom price of Jesus result to the everlasting benefit of all? Does not the scripture at 1 Timothy 2:6 above quoted prove that Jesus gave his life a ransom for all? and is not that a guarantee that all of the human race must have the full benefit of the ransom sacrifice or ransom price? No; such a conclusion is not correct. Some of the human race, the offspring of Adam, are willfully wicked, and such are not benefited by the ransom. If they comply with God's rules concerning the ransom they might become righteous, and then they would receive the benefit of the ransom price. Concerning this Jesus said: "As thou hast given him power over all flesh, that he should give eternal life to as many as thou hast given him. And this is life eternal, that they might know thee the only true God, and Jesus Christ, whom thou hast sent." —John 17:2, 3.

Those persons who refuse to know God and
Christ Jesus cannot receive life. Many persons
to whom the truth is presented and who are
shown God's provision for life and salvation
spurn such truth and say, in substance: "I am
not at all interested. I am satisfied with what I
have." There is no reason to expect Adam to receive life, because he was a willful and deliberate
sinner; nor is there any reason to expect any of
Adam's offspring to receive life who willfully
refuse to hear of God's provision for life. To
give Adam the benefit of the ransom sacrifice
would mean that God would thereby show that
his judgment against Adam was not just; whereas the Scriptures plainly say: 'Justice is the
foundation of God's throne.' (Psalm 89:14) To
give Adam's offspring the benefit of the ransom
sacrifice, which offspring spurn God's provision,
is wholly inconsistent with God's purpose expressed in the Scriptures. The text at 1 Timothy
two above quoted shows that "God is no respecter of persons" (Acts 10:34), and hence the
ransom is for the benefit of all who conform
themselves to God's will or law; and because
there is only one Almighty God, whose name is
Jehovah, there is one mediator between God and
men and that One is the man Jesus, who gave
his life a ransom for all, meaning, of course, as
stated, all who God wills shall be saved and
who comply with the requirements that God has
laid down. There is no authority to say that the
ransom sacrifice automatically operates for the
benefit of all.

The English words *buy, bought, purchase* and
redeem are translated from the Greek *agorazo*

(derived from the word *agora,* meaning "the town square" or "market", and *ageiro,* meaning "gather", as to the town square or market place). Thus *agorazo* literally means to go to market and hence to purchase and redeem that which is sold. As an example: Slaves were bought and sold at the market place; concerning which the word *agorazo* properly is applied. Note here an example of the use of the word, to wit: "Again, the kingdom of heaven is like unto treasure hid in a field; the which when a man hath found he hideth, and for joy thereof goeth and selleth all that he hath, and buyeth that field."—Matthew 13:44.

Many who have tried to interpret the Scriptures have said that the word *field,* used in the foregoing text, symbolizes the entire human race, the wicked and all others. Certainly that is wrong. Mark this: the scripture says "the kingdom of heaven is like", and so on. It is the kingdom of heaven which is bought, and certainly the entire human race is not the kingdom of heaven. Nor is the kingdom of heaven hidden within the folds of the sinful human family. The kingdom of heaven is the hidden treasure, and it is that which is bought. It is the treasure within God's universal organization, which is holy and in no wise sinful. The "kingdom of heaven" is the hidden mystery. (Ephesians 1:20-23; 5:32) "Even the mystery which hath been hid from ages and from generations, but now is made manifest to his saints." (Colossians 1:26) Christ Jesus, by rendering himself in full obedience to his Father's will, became the heir of all things, including the hidden mystery, the kingdom of heaven.

(Hebrews 1:2; Romans 8:16, 17) God made known to Jesus his purpose to have a capital organization, to wit, his government, "the kingdom of heaven," which for ages was a mystery and which mystery was hidden from all others of God's creation until God's due time to reveal it. When Jesus learned of this, he sold his all to become the heir thereof and the head of the kingdom. It was not his human life as the ransom for humanity that bought that estate of the kingdom of heaven; it was his surrender of everything, including human life, to maintain his integrity and faithfulness to God under the greatest pressure even unto an ignominious death; which he did for that field and its hidden treasure. The suffering of Jesus had nothing to do with the purchase price of mankind, but it was by his suffering that he learned obedience and proved his integrity and faithfulness and became the heir of eternal salvation and of the kingdom.—Hebrews 5:8, 9.

The same Greek word, *agorazo,* is translated "bought" in the following text: "Again, the kingdom of heaven is like unto a merchantman, seeking goodly pearls; who, when he had found one pearl of great price, went and sold all that he had, and bought it." (Matthew 13:45, 46) This has the same meaning as the parable stated in the preceding verses forty-three and forty-four. Those two parables include the body members of the body of Christ, because they form a part of the kingdom of heaven. If the purchase or buying that is mentioned in the foregoing text concerning the kingdom of heaven referred to the ransom price the body members would have

no part therein, because they do not have any
part in the purchase of the human race. That the
body members of Christ have a part in the kingdom is true beyond any doubt. (Romans 8:16, 17;
Revelation 1:6; 20:4) Those who faithfully
follow Christ Jesus and become a part of the
kingdom of heaven are first bought by the precious blood of Christ Jesus before they can start
on their way to be made a part of the kingdom.
(1 Peter 1:18, 19) "What! know ye not that your
body is the temple of the holy [spirit] which is
in you, which ye have of God, and ye are not
your own? For ye are bought with a price; therefore glorify God in your body, . . . " (1 Corinthians 6:19, 20; the remaining words in that
twentieth verse are spurious. See *Diaglott*.)
This text refers only to the anointed Christians
as the ones that are bought. This text could
not be construed to mean that it drags along
with those purchased every member of the human family, wicked and otherwise, and that
these are automatically bought. Would a slave
be bought and be given his freedom who refused
to obey his master? Note that the agreement
with Joseph in Egypt by the people was this: that
the people first came to Joseph and asked to be
bought before Joseph would buy them for
Pharaoh. This is a picture of the purchase and
redemption of those of the human race who
come to Christ Jesus to be bought. (Genesis
47:19-23) Those who become members of the
body of Christ first come to Christ Jesus and
agree to do whatsoever is his and the Father's
will. Then his purchase price applies to them,
and they become his and no longer belong to

themselves. They are his bond servants or bond
slaves, thereafter obligated to do his will and
obey his commandments. They were not purchased against their will, but because they desired to be purchased. God's rule is the same at
all times.

Whether the person is called by the Lord and
granted life in the spirit or whether his hope of
life is on the earth, the course of procedure concerning his purchase is exactly the same. The
following text is directed to those of the little
flock: "For he that is called in the Lord, being
a [man's] servant, is the Lord's freeman; likewise also he that is called, being free, is Christ's
servant [that is, the bond servant or slave of
Christ]. Ye are bought with a price; be not ye
the servants of men." (1 Corinthians 7:22, 23)
These were not called until they first surrendered themselves in consecration to do God's will,
and then the purchase or ransom price operated
toward them and they were bought and the Lord
became their owner. Being accepted in the Lord,
such became his bond servants because they
have willingly and voluntarily agreed to be
bought on the Lord's terms. They have sold
themselves to the King.—1 Kings 21:20, 25.

Those who are wicked are not purchased: "But
there were false prophets [in Israel] also among
the people, even as there shall be false teachers
among you [who are Christians], who privily
shall bring in damnable heresies, even denying
the Lord that bought them, and bring upon
themselves swift destruction." (2 Peter 2:1)
Such were first bought, but afterwards became
wicked, denying the Lord and the value of his

blood by which they were bought; and for such there is no salvation, as is plainly stated in the Scriptures. (See Hebrews 6: 4-10; 10: 26-29.)

The Scriptures refer to mature and faithful Christians as "elders", who are bought and redeemed: "And they [the twenty-four elders named as members of the body of Christ] sung a new song, saying, Thou [Christ Jesus] art worthy to take the book, and to open the seals thereof; for thou wast slain, and hast redeemed us to God by thy blood, out of every kindred, and tongue, and people and nation."—Revelation 5: 9.

This scripture could have no application to the wicked, because they are not redeemed unto God. The language of this text shows conclusively that none are automatically redeemed, because the elders were redeemed, as stated, "out of every kindred."

The members of the body of Christ are the ones ransomed and redeemed, as stated, in the following text: "And they sung as it were a new song before the throne, and before the four beasts, and the elders; and no man could learn that song but the hundred and forty and four thousand, which were redeemed from the earth. These are they which were not defiled with women; for they are virgins. These are they which follow the Lamb whithersoever he goeth. These were redeemed from among men, being the firstfruits unto God and to the Lamb."—Revelation 14: 3, 4.

The fact that these were "redeemed from among men" shows that all men were not automatically redeemed. The members of the body

of Christ, here mentioned, first consecrated
themselves by agreeing to do God's will, and
hence asked to be bought. The purpose and provision of God is for the redemption of men without discrimination, but all who are redeemed
must first have faith in God and in Christ Jesus,
and then fully consecrate themselves to do God's
will. This rule of God applies to all. Furthermore, these members of the body of Christ are
"the first-fruits" unto God and Christ; which
proves that there will be others who will see the
privilege of being bought and who will avail
themselves of that privilege by willingly exercising faith in God and in Christ by fully con-
secrating themselves to do God's will.

"EXAGORAZO"

Another Greek word, *exagorazo*, and which is
stronger and more emphatic than *agorazo*,
means "to buy or redeem from; to buy up entirely; to get the whole, all; to ransom; to rescue,
and to release". It is applied both to the redeeming of creatures and to buying back time as to
creatures. Note Galatians 3:13, 14: "Christ hath
redeemed us from the curse of the law, being
made a curse for us; for it is written, Cursed is
every one that hangeth on a tree; that the blessing of Abraham [as to Abraham's seed] might
come on the Gentiles through Jesus Christ; that
we might receive the promise of the spirit
through faith."

Disobedient and unwilling Jews were not redeemed from the curse of the law, neither are
the unwilling Gentiles redeemed from the curse
or bondage of sin. This text says: "That **we**

might receive the promise of the spirit through
faith"; which shows that they that are Christians willingly believe on and follow Christ Jesus. All others of the Jews remain under the
curse of the law. Again, it is written: "But
when the fulness of the time was come, God sent
forth his Son, made of a woman, made under the
law, to redeem them that were under the law,
that we might receive the adoption of sons."
(Galatians 4:4, 5) According to this text only
those of the Jews who 'received the adoption of
sons' are those who were redeemed. This is fully
supported by the scripture, to wit: "He [Jesus]
came unto his own, and his own received him
not. But as many as received him, to them gave
he power to become the sons of God, even to
them that believe on his name: which were born,
not of blood, nor of the will of the flesh, nor of
the will of man, but of God."—John 1:11-13.

It follows that those who did not believe were
not bought, and those who did believe and devoted themselves to Christ were "bought up entirely". That same Greek word, as applied to
buying back of time, is used in the following
text: "Redeeming the time, because the days are
evil."—Ephesians 5:16.

The Greek verb *lyo,* which means simply "to
loosen", is the base or root of the Greek words
rendered "redeemed" in the following texts:
"But we trusted that it had been he which should
have redeemed [*lytro'o*] Israel; and beside all
this, to day is the third day since these things
were done." (Luke 24:21) "Forasmuch as ye
[elect] know that ye were not redeemed
[(Greek) *lytro'o*] with corruptible things, as

silver and gold, from your vain conversation received by tradition from your fathers; but with the precious blood of Christ, as of a lamb without blemish and without spot."—1 Peter 1: 18, 19.

This last scripture is addressed only to those who had fled from Satan's organization and devoted themselves to God by and through Christ Jesus. The Greek word *lytrosis,* which means to ransom or "redemption" by paying over a price, is used in the following text, to wit: "Blessed be the Lord God of Israel; for he hath visited and redeemed [literally: wrought redemption for] his people." (Luke 1: 68) None except those who have become the Lord's are included. Again in Luke 2: 36-38 mention is made only of those who "looked for redemption" through the One whom Jehovah had promised. In Hebrews 9: 12 it is written: "By his own [Christ's] blood, he entered in once into the holy place, having obtained eternal redemption for us." Here the apostle is not classifying himself with the entire human race, but speaking of "us" (9: 24), who have fled to Christ and joyfully consecrated ourselves to do God's will.

Apolytrosis, meaning "to loosen away from", particularly the act of loosening; "the redemption; a releasing on payment of a ransom price; a ransoming," is translated "redemption" and "deliverance", as used in the following text: "And when these things begin to come to pass, then look up, and lift up your heads; for your redemption [(*Diaglott*) deliverance] draweth nigh." (Luke 21: 28) The redemption here is such a deliverance as was experienced by the

Israelites when they were delivered from Egypt
(Exodus 6:6; 15:13; Psalm 106:9-11); also
such as the faithful followers of Christ Jesus
being released from Satan's organization, that
is, Babylon. After 1918 the faithful remnant of
the seed of the Lord's organization were released or delivered from Satan's organization
by the exercise of the Lord's power. (Psalm
107:2, 3; Isaiah 52:9-11; Jeremiah 31:10-12)
"Even the righteousness of God, which is by
faith of Jesus Christ, unto all and upon all them
that believe; for there is no difference: for all
have sinned, and come short of the glory of God;
being justified freely by his grace, through the
redemption that is in Christ Jesus." (Romans
3:22-24) Here again the redemption applies
only to them that have faith and believe, which
results in justification to such believers. Such
are set free or loosened from bondage, and this
applies to none other.

In the following text the same Greek word is
translated "redemption": "Not only they [the
people of good will, the Lord's 'other sheep'],
but ourselves also, which have the firstfruits of
the spirit, even we ourselves groan within ourselves, waiting for the adoption, to wit, the redemption of our body." (Romans 8:23) In this
text it is "our body", of which Christ Jesus is
the Head, that is, The Christ, including Christ
Jesus, the Head, and 144,000 body members,
that experiences redemption or deliverance. The
visible manifestation of this redemption is by
the deliverance of the faithful on earth from the
bondage of Satan's organization, where they
had been captives and prisoners down to 1918,

at which time the Lord came to his temple and gathered the faithful into it. Again those only who are in Christ Jesus are considered in the following text: "But of him are ye in Christ Jesus, who of God is made unto us wisdom, and righteousness, and sanctification, and redemption." (1 Corinthians 1:30) Certainly this does not apply to those who spurn God's provision through Christ Jesus.

At Ephesians 1:7, 14 the same word is used: "In whom we have redemption through his blood, the forgiveness of sins, according to the riches of his grace." "Which is the earnest of our inheritance, until the redemption of the purchased possession, unto the praise of his glory." At verse fourteen the words "purchased possession" here translate the one Greek word *peripoiesis*, the same as used at 1 Peter 2:9, which describes the "people for God's own possession". (*A.R.V.*) The "purchased possession" here mentioned is the body of Christ, and none other. At Ephesians 1:7, 14 "redemption" is limited to those who apply to God for the blood of Christ as the only means of salvation, and who receive the forgiveness of sins and then receive "the earnest" (a hand payment, to bind the bargain) of the spirit. When Satan's organization is destroyed such "purchased possession" experience complete deliverance.

Again, at Colossians 1:14: "In whom we have redemption through his blood, even the forgiveness of sins." The "redemption" here mentioned is not applied automatically to anyone, but only to those who first voluntarily seek and ask for such. It is broad enough to cover all persons that do come to God desiring salvation.

At Hebrews 11:35 the same Greek word is rendered "deliverance", and according to *Young,* "redemption." "Women received their dead raised to life again; and others were tortured, not accepting deliverance; that they might obtain a better resurrection." The faithful ones of old refused to accept any redemption that purchased deliverance from torture and at the price of a compromise with the Devil's agents or organization. When those faithful ones are raised from the dead they will gladly and with intelligence accept redemption through Christ Jesus. They exhibited faith in God and in his promise to send them the Messiah, and they maintained their integrity.

The Greek *lytron,* which means "something to loosen with", that is, a redemption "price", is translated "ransom" in the following text, to wit: "And whosoever will be chief among you, let him be your servant; even as the Son of man came not to be ministered unto, but to minister, and to give his life a ransom for many." (Matthew 20:27, 28) The word *lytron* here is followed by the preposition *anti,* meaning *instead of, corresponding to,* or *in behalf of,* and the last more correctly translates the same. This is the very reverse of the compound word *anti-lytron* at 1 Timothy 2:6. At Matthew 20:28 the *anti* could not mean "exactly corresponding" in price, because the lifeblood of Jesus was not exactly corresponding to the "many", but was "in behalf of" the many. God's law as stated at Deuteronomy 19:21 shows that the life that buys must be the price exactly corresponding to that which was forfeited; and hence the life of Jesus must be equivalent to what Jesus ransoms for the many.

The same matter is correctly stated at Mark 10: 44, 45: "And whosoever of you will be the chiefest, shall be servant of all. For even the Son of man came not to be ministered unto, but to minister, and to give his life a ransom for [*lytron anti*] many." Jesus gave his life a ransom in behalf of many, and he bought for such the full and complete life, with the right thereto, for as many as comply with God's fixed rules relating to salvation. Certainly Jesus did not come to save and to give his life for the willfully wicked. It is true, as written at Romans 5: 8, 10, that Christ died for us while we were enemies. "But God commendeth his love toward us, in that, while we were yet sinners, Christ died for us." "For if, when we were enemies, we were reconciled to God by the death of his Son, much more, being reconciled, we shall be saved by his life." The persons referred to in the word "we" in these texts do not include everyone, but only those who are "called to be saints".–Romans 1: 7.

The epistle of 1 Timothy is addressed to Timothy, who was commissioned and sent forth to instruct those persons who had already made a consecration to do the will of God, which includes, of course, those taken out of the world for Jehovah's name. The sum of the inspired statement of the apostle is this: God is no respecter of persons, but it is his will that 'all men might be saved, and come to a knowledge of the truth, for there is one God and one mediator between God and men, and that one is Christ Jesus, who gave himself a ransom in behalf of all'; meaning, of course, all of those who seek the Lord. The meaning here manifestly is that Christ Jesus is the Mediator of all who have first entered into a covenant to do the will of God. From all the foregoing Scripture texts it is seen that the ransom sacrifice of Jesus does not automatically affect every man, whether he wishes it or not, but only those receive the resulting benefits therefrom who first seek the way of righteousness and believe on God, that He is the Almighty and that the blood of Christ Jesus is the means of salvation, and who then voluntarily agree to do the will of God. Without Christ Jesus, the Mediator, no man could be reconciled to God. Jesus has bought the race with his own blood, and he relieves from the disability of sin only those who are willing to be delivered and saved.

God has shown his mercy to sinful men, the offspring of Adam, and such is the result of his loving-kindness. Therefore says the scripture: "For God so loved the world, that he gave his only begotten Son, that whosoever believeth in him should not perish, but have everlasting life." (John 3: 16) Only those who believe in him are rescued from perishing: "For God sent not his Son into the world to condemn the world; but that the world through him might be saved." (Verse 17) This manifestation of God's mercy is that men "might be saved", and not that they must be saved whether they desire, believe or do otherwise.

Without the ransom sacrifice no man could be saved, because he is a sinner by inheritance from Adam and upon all sinners the "wrath of God", that is, God's just condemnation, falls because of imperfection resulting from sin. God cannot approve an imperfect thing. Not by the exercise of justice, but by the exercise of his loving-kindness God provides that Jesus may buy men and that, when men exercise faith in God and in Christ, such will have the benefit of being released from the bondage of sin and given an individual opportunity to prove their integrity toward God and, so doing, receive salvation to life by and through Jesus Christ. But certainly those who fail or refuse to believe could not have salvation. If they could, then it would mean that the conditions of belief are of no effect. Therefore says the scripture plainly: "The Father loveth the Son, and hath given all things into his hand. He that believeth on the Son hath everlasting life; and he that believeth not the Son shall not see life; but the wrath of God abideth on him."—John 3: 35, 36.

There is no way for man to escape the just punishment of everlasting death except by and through the merit of Christ Jesus applied to and received by him. The doctrine, therefore, of 'a ransom for all regardless of belief' is entirely without Scriptural authority.

The *ransom price* is the valuable thing or price provided for the purchase of mankind, and which price exactly corresponds to that which the perfect man Adam forfeited for himself and lost to all of his offspring.

The *sin offering* is the presentation of and the paying over to Jehovah God of that asset, valuable thing or purchase price. Jesus died on the earth. His lifeblood was poured out as the ransom price. God raised Jesus out of death a spirit and exalted him to heaven, fully clothed with all power and authority to carry out God's purpose. Christ Jesus, the Divine, in heaven, presented to Jehovah God the valuable asset, to wit, his right to human life, as an offering for sin. Such is the sin offering. The act of ransoming includes both the providing of the purchase price and the presentation and paying over of that purchase price. The entire work of providing the valuable asset and paying it over is performed by Christ Jesus according to the will and command of God. It therefore follows that Christ Jesus alone and separate and apart from the members of his body performed the act of ransoming mankind.

The prophetic picture made on the typical atonement day in the sacrifices performed at the tabernacle in the wilderness fully supports the foregoing conclusion. The bullock, which was a type of the man Jesus, was brought into the court of the tabernacle and was slain there, which pictures the earth where Jesus was slain. Israel's high priest, in the type, took the blood of the bullock and carried it into the "holiest of all", corresponding with heaven, and there sprinkled the blood, which pictured the life of the slain man, Christ Jesus. In fulfillment of that part of the picture Christ Jesus, the great High Priest, ascended into heaven itself and presented and paid over the valuable asset, to

Presenting the sacrifice

wit, his right to human life, to God. In the type
the blood was sprinkled on the mercy seat by
the priest seven times. "Seven," being a symbol
of completeness in heaven, shows that the blood
was sprinkled in heaven in completeness by the
Lord himself, that is, that Christ Jesus fully
and completely paid over the purchase price for
the human race. (See Leviticus chapter 16.) The
high priest in the type went alone into the Most
Holy, and no one was permitted to be there with
him.

Note now the text: "But into the second [holi-
est of all], the high-priest alone, once annually,

not without blood, which he offers on behalf of himself, and the sins of ignorance of the people." (Hebrews 9:7, *Diaglott*) "And there shall be no man in the tabernacle of the congregation when he goeth in to make an atonement in the holy place, until he come out, and have made an atonement for himself, and for his household [the priestly anointed class in the type], and for all the congregation of Israel." (Leviticus 16:17) Likewise in the antitype Christ Jesus, the great High Priest, presented the value of his human life, the purchase price, in behalf of the royal house, which God selects, and also for the sins of the people.—Hebrews 9:17, 24.

It has been repeatedly said that the church, that is, the glorified members of the body of Christ, by reason of their sacrifice, have a part in the sin offering; and in support of that theory the following scripture is offered: "Then shall he kill the goat of the sin offering, that is for the people, and bring his blood within the vail, and do with that blood as he did with the blood of the bullock, and sprinkle it upon the mercy seat, and before the mercy seat."—Leviticus 16:15.

Neither the foregoing nor any other scripture sustains the conclusion that the body members of Christ have any part in the sin offering. It is the lifeblood of the man Jesus alone that is the valuable thing, the purchase price, and which price is presented and paid over as a sin offering. What, then, will be asked, does the sacrifice of the Lord's goat and the sprinkling of its blood, as shown in the type, mean, if not sprinkled in behalf of mankind as a part of the

sin offering? It is true that the blood of the
Lord's goat was taken into the Holy the same
as that of the bullock. In the type the goat did
not sacrifice itself, but the sacrifice was done by
the high priest. In the antitype no man sacrifices
himself, but the Lord Jesus, the great High
Priest, does the sacrificing. The meaning of the
sacrifice and sprinkling the blood of the Lord's
goat manifestly is this: That everyone of the
humankind that is called to the "high calling"
must bear the reproaches that fall upon Christ
Jesus and must therefore suffer with him and
die with him as a condition precedent to reigning with him in heaven. In support of this are
the inspired words of the apostle: "Who now rejoice in my sufferings for you, and fill up that
which is behind of the afflictions of Christ in my
flesh for his body's sake, which is the church."
(Colossians 1: 24) "It is a faithful saying: For
if we be dead with him, we shall also live with
him; if we suffer, we shall also reign with him;
if we deny him, he also will deny us." (2 Timothy
2: 11, 12) "For even hereunto were ye called:
because Christ also suffered for us, leaving us
an example, that ye should follow his steps."
(1 Peter 2: 21) In the type the Lord's goat pictured those who are begotten of the spirit and
who therefore as human creatures must die and
must be faithful unto death, that they may participate with Christ Jesus in his kingdom, enjoy-
ing the highest element of life and reigning with
him: "Fear none of those things which thou shalt
suffer: behold, the devil shall cast some of you
into prison, that ye may be tried; and ye shall
have tribulation ten days: be thou faithful unto

death, and I will give thee a crown of life."
(Revelation 2:10) "And they lived and reigned
with Christ a thousand years."–Revelation 20:4.

The following cannot be successfully contradicted, to wit: That God has provided salvation
by and through his Son, Christ Jesus; that the
lifeblood of the man Jesus poured out at Calvary is the purchase price of sinful man, which
price purchased all the right that Adam lost
for his offspring; that such purchase price was
presented in heaven and paid over to God as a
sin offering in behalf of as many as do believe
on the Lord Jesus Christ; that such was done
and performed by Christ Jesus in obedience to
God's will; that Christ Jesus, having paid over
the ransom price, is the owner of all men, and all
receive the benefit thereof who believe and obey;
that life everlasting is the gift of Jehovah God
through Jesus Christ our Lord, because salvation belongs to Jehovah and Christ Jesus is his
means of administering the same; that there is
no other means of gaining life; and that no man
can gain life or receive life everlasting unless
he believes God and believes on the Lord Jesus
Christ and asks for salvation by making an unconditional agreement to do the will of God.

That class of religionists known as the "higher critics" do not believe the Scriptural doctrine
concerning the ransom sacrifice. They do con-
descend to say that Jesus was a great and good
man, but that his death upon the tree means
nothing more than the death of any other man
so far as the purchasing of the human race is
concerned. Being willingly ignorant of God's
provisions for man's salvation, those "higher

critics" are wise in their own conceits and blind
to the truth. (Romans 11:25; 12:16) "Seest
thou a man wise in his own conceit? there is
more hope of a fool than of him." (Proverbs
26:12) The man who desires salvation to life
must learn of God's provision for salvation, because there is no other way to be saved.

Jehovah's revealed purpose is first to ransom
and deliver the church, that is to say, those who
constitute the members of the body of Christ,
which selected ones shall reign with Christ in
his kingdom. Second, after the selection of the
elect ones is completed to the required number,
then follows the work of the Lord in gathering
and delivering his "other sheep", and which latter work is now in progress. Long before the
coming of Christ Jesus to earth as a man God,
by the mouth of his holy prophets, told of His
provision for the salvation of humankind that
would believe and obey him. This matter is of
such vital importance to those who believe that
it appears well to here consider somewhat in
detail the prophetic scriptures written before
the ransom price was actually provided, and
which part of the Holy Scriptures have been
long designated "The Old Testament".

The English word "ransom" (translated from
the French) is from the Latin word *"redemp-
tio"* (French: *rançon*). Thus the two words
ransom and *redeem* are related one to the other,
and such is also true in the Holy Scriptures.
Because the English word *ransom* is used in
our studies, the definition of *ransom* as given by
Webster, the lexicographer, is here set out, to
wit: "Ransom," as a noun, means "act of ran-

soming; a redeeming or releasing of a captive by payment of a consideration. The money, price, or consideration paid or demanded for the redemption of a captured person or persons; a payment that releases from captivity, a penalty, or a forfeit. One who or that which ransoms or redeems". As a verb: "To redeem from captivity, slavery, punishment, or the like, by paying a price; to buy out of bondage. To deliver, as from sin, its penalty, or the like; to be the redeemer of."

The word *redeem* is defined: "To regain possession of by payment of a stipulated price; to repurchase. To ransom, liberate, or rescue from captivity or bondage, or from any obligation or liability to suffer or to be forfeited, by paying a price or ransom. To recover or regain, as pledged or mortgaged property, by the requisite fulfillment of some obligation, as by the payment of what may be due. To rescue; deliver; reclaim."

In the original of the Holy Scriptures various Hebrew words are translated by the words "ransom", "redeem," "redeemed," "deliver," and like words above used. For instance, the Hebrew words *khopher* and *pidhion* are translated "ransom". The Hebrew words *gaal* and *pahdah* are translated "to ransom" and "to redeem". There must be some simple root-meaning of each Hebrew word, making it fitting and usable in all the various connections; that is to say, that of freeing or delivering. Examples are given herein.

The Hebrew word *gaal*, translated "redeemed", is first used in the Scriptures at Genesis 48:16 in connection with Jacob: "the angel which re-

deemed me." The Lord gave command to Moses:
"Wherefore say unto the children of Israel, I
am the Lord, . . . I will redeem you [not with
sacrifices, but] with a stretched out arm." (Exodus 6:6) After crossing the Red sea Moses said
to Jehovah: "Thou in thy mercy hast led forth
the people which thou hast redeemed." (Exodus
15:13) In the following texts the same Hebrew
word is translated "redeemed": "Remember thy
congregation, which thou hast purchased of old;
the rod of thine inheritance, which thou hast redeemed; this mount Zion, wherein thou hast
dwelt." (Psalm 74:2) "Thou hast with thine arm
[not by sacrifice] redeemed thy people, the sons
of Jacob and Joseph." (Psalm 77:15) The prophetic words in the Psalm next quoted are concerning Jesus our Redeemer, to wit: "Draw
nigh unto my soul, and redeem it; deliver me,
because of mine enemies." (Psalm 69:18) Jesus
is Jehovah's duly commissioned King, concerning whom it is written: "Give the king [Christ
Jesus] thy judgments, O God, and thy righteousness unto the king's [Jehovah, the King of
Eternity's] son." "He shall spare the poor and
needy, and shall save the souls of the needy. He
shall redeem their soul from deceit and violence;
and precious shall their blood be in his sight."
(Psalm 72:1, 13, 14) Likewise the same word
appears in the following texts: "Bless the Lord,
O my soul; and all that is within me, bless his
holy name. Who redeemeth thy life from destruction; who crowneth thee with lovingkindness and
tender mercies." (Psalm 103:1, 4) "Let the redeemed of the Lord [the remnant from Satan's
organization] say so, whom he hath redeemed

from the hand of the enemy." (Psalm 107: 2, 3) "Hear the word of the Lord, O ye nations, and declare it in the isles afar off, and say, He that scattered Israel [spiritual Israel, in the year 1918] will gather him [His favored and faithful ones in 1919 and onward], and keep him, as a shepherd doth his flock. For the Lord hath redeemed Jacob, and ransomed him from the hand of him that was stronger than he. Therefore they shall come and sing in the height of Zion, and shall flow together to the goodness of the Lord."—Jeremiah 31: 10-12.

"Jacob" symbolically stands for God's anointed people on the earth, to whom the Lord Jehovah says: "But now thus saith the Lord that created thee, O Jacob, and he that formed thee, O Israel, Fear not; for I have redeemed thee, I have called thee by thy name; thou art mine. Ye are my witnesses, saith the Lord, and my servant whom I have chosen; that ye may know and believe me, and understand that I am he."—Isaiah 43: 1, 10.

Among other scriptures in which the Hebrew word *gaal* is translated "redeemed" is the following: "Sing, O ye heavens; for the Lord hath done it; shout, ye lower parts of the earth; break forth into singing, ye mountains, O forest, and every tree therein; for the Lord hath redeemed Jacob [God's elect people], and glorified himself in Israel. Thus saith the Lord, thy redeemer, and he that formed thee from the womb, I am the Lord that maketh all things; that stretcheth forth the heavens alone; that spreadeth abroad the earth by myself." (Isaiah 44: 23, 24) Likewise in the sixth verse: "Thus saith the Lord,

the King of Israel, and his redeemer the Lord
of hosts; I am the first, and I am the last; and beside me there is no God." (Isaiah 44:6) It was
in the year 1919 that the Lord delivered the
antitypical "Jacob" class, his faithful remnant,
from Satan's organization, and brought them into the kingdom, gathering them into the temple.

A similar use of the word *"redeemed"* appears
in the following text: "Loose thyself from the
bands of thy neck, O captive daughter of Zion.
For thus saith the Lord, Ye have sold yourselves for nought; and ye shall be redeemed
without money." (Isaiah 52:2,3) Note that
these were redeemed without a purchase price.
The remnant have now been delivered or redeemed from Satan's organization and will be
completely free therefrom when the Lord at
Armageddon destroys everything pertaining to
Satan's organization, and then all who survive
shall see the salvation of Jehovah in behalf of
his people. God's anointed remnant have been
free from Satan's organization since recognizing that Jehovah and Christ are the only "higher
powers". They are still surrounded and opposed
by Satan's organization, however, and will be
completely delivered therefrom at Armageddon.
Isaiah 52:9,10: "Break forth into joy, sing
together, ye waste places of Jerusalem; for the
Lord hath comforted his people, he hath redeemed Jerusalem. The Lord hath made bare
his holy arm in the eyes of all the nations; and
all the ends of the earth shall see the salvation
of our God."

Again the remnant is shown as redeemed and
delivered in the following text: "Go ye forth of

Babylon, flee ye from the Chaldeans, with a voice of singing declare ye, tell this, utter it even to the end of the earth; say ye, The Lord hath redeemed his servant Jacob."—Isaiah 48:20.

The faithful are shown as redeemed in the following text: "For the day of vengeance is in mine heart, and the year of my redeemed is come." (Isaiah 63:4) That does not refer to the purchase price, but refers to the deliverance of God's people at the time he executes his wrath upon the enemy.

In the following text a contrast is shown between those who, once enlightened, became unfaithful and who are designated under the symbol of "Ephraim", and those who remain faithful and true to the Lord and who are born in Zion, hence are the children of Zion, God's organization, to wit: "The iniquity of Ephraim is bound up; his sin is hid. The sorrows of a travailing woman shall come upon him [meaning the unfaithful who form the 'evil servant' class]: he is an unwise son [once enlightened and who then takes a wrong course]; for he should not stay long in the place of the breaking forth of children [that is, other children of Zion, beginning in the year 1918 at the coming of the Lord Jesus to the temple, when he began to gather them into his temple]. I will ransom [(Hebrew) *pahdah:* release] them [the faithful who are born in Zion] from the power of the grave: I will redeem them [the children of Zion born from and after 1918] from death: O death, I will be thy plagues; O grave, I will be thy destruction: repentance shall be hid from mine eyes." (Hosea 13:12-14) Instead of this text's referring to the ransom of Adam's offspring by the precious blood of Jesus, it applies to the "new creation". (2 Corinthians 5:17, *Diaglott*) In confirmation of this conclusion that the ones here redeemed are the faithful ones brought into God's organization, the apostle quotes from this very text, to wit: "O death, where is thy sting? O grave, where is thy victory?" (1 Corinthians 15:55) These anointed ones of God were redeemed from death at the time they were justified by Jehovah, following their consecration. The redemption here prophesied by Hosea, however, takes place after the spirit-begotten ones have proved their faithfulness and maintained their integrity toward God and are brought into the temple.

This text could not be properly applied to the purchase of the entire human race by the shed blood of Christ Jesus, since we see that the language of the text refers only to those who have been justified and begotten of the spirit. (John 3:3, 5) The redeemed ones are delivered into the kingdom by being brought into the temple. In 1918 or thereabout Satan attempted to destroy all the consecrated. The "Ephraim" class fell away and became the "evil servant" (Matthew 24:48-51), and God did not permit that class to stay long in Zion; and as to these faithful ones, these were ransomed or delivered from the power of the adversary, who hoped to put them in the grave and destroy them in death. The year 1914 marked the time when Christ Jesus took his power to reign and was sent forth by Jehovah to reign. The war began in heaven and also in the earth. (Revelation 12:7-12) That marked "the beginning of sorrows" upon the earth (Matthew 24:7, 8), and from then until 1919 God's spirit-begotten ones were in much distress; and in the year 1919 the Lord redeemed and delivered the faithful ones from Satan's organization and thus prevented the enemy from overwhelming them. Note further this text that confirms that conclusion: "Be in pain, and labour, to bring forth, O daughter of Zion, like a woman in travail; for now shalt thou go forth out of the city, and thou shalt dwell in the field, and thou shalt go even to Babylon; there shalt thou be delivered; there the Lord shall redeem thee from the hand of thine enemies."—Micah 4:10.

By his prophet Jehovah tells of a "highway", called "the way of holiness", over which the cleansed of the Lord must walk. (Isaiah 35:8-10) Prior to the coming of the Lord to the temple in 1918 the faithful were compelled to mingle with Satan's organization and the faithful believed that the rulers of this wicked world constituted the "higher powers" (Romans 13:1). When the Lord revealed to his faithful ones his capital organization and their relation thereto, then they discerned the true meaning of the "highway" and they immediately began their march thereupon. All the righteous must go thereupon. The remnant must take the lead upon the highway and teach others who are seeking the way to righteousness, that they may know the way to come to God and to Christ Jesus. The "unclean" are not permitted to enter that highway. Who shall go thereupon and go over the highway? The "redeemed" of the Lord; as it is written: "No lion shall be there, nor any ravenous beast shall go up thereon, it shall not be found there; but the redeemed shall walk there."—Isaiah 35:9.

The text last above quoted discloses the persons who are redeemed. In the following texts it appears that it is God's consecrated and devoted ones who are redeemed and that Jehovah God is the redeemer of those who are faithful to him, and that he is not the redeemer of the unbeliever or wicked ones. In support hereof note the following texts: Isaiah 41:14; Isaiah 43:14; Isaiah 44:6, 24; Isaiah 47:4; Isaiah 48:17, 20; Isaiah 49:7, 26; Isaiah 63:16; Jeremiah 50:33, 34.

Jehovah God is the Redeemer of Zion: "For thy Maker is thine husband; The Lord of hosts is his name; and thy Redeemer the Holy One of Israel; The God of the whole earth shall he be called. In a little wrath I hid my face from thee for a moment; but with everlasting kindness will I have mercy on thee, saith the Lord thy Redeemer."—Isaiah 54:5, 8.

The redeemed are brought fully into God's capital organization: "And the Redeemer shall come to Zion, and unto them that turn from transgression in Jacob, saith the Lord." (Isaiah 59:20; 60:16) Job pictures or represents those only who are wholly devoted to God, and as such he uses these words: "For I know that my Redeemer liveth, and that he shall stand at the latter day upon the earth." (Job 19:25) This text shows that the redemption or deliverance takes place in the latter days when Jehovah delivers his anointed people from Satan's wicked organization, particularly the religious element, which Satan uses to oppose, reproach and persecute them. "For their redeemer is mighty; he shall plead their cause with thee."—Proverbs 23:11.

In all the foregoing texts quoted or cited there is no direct mention made of a redemption- or redemptive money price or payment. The clear meaning given to all of such texts is that of liberation, freeing, rescuing, delivering from the hand of the enemy, that is, Satan's organization, including his agents that oppose and persecute God's anointed people. None of the enemy organization are ever redeemed, but, on the contrary, the redemption is always spoken of as from the enemy. It is Jehovah, acting by and through his Chief Executive Officer, Christ Jesus, that accomplishes such liberation, rescuing or deliverance from the enemy. The same Hebrew word *gaal* is translated "redeem" and "redeemed", and used in connection with a purchase price, in the following texts: "If thy brother be waxen poor, and hath sold away some of his possession, and if any of his kin come to redeem it, then shall he redeem that which his brother sold. And if the man have none to redeem it, and himself be able to redeem it [(*margin*) his hand hath attained and found sufficiency]; then let him count the years of the sale thereof, and restore the overplus unto the man to whom he sold it, that he may return unto his possession. . . . And if it be not redeemed within the space of a full year, then the house that is in the walled city shall be established for ever to him that bought it, throughout his generations: it shall not go out in the jubilee. . . . And if a man purchase of the Levites [(*margin*) one of the Levites redeem them], then the house that was sold, and the city of his possession, shall go out in the year of jubilee: for the houses of the cities of the Levites are their possession among the children of Israel. . . . After that he is sold he may be redeemed again; one of his brethren may redeem him: either his uncle, or his uncle's son, may redeem him, or any that is nigh of kin unto him of his family may redeem him; or, if he be able, he may redeem himself. And he shall reckon with him that bought him from the year that he was sold to him unto the year of jubilee; and the price of his sale shall be according unto the number of years; according to the time of an hired servant shall it be with him." (Leviticus 25: 25-50) In the following texts, note that the redeemer was required to add one-fifth extra to the price at which the priests valued the thing to be redeemed.—Leviticus 27: 13, 15, 19, 20, 27, 28, 31, 33.

In the foregoing texts the use of the Hebrew word *gaal* is like that in the book of Ruth, which according to Young's translation reads as follows: "And Naomi said to her daughter-in-law: 'Blessed is he [Boaz] of Jehovah, who hath not forsaken His kindness with the living and with the dead'; and Naomi saith to her [Ruth]: 'The man is a relation of ours; he is of our redeemers.'" (Ruth 2: 20) In the following texts the word "kinsman", as it appears in the Authorized Version of the Bible, is from the same Hebrew word *gaal*, which, according to Young, is in each instance rendered "redeemer". In reading the

Authorized Version substitute the word *redeemer* for *kinsman,* wherever it occurs in these texts, to wit: Ruth 3:9, 12, 13; Ruth 4:1, 3, 4, 6, 8, 14. A similar transaction is described at Jeremiah 32:7-9, wherein the word is similarly used. In the fulfillment of the picture made by Ruth and Boaz, the class represented by Ruth is the remnant of Jehovah brought to the Lord, after his coming to the temple, by Christ Jesus, the Greater Boaz, who applies his ransom merit from and after the year 1922, purchasing them that they might be justified and accepted as a part of his royal organization; which are then brought into his fold and made members of the "body of Christ".

CITIES OF REFUGE

The same Hebrew word *gaal* is used in connection with the cities of refuge and the avenging of the blood of the slain one. In such case something is required to be paid over that is equal to what was lost, that is to say, a life for a life, the same rule that was applied in Deuteronomy 19:21, wherein it is written: "And thine eye shall not pity; but life shall go for life, eye for eye, tooth for tooth, hand for hand, foot for foot." Referring to the cities of refuge, one who slays a murderer is called "the revenger [or redeemer] of blood". In the texts following, the Authorized Version renders the Hebrew word *gaal* "avenger" or "revenger", and Young translates the same Hebrew word "redeemer", to wit: Numbers 35:12, 19, 21, 24, 25, 27. That redeeming of the blood, in each case, does not refer to the blood-bought redemption at Calvary, but to the paying in kind, that is, a retribution paid out to the death-dealing enemies of the Lord at the battle of Armageddon, and which is paid by the antitypical Revenger or Redeemer, Christ Jesus, as an offset to the blood that was spilled by the enemies of the Lord. Otherwise stated, the Revenger or Redeemer, Christ Jesus, squares the account with the enemies of the Lord at the battle of Armageddon.

One who had unawares, unwittingly and without enmity or malice slain another might escape the blood-avenger or redeemer by fleeing to and remaining in the city of refuge until the death of the sin-atoning high priest; that is, antitypically he must flee to God's organization under Christ and there remain under the sin-atoning blood of Christ Jesus, trusting in that shed blood as a means of protection and salvation. Those who in the present time have unwittingly done violence to God's law and against his people may gain redemption from destruction by and through the redeeming blood of the great High Priest, Christ Jesus. In this picture the destruction of the enemy of God at Armageddon is foreshadowed as a redemptive price for those slain by the wicked. Christ Jesus, the great High Priest and Executive Officer of Jehovah, with the value of his sacrifice, provides redemption for those who flee to him for refuge, and he is the Executioner of those who remain in the enemy camp and who because of their wickedness suffer destruction in order to offset the wickedness done by them to the Lord and his people. In both cases there is a freeing or delivering by means of a meeting or squaring the obligation, that is, meeting the penalty for sin.

The redemptive price provided at Calvary was for those who exercised faith in and obedience to the commands of the Lord. The redemption at Armageddon punishes the deserving ones, that is, the ones who have caused damage intentionally or otherwise. Those who have thus damaged or committed violence against God's little ones are indebted or obligated on account of their wickedness, and such are bound to pay and they pay at Armageddon with their lives. They cannot pay the debt to the damaged one, because that one is dead, but they must pay to the dead one's next nearest of kin in flesh and blood. As he who causes the death of the slain one is a debtor, so death must be meted out to that slayer by the slain one's nearest of kin, "the redeemer," and the redeemer removes the debt by exacting the life of the slayer. Note now God's words concerning "Christendom" and all the nations that have willfully violated the everlasting covenant. The account must be squared with all of these, and therefore the Lord says: "The land shall be utterly emptied, and utterly spoiled; for the Lord hath spoken this word. The earth mourneth, and fadeth away; the world languisheth, and fadeth away; the haughty people of the earth do languish. The earth also is defiled under the inhabitants thereof, because they have transgressed the laws, changed the ordinance, broken the everlasting covenant."—Isaiah 24: 3-5.

In the case of the unwitting slayer, life is not exacted of him, but in the type he is covered and shielded by the high priest, and in the antitype by the great High Priest, Christ Jesus, who makes atonement for those who flee to Christ. In the type the malicious, willful and deliberate slayer could in no wise have satisfaction met or accepted for his life by any other means, but his life must be taken by the avenger or redeemer. This is done upon the wicked by the great Redeemer at Armageddon. This well pictures and foretells the fact that the sacrificed life of the man Jesus does not stand as an atonement for or ransom for the willfully wicked who spurn God and his provisions for salvation. Such as die at Armageddon under such conditions of willful wickedness certainly will never have a redemption. (Numbers 35:30-33) All the Scripture texts wherein the Hebrew word *gaal* is used prove that in no case are the wicked redeemed, but that only the Lord's poor and needy are redeemed. By "poor and needy" is meant those who come to a realization of their own utter inability to save themselves and who desire to be saved, who exercise faith in God and in Christ Jesus, and apply to Christ Jesus to be saved or redeemed. All those who are wicked and refuse to accept God's provision for salvation abide under the condemnation resulting from Adam's sin: "The wicked shall be turned into hell, and all the nations that forget God."—Psalm 9:17.

TO COVER

The Hebrew word *khopher* is also translated "ransom". It is derived from the Hebrew *khaphar,* which means "to cover". It first appears in the Bible at Genesis 6:14, wherein

God said to Noah: "Make thee an ark of gopher wood: rooms shalt thou make in the ark, and shalt pitch it within and without with pitch [*khopher*]." This same word describes the cover charge or covering price concerning the owner of a death-dealing ox in the following text, to wit: "But if the ox were wont to push with his horn in time past, and it hath been testified to his owner, and he hath not kept him in, but that he hath killed a man or a woman; the ox shall be stoned, and his owner also shall be put to death [for willful negligence in not responding to the notice given]. If there be laid on him [the owner] a sum of money [*khopher;* a price to cover the damage; according to Young: an atonement], then he shall give, for the ransom of his life, whatsoever is laid upon him."—Exodus 21 : 29, 30.

As it appears that the payment of a money ransom was allowed only because the owner of the ox was not the deliberate and direct slayer of the one who was killed, but had been indirectly the cause of death by reason of his negligence, a cover charge or atonement money was taken.

After the census of the Israelites was taken, a ransom was to be paid, as stated in the following text: "When thou takest the sum [census] of the children of Israel, after their number, then shall they give every man a ransom [(Hebrew) *khopher*] for his soul unto the Lord, when thou numberest them; that there be no plague among them when thou numberest them. This they shall give, every one that passeth among them that are numbered, half a shekel after the shekel of the sanctuary: (a shekel is twenty

gerahs:) an half shekel shall be the offering of
the Lord."—Exodus 30:12, 13.

Certainly the ransom named in this text was
not a "corresponding price". The *Septuagint*
renders the Hebrew by the Greek word *lytron,*
which is translated into the English "ransom".
This shows that the English word "ransom" in
itself does not at all times mean "an exact corresponding price". Not all ransoms are a corresponding price; but that of Christ Jesus, that is,
his own precious blood, was and had to be a
corresponding price because such was required
to purchase for Adam's offspring that which
Adam had lost for them.

In the following text in which the word "ransom" appears the translation is from the Hebrew *khopher* and has often been improperly
applied to mankind in general, to wit: "If there
be a messenger with him, an interpreter, one
among a thousand, to shew unto man his uprightness; then he is gracious unto him, and
saith, Deliver him from going down to the pit;
I have found a ransom [an atonement (*Young*)].
He will deliver his soul from going into the
pit, and his life shall see the light."—Job
33:23, 24, 28.

In this prophetic picture Job represents the
faithful followers of Christ Jesus, and the covering ransom is found in the advocacy of Christ
Jesus, who is called in this scripture the Messenger or Interpreter. In the year 1918 the antitypical Job class, the faithful followers of Christ
Jesus whom Job represented, were in great distress because of oppression heaped upon them
by the enemy. In that year the Lord Jesus came

to the temple of Jehovah God. The holy spirit
that had been the guide of God's people, having
performed its functions, was taken away, and the
Lord Jesus himself, being present, represented
his people and advocated in their behalf before
Jehovah God, that is, in behalf of those who had
fallen into distress because of their failure to
properly use their lips in proclaiming the truth.
That class is pictured in the prophecy of Isaiah,
wherein they cried unto the Lord and the Lord
heard them and relieved them. (Isaiah 6:6, 7;
12:1) The faithful who thus cried unto the Lord
are the ones who found a covering ransom in
the advocacy of Christ Jesus. Certainly this did
not apply to the "evil servant" class. Only the
faithful remnant were spared from going down
into the pit, because for them there was a covering. This text has heretofore been applied as a
"restitution" text, that is, to the 'people that
will be restored in the days of Christ's reign'.
But the application in this manner is not correct.
It was the faithful who found an atonement or
deliverance by and through their Advocate,
Christ Jesus.

EXCLUDED

That there are those who are excluded from
the beneficial results of the ransom is fully
shown from the following scriptures. It appears
from the context that the unransomed cases appear before and down to the time of Armageddon, and not beyond Armageddon and during
the thousand-year reign of the King, Christ
Jesus. The provision in relation to the city of
refuge is in point of proof, showing that God

foretold by this prophetic picture that there are those for whom satisfaction or atonement cannot be made. The text in point reads: "Moreover, ye shall take no satisfaction [atonement (according to Young's translation)] for the life of a murderer, which is guilty of death; but he shall be surely put to death. And ye shall take no satisfaction [atonement] for him that is fled to the city of his refuge, that he should come again to dwell in the land until the death of the priest." —Numbers 35:31, 32.

Not even the atonement of the great High Priest, Christ Jesus, could cover the malicious, willful and deliberate man-slayer. Also those receiving the sin-atoning merit of the great High Priest before Armageddon and who get out from under the covering thereof could not hope for any chance of salvation during or after Armageddon, and during the reign of Christ. The prophet Samuel applies this same rule, as noted in 1 Samuel 12:3, *margin:* "Behold, here I am: witness against me before the Lord, and before his anointed: whose ox have I taken? or whose ass have I taken? or whom have I defrauded? whom have I oppressed? or of whose hand have I received any bribe [(*margin*) ransom] to blind mine eyes therewith? and I will restore it you." Thus it is seen that some are completely excluded from the benefit of the ransom sacrifice.

God's servant Elihu, in the picture relative to Job, spoke with authority announcing God's fixed rule, when he said: "But thou hast fulfilled the judgment of the wicked: judgment and justice take hold on thee. Because there is wrath, beware lest he take thee away with his stroke:

then a great ransom [atonement (*Young*)] cannot deliver thee." (Job 36:17, 18) Men of great wealth, either of money or of position, influence and honor amongst men, such as the exalted clergy or their rich "principal of the flock", think themselves especially favored of God and Christ and rely for safety upon their own wealth, honor and position. But what is the end thereof, according to the Scriptures? "They that trust in their wealth, and boast themselves in the multitude of their riches; none of them can by any means redeem his brother, nor give to God a ransom [atonement (*Young*)] for him; (for the redemption of their soul is precious, and it ceaseth for ever;) that he should still live for ever, and not see corruption." (Psalm 49:6-9) Such men die like brute beasts, because they have no standing above the beast: "Man that is in honour, and understandeth not, is like the beasts that perish."—Psalm 49:20.

In the following texts the word for "envy" (*Strong's*) is translated in the Authorized Version "jealousy". "For jealousy [envy] is the rage of a man; therefore he will not spare in the day of vengeance. He [Christ Jesus, the great High Priest] will not regard any ransom [atonement]; neither will he rest content, though thou givest many gifts [from human priests or clergy or intermediary, whether paid for 'purgatory' prayers or otherwise]."—Proverbs 6:34, 35.

Nor can such provide for or purchase their life by throwing their gold into the streets. Their deliverance cannot be bought by themselves in any manner. Man's riches cannot ransom him: "There is that maketh himself rich, yet hath

nothing: there is that maketh himself poor, yet
hath great riches. The ransom [which the guilty
would pay] of a man's life are his riches [which
Jehovah rebukes]: but the poor [of the Lord,
who are poor in their own estimation, relying
solely upon the Lord] heareth not rebuke."—
Proverbs 13: 7, 8.

The wicked become the ransom for the righteous in certain conditions. And how? "The
wicked shall be a ransom [atonement (*Young*)]
for the righteous, and the transgressor for the
upright." (Proverbs 21:18) This scripture applies at Armageddon. In the expression of Jehovah God's wrath through Christ Jesus at that
time the wicked and willful transgressors must
be put to death as the price of freedom for the
righteous and upright, to the end that the righteous and the upright may be delivered from the
abuse and oppression by the wicked and willful
transgressors. By the death of the willfully
wicked transgressors they ransom the righteous.
The reason is, because the wicked and transgressors will not submit to any other arrangement
for the freedom of the righteous and the Lord
enforces this remedy against them. In support
of this, note Isaiah 43: 1, 3, 4: "But now thus
saith the Lord that created thee, O Jacob, and
he that formed thee, O Israel, Fear not; for I
have redeemed thee, I have called thee by thy
name; thou art mine. For I am the Lord thy
God, the Holy One of Israel, thy Saviour: I gave
Egypt for thy ransom [atonement], Ethiopia
and Seba for thee. Since thou wast precious in
my sight, thou hast been honourable, and I have
loved thee: therefore will I give men [the wicked

men] for thee, and people [the transgressors] for thy life."

The religious Israelites conspired together to kill Jeremiah, God's faithful servant and prophet. Likewise the present-day religionists and their allies conspire together to kill Jehovah's witnesses, of whom the prophet Jeremiah was a type, example or pattern. At the direction of the Lord, God's prophet records the purpose of Jehovah concerning such: "For they [the religious conspirators] have digged a pit to take me [God's anointed], and hid snares [traps laid by the clergy and their religious allies against Jehovah's witnesses] for my feet [the 'feet' of Christ Jesus, the last members on earth]. Yet, Lord, thou knowest all their counsel against me to slay me: forgive not their iniquity [thou dost not cover over their iniquity (*Young*)], neither blot out their sin from thy sight; but let them be overthrown [at Armageddon] before thee: deal thus with them in the time of thine anger." (Jeremiah 18: 22, 23) This shows that such conspirators do not have the benefit of the ransom sacrifice at Armageddon or thereafter.

The sons of Eli, the high priest of Israel at Shiloh, were wicked; and those wicked sons pictured "the man of sin", made up of the "evil servant", the religious persecutors of God's people, and allies, and concerning such it is written: "For I have told him that I will judge his house for ever for the iniquity which he knoweth; because his sons made themselves vile, and he restrained them not. And therefore I have sworn unto the house of Eli, that the iniquity of Eli's house shall not be purged with sacrifice nor offering for ever." (1 Samuel 3:13, 14) What befell Shiloh pictures what shall shortly come to pass upon the religionists of "Christendom", and this is shown by Jeremiah 7:14: "Therefore will I do unto this house, which is called by my name, wherein ye trust, and unto the place which I gave to you and to your fathers, as I have done to Shiloh."

The Scriptures written under inspiration by the apostles fully corroborate this conclusion, that there is no ransom for those who are knowingly wicked and who purposely persecute others because of the faithfulness of such others in their devotion and service to the Lord. (Hebrews 6:4-6) "For if we sin wilfully after that we have received the knowledge of the truth, there remaineth no more sacrifice for sins, but a certain fearful looking for of judgment, and fiery indignation, which shall devour the adversaries. He that despised Moses' law died without mercy under two or three witnesses; of how much sorer punishment, suppose ye, shall he be thought worthy, who hath trodden under foot the Son of God, and hath counted the blood of the covenant, wherewith he was sanctified, an unholy thing, and hath done despite unto the spirit of grace?"—Hebrews 10:26-29.

FIRSTBORN

The Hebrew word *pahdah* is rendered "ransom". It means "to let go; to let loose; to ransom". This word is used at Exodus 13:13, 15, and is rendered in the Authorized Version of the Bible "redeem", and according to Young is translated "ransom". To Moses Jehovah said:

"And every firstling of an ass thou dost ransom with a lamb; and if thou dost not ransom it, then thou hast beheaded it; and every first-born of man among thy sons thou dost ransom. Yea, it cometh to pass when Pharaoh hath been pained to send us away, that Jehovah doth slay every first-born in the land of Egypt, from the first-born of man even unto the first-born of beast; therefore I am sacrificing to Jehovah all opening a womb who are males, and every first-born of my sons I ransom." (Young's translation) This shows that the original firstborn of Israel in Egypt were ransomed from death at the hand of God's destroying angel although a "correspondent price" was not given.

Referring again to the man who owned an ox that killed a man and against whom the obligation rested as the owner, it is written: "If there be laid on him [that is, the owner of the ox] a sum of money [as a penalty], then he shall give, for the ransom of his life, whatsoever is laid upon him." (Exodus 21:30) In such a case his ransom is from the penalty of death; that is to say, he paid a sum of money instead of paying by his life.

There is nothing in the typical picture that foreshadows or foretells that Jehovah provides a ransom or redemption for all human creatures down to and including the wicked individuals; and therefore the conclusion must be that during the thousand-year reign of Christ the willfully wicked will not be brought back from death. Note that before the coming of Jesus the "ransom" or "redemption" spoken of in the Scriptures applied as follows: To Israel (Jacob) as

shown at Deuteronomy 7:8; 13:5; 21:8; Psalm
25:22; 1 Chronicles 17:21; applied to "thine
inheritance" (Deuteronomy 9:26); applied to
David, out of adversity and distress (2 Samuel
4:9; 1 Kings 1:29); applied to "my soul"
(Psalm 49:15); to "his soul" (repentant ones)
(Job 33:27, 28); to Christ Jesus (Psalm
69:18-20); to the remnant, already justified
by faith through the ransom price of Christ
Jesus, and now needing deliverance from the
strong enemy (Jeremiah 15:21), which latter
text reads: "And I will deliver thee [the remnant, represented in Jeremiah] out of the hand
of the wicked, and I will redeem [have ransomed (*Young*)] thee out of the hand of the
terrible."—Jeremiah 15:21.

The following texts apply exclusively to those
who have previously been bought with the precious blood of Christ Jesus but now have the
promise of deliverance from the enemy: Isaiah
35:10; Isaiah 51:11; Isaiah 1:27; Jeremiah
31:11, 12; Hosea 13:14. "I will hiss for them,
and gather them [to the temple, that is, Zion];
for I have redeemed them [from Babylon, Satan's organization]: and they shall increase as
they have increased."—Zechariah 10:8.

BRINGING BACK

It has been held by many that the Scriptures
guarantee that "all must come back from the
dead" at Christ's return and during his thousand-year rule. (*Studies in the Scriptures*, Volume Five, pages 478-486) That conclusion does
not appear to have support in reason or in the
Scriptures. No one will receive the benefit of the

ransom sacrifice or ransom price that has been paid unless he willingly avails himself of that privilege. It appears, then, that God would bring back from death only those who could and possibly would avail themselves of the ransom when coming to a knowledge of the truth, because the ransom is available only for such, and not those who have no desire to be reformed or saved. The gift of God is not forced upon unwilling creatures.

Let it be fixed in mind that in the redemption of mankind by the blood of Christ Jesus the attribute of justice is not involved. If the divine rule of justice alone is invoked and applied, then the entire human race must perish because of sin and imperfection. It is the attribute of love that is involved. Mercy is the result of the exercise of God's loving-kindness. From the viewpoint of justice God is under no obligation whatsoever to ransom sinful men, nor is God obligated to extend his mercy to every creature regardless of whether that creature desires and seeks mercy. With the two sons of Isaac God made a prophetic picture showing his foreknowledge of the class of persons who seek the way of righteousness and life, and also of that class that takes exactly the opposite course. It is written:

"As it is written: Jacob have I loved, but Esau have I hated." (Romans 9:13) "Jacob" here represents that class that seek the Lord and find him and faithfully serve him; and such God loves. "Esau" represents the unfaithful class, who do not regard God's gracious provision for mankind. God foreknew those two classes, and he so foretold the same, because he foreknows everything: "Known unto God are all his works, from the beginning of the world." (Acts 15: 18) Surely God foreknew those human creatures who shall spurn his proffered blessings of life, and he foreknew the class that would gladly accept his gracious provision. It follows, then, that those who have no desire to know God and Christ Jesus, and no desire to receive God's blessings through Christ Jesus, on such He will not have mercy, and God will not force his mercy upon them. Could it be argued that justice toward all would require God to force his mercy upon all, even though he knows in advance that such persons would reject his loving-kindness? Certainly not. Justice is righteousness, and injustice is unrighteousness. The argument advanced by the inspired Word of God is: "What shall we say then? Is there unrighteousness with God? God forbid. For he saith to Moses, I will have mercy on whom I will have mercy, and I will have compassion on whom I will have compassion. So then it is not of him that willeth, nor of him that runneth, but of God that sheweth mercy." (Romans 9: 14-16) This statement is made in connection with the challenge of the Devil made to Jehovah God, and thus God discloses His purpose to extend his mercy toward those who hear the testimony and prove their integrity toward Jehovah. To hold that because God is just he is under obligation to extend mercy to everyone is entirely inconsistent and wrong. To hold that because of justice God is bound to give every creature the benefit of salvation by the ransom sacrifice is wrong, and

wholly unsupported either by reason or by the
Scriptures. To hold that God is obligated to save
all men in order to fully prove his supremacy
is entirely wrong and unsupported by any authority.

The challenge of the Devil raised the question of God's ability to put any man on earth
who willingly would remain faithful and true
to God when he was subjected to the test im-
posed by the Devil. Concerning that challenge
all the evidence abundantly shows that God has
proved Satan a liar and has proved his own
supremacy beyond any question of doubt, in this,
that many men up to the present time have maintained their integrity toward God. At Armageddon God will completely wipe out everything
that Satan has brought forward in opposition
to God, and therefore will completely establish
His own supremacy. Whosoever, therefore, willingly avails himself of God's gracious gift will
be blessed with life, and he will have an opportunity of proving that Satan's wicked challenge
is a defamation of God's name and His word,
and that Satan is a liar and God is true. Men
have gotten themselves into great difficulty concerning the ransom by proceeding upon the
theory that the question of justice is involved.

When God sentenced Adam to death justice
required the forfeiture of Adam's life. When
Adam went down into the dust from which he
came justice was completely satisfied. Justice
has been satisfied at all times since, so far as
Adam was concerned, Adam's offspring justly
came under condemnation by inheritance, but,
not being under direct judgment themselves,

God could consistently extend his mercy toward them. It was not a question of satisfying justice by the death of another perfect man, and the death of Jesus was not for the purpose of satisfying justice. If Jehovah would accept the perfect life of Christ Jesus in satisfaction of justice, that would mean that either the judgment against Adam was not satisfied or else the life-blood of Jesus poured out was a double satisfaction; which would be entirely inconsistent and impossible with Jehovah God.

Viewing the matter now from the point of love: God unselfishly provided, and, without a doubt, Jesus agreed with Jehovah, that he should become a man, and that he should lay down his life and that perfect human life laid down would be equivalent to what Adam's offspring would have been entitled to and would have received from their father Adam. When that equivalent, to wit, the perfect human life of Jesus and the right thereto, is presented to Jehovah God in heaven, it constitutes and constituted the purchase price of all the rights which Adam's offspring had lost by reason of Adam's sin. Therefore Christ Jesus' receiving life as a spirit creature and paying over his right to life as a human creature made him by right of purchase the owner of every one of Adam's offspring that would comply with God's requirements, to wit: have faith in God and in Christ Jesus, and meet the rules subsequently made to govern all who take that step of faith. The ransom sacrifice of the Lord Jesus Christ is a price exactly corresponding to what Adam lost; but it is not a substitute for Adam, nor was it given for the purpose of satisfying justice, but was given as a purchase price. Jehovah God makes Jesus "the Everlasting Father", that is to say, the one who administers life everlasting. But upon what condition? That men comply with God's requirements. (Isaiah 9:6) Hence it is written that 'life is the gift of God through Jesus Christ our Lord'. (Romans 6:23) A gift cannot become operative except by the meeting of the minds of the giver and the receiver. Otherwise stated, the offer must be made, and the one to whom it is offered must willingly accept that offer. It follows, then, that the man to whom the offer is made available and who refuses or fails to accept that offer, the gift does not operate toward him. Consequently the ransom sacrifice inures to the benefit of only those who ask for and willingly receive its benefits.

As stated in the Scriptures, all men have come under condemnation, which must result ultimately in death unless provision is made for redemption. (Romans 5:12) God has graciously provided and placed before mankind the way of escape from death and hence the way to obtain life everlasting. Men must choose either to remain under condemnation that justly rests upon them or to avail themselves of the loving-kindness and mercy of God and seek and willingly accept God's gracious provision of salvation by which man obtains life. The way of escape from death and the way to everlasting life are by and through Christ Jesus. God laid him as the foundation, and there is no other way and no other name whereby man receives life. Only those who believe that God has made such provision and that Christ Jesus is the means of salvation can possibly be saved. During the centuries past many have been brought face to face with God's provision for life and have willfully and deliberately spurned the same. They have died in their sins, that condemnation abiding upon them. It is not reasonably possible that God will bring them back and give them another chance to reject his gracious offer of life.

What is here said is not in the least contrary to or out of harmony with the Scriptural declaration uttered by John the Baptist concerning Jesus, to wit: "Behold the Lamb of God, which taketh away the sin of the world." (John 1: 29) This emphatic declaration cannot be construed to mean that Jesus removes the sin of all those of the world who refuse to avail themselves of the opportunity but who willingly choose the way of wickedness, which means absolute death. In times past there have been many, and there are yet many of such. The words of Jesus are emphatic, to wit: "For God sent not his Son into the world to condemn the world; but that the world through him might be saved. He that believeth on him is not condemned; but he that believeth not is condemned already, because he hath not believed in the name of the only begotten Son of God."—John 3: 17, 18.

When Jesus was on the earth he vigorously condemned the Pharisees and their religious allies, telling them that they were the offspring of the Devil and worthy of death. To hold that the ransom sacrifice would apply to such opposers of the Lord and his kingdom would be to deny the sincerity and truth of Jesus' condemna-

tion of such wicked ones. The loving-kindness
and mercy of Jehovah is extended to all men
who willingly and voluntarily believe God and
faithfully serve him and his beloved Son, Christ
Jesus: "Whoso is wise, and will observe these
things, even they shall understand the loving-
kindness of the Lord."—Psalm 107:43.

There is a class of clergymen throughout
"Christendom", wise in their own conceit, who
adopt the words of the bishop of Birmingham,
who says: "The story of the sin and fall of
Adam, and redemption by Christ Jesus, is folk-
lore." Those men are known as "higher critics"
and deny that there is any value in the shed
blood of Jesus. They have an opportunity to
know of God's provision of salvation, and willfully and deliberately shun the same and lead
others into the same error. Those higher critics
pose before the people as preachers of righteousness. They call themselves "doctors of
divinity", "clergymen," "bishops," and other
high-sounding titles. They are religionists and
leaders in religious organizations. They have
substituted the doctrines of men for the Word
of God, and thus they have made the Word of
God of none effect. (Matthew 15:6-9) The people must choose either to follow these human
leaders of man-made organizations or else to
accept the Word of Jehovah God and the Lord
Jesus Christ. To follow religionists who thus
deny God's Word, therefore, means that all who
do, remain under the condemnation that came
upon them by inheritance, and are subjects of
God's wrath. To disregard these worldly-wise
men and give full heed to the Word and admoni-

tion of Jehovah and his Son, Christ Jesus, means to find life. The scripture upon this point is emphatic: "He that believeth on the Son hath everlasting life: and he that believeth not the Son shall not see life; but the wrath of God abideth on him." (John 3:36) All by inheritance being under condemnation, and God having provided the one way to get out, there is no other way, and therefore Jesus says: 'This is life eternal, to know thee the only true God, and Jesus Christ, whom thou hast sent.' (John 17:3) Surely, then, everyone who has a desire for life will eagerly seek to know what God requires of man in order to receive life everlasting.

CHAPTER V

REQUIREMENTS

EVERY sane person desires to live. Life everlasting in a state of perfect peace and happiness, what more could one desire? The time has come for sincere persons to live for ever on the earth if such will comply with God's requirements. From and after Armageddon the kingdom of God will be in full control of the earth. Concerning the result to obedient human creatures it is written: "And God shall wipe away all tears from their eyes; and there shall be no more death, neither sorrow, nor crying, neither shall there be any more pain: for the former things are passed away." (Revelation 21:4) The human race has been afflicted with sickness, sorrow and death for such a great period of time that many find it difficult to believe that conditions will ever change. Let each one satisfy himself on this point by giving diligence to learn the truth. God's arrangement is that there is a time for everything; and now is the time for people of good will to learn the way to life everlasting.—Psalm 16:11.

In the preceding chapters the indisputable facts are submitted proving that death is the result of sin, which comes upon all men by inheritance; that to Jehovah God belongs salvation; that the greatest crisis of all time is at hand, when the wicked will be destroyed at Armageddon and when those who seek righteousness and meekness may be spared in that great disaster; that salvation from death, and life for ever in happiness, are open to the obedient ones; and that therefore a great emergency now confronts those who shall form the "great multitude". In order to gain life everlasting one must conform oneself to God's requirements. What is revealed by the Scriptures as that God requires of man?

FAITH

All who would receive the gracious gift of life must please God. Faith is the first requirement. "But without faith it is impossible to please him: for he that cometh to God must believe that he is, and that he is a rewarder of them that diligently seek him." (Hebrews 11:6) That means that the ones who desire to live must believe first that God is the Almighty, whose name is Jehovah, that he is the Supreme One, and that he is the rewarder of them that diligently seek him. Their desire is to be in harmony with the Almighty God. His provision for life is by and through Christ Jesus. Therefore Jesus says: "I am the way, and the truth, and the life; no man cometh unto [God] the Father, but by me." (John 14:6) "And this is life eternal, that they might know thee the only true God, and Jesus Christ, whom thou hast sent." (John 17:3) Jesus buys every one of the human race that asks to be bought; and, being bought, that is to say, receiving the benefit of the ransom price paid for man, the bought ones become the bond servants of the Lord, and therefore Jesus

says: "If any man serve me, let him follow me."
(John 12:26) The first requirement, therefore,
is to believe in God, the Almighty, believe in the
Lord Jesus Christ as man's Redeemer or purchaser, and then to follow Jesus. The man
proves his belief by the course of action he takes.

CONSECRATION

The next requirement to be met is to do the
will of Almighty God, because that is what Jesus always does; as it is written: "Then said
he [Jesus], Lo, I come to do thy will, O God.
He taketh away the first, that he may establish
the second." (Hebrews 10:9) "I delight to do
thy will, O my God; yea, thy law is within my
heart." (Psalm 40:8) Imperfect man is selfish
and desires to do his own will; but, having believed on God and Christ Jesus, that man then
must voluntarily surrender his own selfish will,
agreeing to do whatsoever is God's will concerning him. That means consecration of the man by
agreeing to serve Jehovah God through Christ
Jesus; and such consecration must be unconditional, that is to say, the person must gladly
forego the doing of his own selfish will and way
and diligently seek to know and to do what is
the will of Jehovah God. What, then, is the will
of God concerning the Lord's "other sheep" who
will constitute the great multitude? They must
gather themselves together unto the Lord.
(Zephaniah 2:1) Such are either directly or indirectly in or under the influence of the religious
organization of Satan, which is called "Babylon"; and that organization the person must
abandon. As shown by the typical city of refuge,

such person must flee to Christ, the Head of
God's organization, and there find refuge until
the crisis or emergency of Armageddon is
passed. That person must recognize Christ Jesus as the "bread of life"; and as the people of
Egypt asked Joseph to buy them so that they
might not die, so now the Lord's "other sheep",
who will form the great multitude, must ask
Christ Jesus, the Greater Joseph, to buy them
and feed them upon the "bread of life" that they
may not die. They must see that God's kingdom
under Christ is the only means of escape from
the crisis, and the only place of protection and
salvation. The religious institutions are snares
into which Satan draws men and entraps them;
and the one who would live must avoid such
snares and give himself entirely into the possession and protection of Christ Jesus.

The person who believes that Jehovah God is
supreme and that Christ Jesus is God's Executive Officer, great High Priest and King, and
Redeemer of man, is therefore anxious to know
and do the will of God. Belief does not mean
merely a mental conception of the fact that God
is supreme and that Christ Jesus is the Redeemer, but it means to acknowledge the same
and to act accordingly: "That if thou shalt confess with thy mouth the Lord Jesus, and shalt
believe in thine heart that God hath raised him
from the dead, thou shalt be saved. For with
the heart man believeth unto righteousness; and
with the mouth confession is made unto salvation. For the scripture saith, Whosoever believeth on him shall not be ashamed."—Romans
10:9-11.

Fleeing from Satan's organization and seeking refuge under Christ's organization means that such a one acknowledges the Lord Jesus Christ and asks Christ to take him in. He is not ashamed to confess before others his full confidence in God and Christ Jesus; and so he makes it known to others that he has taken his stand on the side of God and Christ and has voluntarily agreed to do the will of God. The heart is the seat of motive; and, therefore, when a person believes on the Lord, he is moved to make known to others that he has fled to Christ Jesus and has taken his stand on the side of the Lord and wishes to acknowledge that he has agreed to do the will of God. He seeks protection at the hand of Christ Jesus and calls upon the Lord for protection and salvation: "For whosoever shall call upon the name of the Lord shall be saved." (Romans 10:13) Being received by the Lord and under his protection, such person is in line to be saved from the devastation of Armageddon. God is always right, and the man who is guided by the will of God is always in the right way. The will of God is his expressed and perfect law concerning men: "The law of the Lord is perfect, converting the soul: the testimony of the Lord is sure, making wise the simple. The statutes of the Lord are right, rejoicing the heart: the commandment of the Lord is pure, enlightening the eyes." (Psalm 19:7, 8) "Thy testimonies that thou hast commanded are righteous and very faithful. Thy word is very pure: therefore thy servant loveth it. Thy righteousness is an everlasting righteousness, and thy law is the truth."—Psalm 119:138, 140, 142.

SANCTIFICATION

The next necessary step to take is that of sanctification. The proper understanding of "sanctification" and "sanctified" is quite essential in order that one may appreciate his relationship to God. There is first here set out the definitions of the following words as given by worldly lexicographers:

"SANCTIFICATION: The act of sanctifying; being sanctified.

"SANCTIFIED: Made holy.

"SANCTIMONIOUSNESS: Making a show of sanctity; assumed or hypocritical devoutness."

It is therefore seen from the foregoing definitions that there is a real sanctification and an assumed sanctification.

The Scriptures give the correct definitions. In the Scriptures the words "sanctification", "sanctify," "sanctified," and the word "holy" are all from the same Greek root word. God said to the Israelites, whom he had chosen for his typical people and with whom he made a covenant: "For I am the Lord your God; ye shall therefore sanctify yourselves, and ye shall be holy; for I am holy." (Leviticus 11:44) The inspired apostle quotes these words: "As obedient children, not fashioning yourselves according to the former lusts in your ignorance. Because it is written, Be ye holy; for I am holy." (1 Peter 1:14, 16) God is holy, since he is devoted exclusively to righteousness, hence wholly, entirely and fully righteous, or "holy". The Devil is wholly or completely devoted to wickedness, which is the very opposite of righteousness. To those who have taken the side of God the admonition is given: "But as he which hath called you is holy, so be ye holy in all manner of conversation [course of action]."—1 Peter 1:15.

There are those who profess to be on the Lord's side but who are in fact on the side of God's enemy, the Devil. Such persons are properly said to be sanctimonious, hypocritically holy, because they have an outward appearance of being one thing, when in fact they are the very opposite thing. Religionists are sanctimonious, but a real Christian is sanctified and holy, because the Christian is entirely on God's side. Religion breeds sanctimoniousness. "Christianity" means to be sanctified. The religious leaders of Israel, known as Pharisees, had the outward appearance of sanctity, but they were in fact hypocrites, and Jesus so identified them. To the people Jesus said of and concerning the Pharisees, the religious leaders: "Do not ye after their works. . . . For they bind heavy burdens, and grievous to be borne, and lay them on men's shoulders; but they themselves will not move them with one of their fingers. But all their works they do for to be seen of men: they make broad their phylacteries, and enlarge the borders of their garments, and love the uppermost rooms at feasts, and the chief seats in the synagogues, and greetings in the markets, and to be called of men, Rabbi, Rabbi. . . . And call no man your father upon the earth; for one is your Father, which is in heaven."—Matthew 23:3-9.

Then Jesus, addressing himself to the religious leaders who had made God's Word of no effect by their traditions, said: "Woe unto you, scribes and Pharisees, hypocrites! for ye make clean the outside of the cup and of the platter, but within they are full of extortion and excess." "Even so ye also outwardly appear righteous unto men, but within ye are full of hypocrisy and iniquity." (Matthew 23:25, 28) A like condition of sanctimoniousness is plainly seen among the present-day religious leaders.

"Sanctified," applied according to the Scriptures, means to be completely devoted to God and his kingdom, therefore holy, as God and Christ Jesus are holy. The Lord is wholly and completely devoted to righteousness; as it is written: "Righteous art thou, O Lord, and upright are thy judgments. Thy righteousness is an everlasting righteousness, and thy law is the truth." (Psalm 119:137, 142) To be righteous means to be right: "The statutes of the Lord are right, rejoicing the heart: the commandment of the Lord is pure, enlightening the eyes." (Psalm 19:8) "For the righteous Lord loveth righteousness; his countenance doth behold the upright." (Psalm 11:7) "Thy righteousness is like the great mountains"; that is, solid and everlasting. (Psalm 36:6) "Thy righteousness also, O God, is very high, who hast done great things: O God, who is like unto thee!" (Psalm 71:19) "His work is honourable and glorious: and his righteousness endureth for ever." (Psalm 111:3) The Lord Jesus is like his Father Jehovah; that is, entirely righteous. Of him it is written: "Thou lovest righteousness, and hatest wickedness: therefore God, thy God, hath anointed thee with the oil of gladness above thy fellows." (Psalm 45:7) Christ Jesus is the great Judge and King, who shall reign and rule in righteousness. (Isaiah 32:1; Psalm 96:13; Acts 17:31) Jehovah God is holy: "Exalt the Lord our God, and worship at his holy hill: for the Lord our God is holy." (Psalm 99:9) "The Lord is righteous in all his ways, and holy in all his works." (Psalm 145:17) Concerning the Lord Jesus it is written: "Who is holy, harmless, undefiled, separate from sinners."—Hebrews 7:26.

Christ Jesus is the Head of the "holy nation", that is to say, God's kingdom, which is devoted exclusively to righteousness and to the carrying out of Jehovah's purpose. (1 Peter 2:1-10) Every creature that pleases God and receives God's approval must be holy, that is to say, unreservedly devoted to God and to his kingdom, which is righteous. Therefore every one of such must be sanctified. That does not mean that the person is perfect in the flesh, but it does mean his heart devotion is unreservedly for the Lord. The faithful men of old from Abel to John the Baptist, including the holy prophets, were not perfect in their organism or flesh, but they were wholly and unreservedly devoted to Jehovah God, and therefore God's invisible power, his holy spirit, guided them in the right way, and they wrote accordingly. (2 Peter 1:21) The words for "holy spirit" are improperly translated "holy ghost" in many versions of the Bible. Wherever the words "holy ghost" appear, they mean "holy spirit". The sum total of the matter is that every creature who receives God's approval and is granted life everlasting, must be holy: wholly, completely, uncompromisingly and unreservedly devoted to that which is right and righteous; and therefore he is sanctified. Those who take their stand on the side of God, his King and his kingdom, must thenceforth be completely devoted to God and his kingdom and must avoid compromising with the world, which is the Devil's organization.

"Sanctification" is the act of sanctifying. The man who has agreed to do the will of God and has taken his stand by declaring himself for God and his kingdom must then act to the sanctifying of himself, which means that he sets himself to the task of fully performing his agreement to do the will of God. It will not do merely to agree, but he must perform his agreement. The Scriptural account of "the house of the Rechabites", that is, of the Jonadabs, is a striking example. Those men solemnly agreed that they would drink no wine and that they would dwell in tents. There was no evil in the drinking of a moderate amount of wine nor in the living in houses, but they agreed to do otherwise, and to them the important thing was to keep that agreement and perform it. They did faithfully keep their agreement, and because of that fact God said concerning them: "Jonadab the son of Rechab shall not want [that is, shall not fail of] a man to stand before me for ever." (Jeremiah 35:19) The faithful keeping of the agreement is what God approves. To be sanctified, therefore, means that the man who has agreed to do God's will sets himself faithfully to the task of performing his agreement, and hence sets himself aside and devotes himself wholly to that which is right and righteous. The man who takes the step of setting himself to the task of doing God's will is set to work by the Lord to do God's will and thus to maintain his integrity toward God.

How is man sanctified? Jesus answers in these words, addressed to Jehovah: "Sanctify them through thy truth: thy word is truth." (John 17:17) It is therefore impossible for any kind of religious ceremony to sanctify one to God. The clergy of the religious organizations can do nothing to sanctify a man to God. Sanctification is solely between the individual, who has agreed to do the will of God, and the Lord, who sets the man to work to prove his agreement. The man must learn what is the will of God toward him: "For this is the will of God, even your sanctification, that ye should abstain from fornication." (1 Thessalonians 4:3) In this text the word "fornication" means illicit relationship, whether between individuals or between a Christian and the world. The one who has agreed to do God's will is precluded from mixing up with or compromising with the world, or the Devil's organization; and to do so means an illicit relationship described as fornication or adultery. "Ye adulterers and adulteresses, know ye not that the friendship of the world is enmity with God? whosoever therefore will be a friend of the world, is the enemy of God."—James 4:4.

Satan is the god or invisible ruler of this wicked world, which world will be destroyed at Armageddon. (2 Corinthians 4:4; John 12:31;

14: 30) The consecrated and sanctified one must be entirely or wholly on the side of God and his kingdom and wholly or completely against the Devil and his organization. Such sanctified one must "study to show [himself] approved unto God", and not be ashamed or apologetic in doing the work which God has given him to do. (2 Timothy 2: 15) For the aid and comfort and hope of those who have taken their stand on the side of God and his kingdom the Scriptures have been provided by the Lord, and in these last days the Lord makes them to be understood and causes publications to be circulated among the people to aid them in understanding. For that purpose study classes are organized and carried on for the study of God's Word, that those who have made an agreement to do God's will may learn the right way.

The "other sheep" of the Lord, which he is now gathering, flee from Satan's organization and seek refuge in the Lord's organization and, having thus taken their stand on the side of the Lord, they cannot remain idle or indifferent. As the "strangers" among the Israelites were required to obey the law which God had given to Israel, so now the Jonadabs, or "other sheep", are required to obey. (Exodus 12: 48, 49) The "other sheep", who will compose the great multitude, have now become the "companions" of Jehovah's witnesses on earth, and the same law of God is the rule of action for both. They must be active in doing what the law of God commands to be done.

THINGS REQUIRED

As Jehovah has shown his witnesses, the remnant, so has he shown his "other sheep", who have consecrated and sanctified themselves to God, what is required, and therefore to all such he says: "He hath shewed thee, O man, what is good; and what doth the Lord require of thee, but to do justly, and to love mercy, and to walk humbly with thy God?"—Micah 6:8.

"To do justly" means to do what is right and righteous. The "other sheep" are specifically commanded to "seek righteousness", and therefore they must be diligent to ascertain what is righteousness in the sight of God. Jehovah deals justly with all, and never unjustly with any. To do justly, then, means to know God and his way and walk therein and do justly towards all; avoid everything that is unjust toward another. "Open thy mouth, judge righteously, and plead the cause of the poor and needy." (Proverbs 31:9) The poor and needy are particularly those who seek the Lord and hence who show a sincere desire to learn the truth. Concerning those who have God's approval it is written: "He that walketh righteously, and speaketh uprightly; he that refuseth the gain of exactions; that shaketh his hands free from holding a bribe; that stoppeth his ear from hearkening to deeds of blood, and shutteth his eyes from giving countenance to wrong." (Isaiah 33:15, *Rotherham*) "For the grace of God that bringeth salvation hath appeared to all men, teaching us, that, denying ungodliness and worldly lusts, we should live soberly, righteously, and godly, in this present world."—Titus 2:11, 12; 2 Corinthians 4:1, 2; 2 Corinthians 7:1.

One who has made a covenant to do the will of God must perform that covenant faithfully, and justice and righteousness requires such. That is of first importance; as it is written: "In the way of righteousness is life; and in the pathway thereof there is no death." (Proverbs 12:28) "The Lord . . . loveth him that followeth after righteousness." (Proverbs 15:9) Every person who is truly on the side of God and his King has a sincere desire to do good unto all who will receive that which is good: "As we have therefore opportunity, let us do good unto all men, especially unto them who are of the household of faith." (Galatians 6:10) Such is the right course to pursue. "Withhold not good from them to whom it is due, when it is in the power of thine hand to do it." (Proverbs 3:27) All acts of injustice are iniquity, or lawless, because contrary to God's command. Those persons who are under Satan's control do unjustly toward others. Those who are on the side of God and his King take exactly the opposite course, and hence do right toward others. It is not the duty or even the privilege of those who are on the side of God to demand justice of others, but they must likewise do justly toward others. The one who deals unjustly with others God will duly recompense in his own good way.

God requires those on his side to love mercy. "Love" is the perfect expression of unselfishness. "Mercy" is the result of loving-kindness exercised toward another who is not justly entitled thereto. "To love mercy," therefore, means to unselfishly do good to others, even though such others are not entitled to receive goodness: "Who is a God like unto thee, that pardoneth iniquity, and passeth by the transgression of the remnant of his heritage? he retaineth not his anger for ever, because he delighteth in mercy." —Micah 7:18.

When Jehovah God sent his beloved Son to earth that he might save man from perishing God thereby showed great mercy toward man. All men, being imperfect because of inherited sin, would justly go into death; but in the exercise of his unselfishness or loving-kindness God shows mercy to those who believe on the Lord Jesus Christ and thus saves them from perishing. (John 3:16, 17) "God is love." (1 John 4:8) Therefore he is wholly unselfish. "For thou, Lord, art good, and ready to forgive; and plenteous in mercy unto all them that call upon thee. But thou, O Lord, art a God full of compassion, and gracious; longsuffering, and plenteous in mercy and truth." (Psalm 86:5, 15) The person who oppresses another, and particularly the poor, because he has the power to do so, is not merciful and is therefore a reproach to Jehovah's name. (Proverbs 14:31) The man who loves mercy delights to show kindness and mercy to another, and that without any hope or expectation of personal or pecuniary gain. If the one who has done wrong shows a contrite spirit, then it is the privilege of the other one, who has been the victim of the wrongdoer, to show mercy to the wrongdoer. Teaching his disciples the right and proper course, Jesus said to them: "Blessed are they which do hunger and thirst after righteousness: for they shall be filled. Blessed are the merciful: for they shall obtain mercy."—Matthew 5: 6, 7.

WITH GOD

Another thing God requires of man is, "to walk humbly [(*margin*) humble thyself to walk] with thy God." That means to pursue a course that God marks out for the ones who are in a covenant to do his will. 'To walk with God' means to go in the way God goes, which is always righteous. How is weak man to know the way of God? Man ascertains the will and the way of God by informing himself of the truth as set forth in the Bible, and thus he is guided in the right way: "Thy word is a lamp unto my feet, and a light unto my path." (Psalm 119: 105) "The meek will he guide in judgment, and the meek will he teach his way." (Psalm 25: 9) The reasoning faculties of imperfect man necessarily are imperfect, and therefore he unwittingly takes the wrong way; which is often the result of yielding to his own process of reasoning. Therefore it is written: "Trust in the Lord with all thine heart; and lean not unto thine own understanding. In all thy ways acknowledge him, and he shall direct thy paths." (Proverbs 3: 5, 6) Without a knowledge of what God has put in his Word no one can learn God's way. The religious institutions have kept the Bible away from the people and therefore have induced the common people to rely upon what the priests or clergymen tell them to do. The result is that many sincere persons are totally ignorant of God's will and ignorant of his righteous way. Now God brings to the attention of the people the Bible and the meaning thereof, that they may learn the righteous way, and the clergy fight against the people's gaining this knowledge. Now God commands his faithful witnesses to carry to the people an explanation of his Word, that they may learn the way of salvation. Those who receive such favor from the hand of the Lord and who devote themselves to a study of his Word rejoice and truly say: "O how love I thy law! it is my meditation all the day. Thou, through thy commandments, hast made me wiser than mine enemies: for they are ever with me. I have more understanding than all my teachers: for thy testimonies are my meditation. How sweet are thy words unto my taste! yea, sweeter than honey to my mouth! Through thy precepts I get understanding: therefore I hate every false way." (Psalm 119: 97-99, 103, 104) Never has it been so vitally necessary for the people to learn God's law as it is at the present time, because now the Lord is gathering his "other sheep", who must be teachable and who must seek righteousness in order to escape the emergency and disaster of Armageddon.

OBEDIENCE

God requires obedience to his commandments from every one that agrees to do His will. To obey means to receive salvation unto life. To disobey means destruction. The Lord Jesus blazed the way of obedience that every creature who receives life everlasting must follow. Disobedience is rebellion against God and is the sin that finds no forgiveness. Lucifer disobeyed by rebelling against God. His end will be complete destruction. (Ezekiel 28:19) Many religious leaders knowingly and willfully disobey God, and their end is the same. Jesus was fully obedient to every law of God, and he lives for ever and occupies the highest place next to Jehovah. While undergoing the most severe suffering Jesus was always obedient. By reason of his full obedience he received the greatest honor of all creatures. In this connection the rule is announced that every creature that receives life everlasting must be fully obedient unto God: "Though he were a Son, yet learned he obedience by the things which he suffered; and being made perfect, he became the author of eternal salvation unto all them that obey him."—Hebrews 5:8, 9.

Since God has committed into the hand of Jesus the full power and authority to carry out his purpose, every creature that lives must be obedient to Christ Jesus. Therefore 'to walk with God' means joyfully to submit to His will and follow faithfully the course that Jesus has marked out. The "other sheep" of the Lord must render themselves in full obedience unto the Lord. In every instance cited in the Scriptures willful disobedience of God leads the disobedient ones into destruction. The importance of obeying God cannot be overstated. For this reason one who really is devoted to God will always be diligent to obey God rather than men.

FEAR

Satan the Devil is God's great adversary and also man's worst enemy. Satan uses fraudulent and deceptive means to ensnare the people. Religion is one of his chief means by which he ensnares them. Satan is the author of religion, and men are made religious teachers, and the Devil uses men to put fear into the minds of others that they might be ensnared by religion. The religious teachers induce men to fear "eternal torment" if they do not obey the teachings of the religious system. They teach men that all imperfect ones must spend a time in "purgatory", the duration of which may be long or short in proportion to the ability of that man's friends to contribute to the priest to get him out. Both "eternal torment" and "purgatory" are inventions of the Devil and are promulgated by men as his representatives, and both serve as a great means of deception and as a defamation of God's name.

Fear, then, is the chief means by which men are drawn into these organizations. The Scriptures fully disprove the "eternal torment" and "purgatory" doctrines. Many sincere persons fear to disobey the commands of the priests or the clergymen of the religious organizations. That fear of man is a means of ensnaring others; as it is written: "The fear of man bringeth a snare." (Proverbs 29:25) Religion, being an invention of the Devil, turns men away from God. The people were long ago warned that religion would ensnare them, and it has ever been so: "And thou shalt consume all the people which the Lord thy God shall deliver thee; thine eye shall have no pity upon them; neither shalt thou serve their gods; for that will be a snare unto thee. The graven images of their gods shall ye burn with fire; thou shalt not desire the silver or gold that is on them, nor take it unto thee, lest thou be snared therein; for it is an abomination to the Lord thy God."—Deuteronomy 7:16, 25; Judges 2:3.

To safeguard men from the snares of the Devil which are laid by causing men to fear other creatures, God commands that those who agree to do His will shall fear God, and not creatures. Then God states the meaning of fear concerning him: "The fear of the Lord is to hate evil; pride, and arrogancy, and the evil way, and the froward mouth, do I hate." (Proverbs 8:13) The Devil is the chief of the wicked, and therefore the way of the Devil and his agents is wicked, and all righteous men must hate such wickedness, and those on the side of God and his kingdom do hate wickedness. God's law is right, and the wise person fears to take a course contrary to God's law. When one comes to know God he fears to disobey God. Therefore the fear of God is the beginning of knowledge and of wisdom. (Proverbs 1:7; 9:10) The fear of God is a real protection to all of those who have agreed to do his will. The prophet under inspiration from God asks: "Whence then cometh wisdom? and where is the place of understanding? And unto man he said, Behold, the fear of the Lord, that is wisdom; and to depart from evil is understanding."—Job 28:20, 28.

The rulers of the nations of the earth are moved by their fear of man and man-made powers. Worldly leaders are now in the state particularly mentioned by the Lord, to wit: "Men's hearts failing them for fear, and for looking after those things which are coming on the earth." (Luke 21: 26) It was fear that induced the rulers to form the League of Nations; and hence they acted under the direction of Satan. God warned his people to have nothing to do with such a confederacy of nations, but that they should fear God; and his promise is that to them he will be a sanctuary. (Isaiah 8: 12, 13) The League of Nations has failed to bring about peace, but it has accomplished the Devil's purpose.

The Devil set a snare in which to catch the people, and out of that League of Nations have grown the totalitarian governments, that is to say, the total power vested in one dictator; and now all the nations are headed right into that same snare. The political leaders of the earth have great fear, and, they desiring some assurance from some power, the Devil and his wicked angels induced them to believe that they can find such consolation through the Papal Hierarchy. Hence the political leaders of the nations visit and send ambassadors to Vatican City and there take the advice of religious leaders and in this manner the Devil leads the political rulers fully into his trap. In this the political rulers follow the same course that King Saul took after God had rejected him. He went to the witch of Endor, the representative of the Devil, which witch spoke as a medium of the wicked spirits. She gave bad advice to Saul. (1 Samuel 28: 7-25) Even so now the worldly rulers hasten to take advice of the Roman Catholic Hierarchy, and particularly the pope, and from that source they receive bad advice, as they will shortly come to

know at Armageddon. Both the political and
religious leaders are blind and find themselves
in the same class named by the Lord when he
said that they would "both fall into the ditch",
meaning destruction. (Luke 6 : 39) The rulers of
the nations know that the witnesses of Jehovah
are proclaiming within their hearing the facts
concerning the approaching disaster of Armageddon. They do not want to hear God's warning, because it is bad news to them. Hence they
willingly join the religionists in the persecution
of Jehovah's witnesses, and because of their
fear they rush off to the pope, hoping to there
find some consolation. Exactly as God foretold
by his prophets, these worldly rulers form
leagues and build strong cities, hoping thereby
to protect themselves. They put the state above
God and even indulge in the persecution of little
children to compel them to recognize the state
above God, and the Devil induces them to use
this as a means of persecution of Jehovah's true
witnesses.

"HIGHER POWERS"

Are not all persons commanded to obey the
"higher powers"? and are not the rulers in the
various nations the "higher powers"? All who
have agreed to do the will of God must obey and
be subject to the "higher powers"; as it is written: "Let every soul be subject unto the higher
powers. For there is no power but of God; the
powers that be are ordained of God. Whosoever
therefore resisteth the power, resisteth the ordinance of God; and they that resist shall receive
to themselves damnation."—Romans 13 : 1, 2.

But the "higher powers" herein named are not the kings and dictators and presidents or other political rulers of the nation, nor are the religious leaders any part of the "higher powers". Not one of them represents God and Christ Jesus, but, on the contrary, they are under the control of Satan, who is the invisible ruler of this world. (2 Corinthians 4:4) Further instructing those who would know the right way, the scripture reads: "For rulers are not a terror to good works, but to the evil. Wilt thou then not be afraid of the power? do that which is good, and thou shalt have praise of the same; for he is the minister of God to thee for good. But if thou do that which is evil, be afraid; for he beareth not the sword in vain: for he is the minister of God, a revenger to execute wrath upon him that doeth evil."—Romans 13:3, 4.

Everyone knows that the rulers of this world are evil and do many evil things and, instead of aiding good works, they persecute those who do good works. This shows that they are not the "higher powers" mentioned in the Scriptures. Who, then, are the "higher powers"? Jehovah God is supreme, and Christ Jesus is his Chief Officer, to whom he has committed full power and authority to carry out his purpose; and therefore the "higher powers" are Jehovah God and Christ Jesus. (Matthew 28:18) The scripture above quoted concerning the "higher powers" is addressed specifically to those who have agreed to do God's will and whom God has accepted and called into his organization. (Romans 1:7) God is not dealing with the rulers of this world, nor authorizing them to represent him.

Concerning the "higher powers", as above mentioned, he is instructing those who are on the side of the kingdom, and them alone, and shows that Christ is "the minister of God" and "revenger to execute [God's] wrath upon him that doeth evil". Christ Jesus is the "King as supreme" in the organization of God, and is so named in the following scriptures: "Submit yourselves to every ordinance of man for the Lord's sake: whether it be to the king, as supreme; or unto governors, as unto them that are sent by him for the punishment of evil doers, and for the praise of them that do well." (1 Peter 2: 13, 14) "Governors," in the foregoing text, means the apostles of Jesus Christ, who were given specific power in the organization of the Lord. God's organization alone is included in the following text: "Obey them that have the rule over you, and submit yourselves: for they watch for your souls, as they that must give account; that they may do it with joy, and not with grief; for that is unprofitable for you." (Hebrews 13: 17) That text has no reference whatsoever to worldly organizations. Surely such wicked men as Hitler and Mussolini and Stalin, all of whom are against God and Christ Jesus, do not "watch for your souls", but rather attempt to destroy those who are on the side of Christ the Lord. In the foregoing text (1 Peter 2: 13), "every ordinance of man" is limited entirely to those who are on the Lord's side and in his organization. When the Lord sent the apostles forth to establish congregations of Christian people he committed to those apostles authority to make certain "ordinances" or rules, and therefore the faithful apostles were "governors" in the Lord's organization, and the rules promulgated by such are to be obeyed, and these rules are written in the Scriptures. (For an extended examination of this matter concerning the "Higher Powers" see *The Watchtower,* 1929, pages 163-169, 179-185.)

IMAGES, MEN, FLAGS

Should a Christian obey the law of the land where he lives? Yes; unless the law of the land is directly opposed to the law of God. As an example, taxes are required to be paid for the legitimate expense of the state. Jesus said: "Render therefore unto Cæsar [Cæsar symbolically standing for the state] the things which are Cæsar's, and unto God the things that are God's." (Matthew 22:18-21) Following that rule announced by the Lord, the Christian should obey every law of the state that is not in conflict with the law of God; but when obedience to any law of the state would operate as forcing the Christian to violate God's law, then the law of God takes precedence over the law of the state and the law of God must be obeyed rather than the law of man or that of the state.

A state or government in which all the activities of the people are within the control of a dictator, that ruling power constitutes a "totalitarian state or government". Under such the people are regimented or formed into classes, and all their individual privileges are fixed by the state, if they have any at all. Germany is such a government under the rule of a dictator. In that land all the people are required to give a specific salute and to exclaim "Heil Hitler", which means, "Salvation and protection come from Hitler." A person who is in a covenant to do the will of Almighty God could not obey that law of the German state, which demands him to give a specific salute and repeat the words above mentioned, for the reason that to do so is a flagrant violation of God's specific command, as recorded at Exodus 20:2-5. "Salvation belongeth unto Jehovah," and not to any man, and a Christian who denies this and obeys the state rather than God takes the course leading to certain destruction.

An image, as defined by the Scriptures, means a "representation, a figure, a symbol; that is, something that stands for and in the place of another". It is defined by Webster thus: "Something that represents another; a symbol; a representation." "Bowing down," as used in the Scriptures, means to do reverence, obeisance; to worship. It is the purpose of the Devil to cause men to reproach God's name that destruction of man may result. For the specific protection of those who have agreed to do God's will the Most High gives this commandment: "Thou shalt have no other gods before me. Thou shalt not make unto thee any graven image, or any likeness of any thing that is in heaven above, or that is in the earth beneath, or that is in the water under the earth: thou shalt not bow down thyself to them, nor serve them: for I the Lord thy God am a jealous God, visiting the iniquity of the fathers upon the children unto the third

and fourth generation of them that hate me."
—Exodus 20: 3-5.

The salute to the dictatorial ruler, as above
mentioned, the bowing down to images or worshiping such, attributes to whatsoever that
image represents the quality of protection and
salvation, and is therefore a clear violation of
God's law; and hence the one devoted to Jehovah cannot obey and will not obey a law of a
state that requires him to violate God's law.

The Israelites were in a covenant to do the
will of God, and they were a typical people.
Satan had established religion amongst the nations and endeavored to draw the Israelites
away from God by means of religion. The faithful servant and prophet of Almighty God, at
the command of Jehovah God, gave utterance
to these words: "Be ye therefore very courage-
ous to keep and to do all that is written in the
book of the law of Moses, that ye turn not aside
therefrom to the right hand or to the left; that
ye come not among these nations, these that
remain among you; neither make mention of the
name of their gods, nor cause to swear by them,
neither serve them, nor bow yourselves unto
them: but cleave unto the Lord your God, as
ye have done unto this day." (Joshua 23: 6-8)
Thus the command of the Lord not to bow down
to anything that represented the Devil was emphasized, and all who follow the Lord must obey
God, and not obey man.

In the beginning Lucifer was appointed as a
god or invisible overlord of man, and when he
rebelled his name was changed to "Satan" and
"Devil" (Ezekiel 28: 13-15; Isaiah 14: 12-15),

but his power to control men was not taken away. Therefore Satan is the "god" or invisible ruler of the wicked world, and the Scriptures plainly so state. (John 12:31; 14:30; 2 Corinthians 4:4; Psalm 110:1, 6) The above scriptures and the extraneous evidence show that the nations of the world are under the control of Satan. (James 4:4; 1 John 5:19, *A.R.V.*) Flags of the various nations represent the government and what the government stands for. The law of the nation or government that compels the child of God to salute the national flag compels that person to salute the Devil as the invisible god of the nation. The Christian, therefore, must choose to yield to God's enemy or to remain faithful and true to Almighty God. No one for a moment can doubt the fact that the Hitler government is against Jehovah God. No Christian could salute the German swastika without violating God's law.

But is the saluting of the American flag by a Christian or one in a covenant to do God's will a violation of God's law? Most emphatically yes, for the reason that protection and salvation are thereby attributed to the nation, whereas the protection and salvation to the Christian come from the Lord. In the flag itself there is no harm. It stands, however, for the ruling power of the government, all of whom are against Jehovah God and his kingdom under Christ. Not a single officer in the American government is for God's kingdom under Christ Jesus. The child of God, who has made a solemn covenant to be in full harmony with Jehovah and his kingdom, must look to Jehovah's kingdom alone for protection and salvation. When he salutes a flag of a worldly government he repudiates his covenant with Jehovah; and that means his destruction, because he thereby becomes a 'covenant breaker worthy of death'.—Romans 1: 31, 32.

The real question is this: Is a person who is a Christian to fear the things that the governments of this world stand for? or is that person to fear Jehovah God and his kingdom under Christ? If the judges of the courts really understood what it means to be for Jehovah God and his kingdom and to be fully on the side of God and his King, and if they desired to be on the side of Jehovah and his kingdom, they would immediately resign as justices of worldly courts and declare themselves wholly for God's kingdom.

Judges of courts who have ruled that compulsory flag-saluting is right concerning a Christian doubtless sincerely believe that the flag stands for righteousness; but the facts show exactly to the contrary. Today God's kingdom is here and Christ Jesus is present and has taken his power and begun his reign while Satan is in control of the earth. All the nations of the earth are against God and his kingdom. It is therefore impossible for a person to be in full accord with the governments of this world and at the same time to be in full harmony with God's kingdom under Christ. He must serve one or the other of the masters, and there can be no compromise. The difficulty with judges and other officers is that they do not see or understand what God's kingdom is or means. The true Christian knows that he cannot be for God and his kingdom and at the same time agree his protection and salvation come to him from the governments of this world. To salute a flag of the nation in effect says: "I look to what that flag stands for and represents for my protection, comfort and salvation." It is impossible for the child of God to say that and at the same time remain true to God, because the Christian knows that the government for which the flag stands will soon go down at the battle of Armageddon and that the Lord will destroy every vestige of Satan's organization. Hence that worldly government for which the flag stands could not be for the protection and salvation of the one who serves God. But does the flag of the United States stand for anything more or mean anything more to those who salute it than mere respect for the government under which they live? Yes, it means much more. If the saluting of the flag meant merely this: "By saluting the flag I will obey every law of the land that is not contrary to God's law," then everyone could salute it with absolute impunity. As to what the flag does mean, let the worldly authorities for themselves speak, as follows:

"The flag, like the cross, is sacred. Many people employ the words or term 'Etiquette of the Flag'. This expression is too weak, too superficial, and smacks of drawing-room politeness. The rules and regulations relative to human attitude toward national standards use strong, expressive words, as, 'Service to the Flag,' 'Respect for the Flag,' 'Reverence for the Flag,' 'Devotion to the Flag,' 'Behavior Towards the

Flag.' "—*Encyclopedia Americana,* Volume 11, page 316.

Continuing the definition, the colors are defined as follows: "White signifies Purity and Innocence; Red, Hardiness and Valor; Blue signifies Vigilance, Perseverance and Justice."

Another authority says: "America was settled by lovers of liberty. America expects those who come here to love and revere and defend the flag which protects them. It is the emblem of a free people."—Manual of Information, National Society of the Daughters of the American Revolution.

If the flag is a symbol of a free people, then to *compel* a person to salute it flatly contradicts that claim. If a man is free, then he is free to believe what God's Word means to him. But if the courts can say that God's Word does not mean to that sincere man what he conscientiously believes it to mean, then the man is not free to exercise his own understanding of the Word of God.

Does not the state have the complete power to compel its citizens to obey every law it makes? Most emphatically, No. If a state enacts a law that is in direct conflict with God's law, the person who is in a covenant to do the will of God cannot properly obey such law of the state, and certainly he could not properly be compelled to violate God's law. Jehovah God is supreme, and his law is above all law of any or all nations of the earth. That question was raised and settled many centuries ago, according to the will of God. The worldly government called "Babylon" held as prisoners many Israelites that had been tak-

en away from Palestine. Babylon enacted a law
which demanded that all the people should bow
down before an image at the giving of a certain
signal. Three Israelites who were devoted to
God, being in a covenant with him, refused to
bow down to that image. They were told that
such refusal meant that they would be cast into
a fiery furnace; and to that they replied to the
king: "We are not careful to answer thee in this
matter. If it be so, our God, whom we serve, is
able to deliver us from the burning fiery furnace; and he will deliver us out of thine hand,
O king. But if not, be it known unto thee, O king,
that we will not serve thy gods, nor worship the
golden image which thou hast set up."—Daniel
3:16-18.

Those men were then bound with fetters and
cast into a fiery furnace, and God rewarded their
faith and delivered them from the fiery furnace
without even a scorch on their clothing. Thus
God demonstrated that his law is far above the
law of man and that those who obey his law shall
receive salvation and those who violate it shall
be destroyed. The men who cast these three
faithful ones into the furnace were destroyed.
The faithful were preserved alive. (See Daniel
3:15-28.)

A further example showing the will of Almighty God in this matter and the proper course
for those in a covenant with God to take, is the
following: The apostles of Jesus Christ were
arrested and arraigned before the courts for
preaching the gospel concerning Jesus Christ,
and the judges of the courts threatened them
with dire punishment if they refused to cease

preaching; and their reply to the court was this: "Whether it be right in the sight of God to hearken unto you more than unto God, judge ye." "We ought to obey God rather than men." (Acts 4:19; 5:29) The child of God has no alternative. He cannot compromise and live. His salvation depends upon full and complete faithful obedience to God.

Refusing Devil worship

"FEAR THEM NOT"

In Germany many persons are imprisoned and some have been killed who refused to salute the swastika flag and "heil Hitler". They preferred death for doing right (because they know the Lord will resurrect them, if they do right) rather than destruction, from which there is no resurrection. If an American law required everyone to salute the flag, would it not be better to salute it rather than be imprisoned or killed? Each person must answer that question for himself. The act of saluting the flag is not an offense; but the one who has made a covenant to do God's will, and who then acts in disobedience to God's will, commits a wrong leading him into destruction. Those who desire to salute flags should do so, but those who have agreed to serve Jehovah God must obey him if they would live at all. The state may imprison and may even kill those who disobey its law concerning the flag-saluting, but those who die because of their faith and obedience to God are assured of a resurrection, whereas he that dies at the hands of God's Executioner, because that person is unfaithful to God, cannot have a resurrection. The state can kill only the body, but has no power to bring one out of death. Only God has the power of resurrection. Therefore Jesus said: "And ye shall be hated of all men for my name's sake [because of your faithfulness to the Lord]; . . . And fear not them which kill the body, but are not able to kill the soul; but rather fear him which is able to destroy both soul and body in hell [*Gehenna;* meaning complete destruction from which there is no resurrection]." (Matthew 10: 22, 28) To disobey God is sin, and the penalty thereof is death; but to obey God by faithfully keeping one's covenant means life everlasting. (Romans 6: 23) It is therefore far better to obey God and suffer for righteousness' sake than to disobey and lose everything. (1 Peter 4: 13, 16) For centuries faithful men have suffered because of complete devotion to God, and such men have God's assurance of his everlasting approval and blessing. The true follower of Christ Jesus, therefore, obeys God at all times, and by obeying God he is certain to do no wrong to his fellow man.

Why is such a strenuous effort put forth in these "last days" to compel the people, and particularly school children, to salute the flag and sing so-called "patriotic" songs? The Scriptures answer that these are evil days, perilous times, when the Devil is desperately attempting to turn all men against God because he knows that his time is short. (Revelation 12:12; 2 Timothy 3:1-5) For more than 150 years the people of America have gotten on without being compelled to salute the flag, but now in these last days of peril Satan is determined to break down all obedience of men to Almighty God in order that he might bring about their destruction. The totalitarian or dictatorial rule is the scheme of the Devil, and compulsory flag-saluting is one of the means of dictatorial rule to break the courage of the people, and to regiment them and control them. The religious leaders, and particularly the clergy of the Roman Catholic system, put fear in the minds of the people and compel them to obey the political rulers. The clergy and the politicians and their allies instill fear into the minds of the people and thus make them the victims of the Devil's snare. "The fear of man bringeth a snare; but whoso putteth his trust in the Lord shall be safe."—Proverbs 29:25.

There are two masters: Jehovah God, the Master over all who desire righteousness; and the Devil, over those who are against God. "No man can serve two masters: for either he will hate the one, and love the other; or else he will hold to the one, and despise the other. Ye cannot serve God and mammon." (Matthew 6:24) The rule that should be followed, then, is this: Obey every law of the state that is in harmony with God's law, because that is right. If you are trusting in Jehovah God and his kingdom, obey his law always, because He is supreme.

ADVERTISING THE KINGDOM

The obligation which God's law lays upon men should be met and performed voluntarily and gladly. Jesus said: "I delight to do thy will, O my God; yea, thy law is within my heart." (Psalm 40:8) Such is the rule that the followers of Jesus must obey, and thus always delight to do the will of God. The "strangers" amongst the typical people of God pictured the present-day Jonadabs, the "other sheep" of the Lord now on earth. The strangers were required to obey the law which God gave to Israel. The same rule applies to the Jonadabs or "other sheep" today. The Lord commands, in Matthew 24:14, that this gospel of the kingdom must be preached unto the nations. The Jonadabs, or "other sheep", are under obligation to obey this commandment of the Lord. At Revelation 22:17 the Jonadabs or "other sheep" are the ones who hear the message from the Lord and the remnant, his witnesses on the earth, and they are commanded to say to other people to "come" and learn of God and his kingdom. It is therefore the duty of the "other sheep" of the Lord, the "companions" of the remnant, to carry the message of the kingdom to the people and to inform them of God's purpose to vindicate his name at Armageddon and to grant salvation to life to all of those who obey his commandments.

The Jonadabs or "other sheep" have declared themselves for Jehovah and his kingdom. It is therefore their privilege and their obligation to give all their support to God's kingdom, and that means their time, their energy, their money, and everything, to advance the kingdom interest. To be sure, the Lord does not need the support of any creature; but those who do voluntarily support his kingdom show their devotion to him. After providing the necessary material things for oneself and one's dependent ones, then if he is in a covenant with the Lord it is his privilege and duty to use his substance to further the interest of the Lord's kingdom.

The Lord has commanded his people to carry the message of warning to the world. He has provided books, magazines, phonographs and other means of preaching the gospel or carrying the message to them, and thus the Lord has made it possible for every one that loves him to have some part in advertising the King and kingdom. It is the privilege and obligation of the Jonadabs, or those who will form the great multitude, to avail themselves of all opportunity to thus bear witness to others of and concerning the kingdom. The religionists and their political allies will attempt to keep the "other sheep" of the Lord from hearing the truth or engaging in the publication of the kingdom message; but let none of them fear what man or devil may do to them. With joy obey the Lord, and live.

BAPTISM

Is baptism required of everyone who is in a covenant to do the will of God? Yes, because baptism or immersion in water is a symbol outwardly testifying that the person thus immersed has surrendered his selfish will to do God's will. To such God provides protection. Immersion in symbol says: 'I have put myself entirely under the command of Almighty God, and by His grace I will do his will.' It is to such that God furnishes his protection and guidance. Before entering upon his work Jesus presented himself to John to be baptized, and John objected, and Jesus in reply said: "Suffer it to be so now: for thus it becometh us to fulfil all righteousness." (Matthew 3: 15-17) Jesus was then baptized; and when he came up out of the water, God gave an outward demonstration of His acceptance of Jesus.

Those who went into the ark with Noah thereby showed that they had agreed to do God's will as made known to them by Noah. They were baptized unto Noah and were thus saved from the flood. 1 Peter 3: 20, 21: "Which sometime were disobedient, when once the long-suffering of God waited in the days of Noah, while the ark was a preparing, wherein few, that is, eight souls, were saved by water. The like figure whereunto, even baptism, doth also now save us, (not the putting away of the filth of the flesh, but the answer of a good conscience toward God,) by the resurrection of Jesus Christ."

When the Israelites left Egypt under the command of Moses, all of them agreed thereby to obey Moses as God's representative; and Moses was a type of Christ. They followed Moses

across the dry bed of the Red sea, made possible
by God's miracle. They were thus hidden or immersed in the cloud and the sea. "Moreover,
brethren, I would not that ye should be ignorant,
how that all our fathers were under the cloud,
and all passed through the sea; and were all
baptized unto Moses in the cloud and in the sea."
(1 Corinthians 10: 1, 2) When John the Baptist
came as the representative of the Lord he commanded the Israelites to repent of their sins
against the law covenant and to be baptized.
(Matthew 3: 1-11) Those who did repent and
were baptized testified thereby that they had
changed their course of action and that they
would no longer be guided by their own selfishness and would gladly obey the will of God.
Those who had not violated the covenant but
had been faithful to God had no need to be
baptized.

Baptism, therefore, symbolically and outwardly testifies to an agreement to do God's
will. In the picture concerning the cities of refuge the "other sheep" of the Lord are shown as
fleeing unto the Lord's organization, thereby
agreeing to do his will. They are thus hidden or
immersed under and unto the organization of
the Lord. Those who followed Moses through the
waters of the Red sea and under the canopy of
the cloud overhead were thus "baptized unto
Moses" in the sea and the cloud and were thus
protected from the expression of God's wrath
against the Egyptians, representing the Devil's
organization. Likewise those who followed Noah
into the ark and remained there were hidden or
immersed and thereby baptized unto Noah. Both

Moses and Noah pictured The Christ, the royal
organization of Jehovah God. Therefore even
the Jonadabs at this present time experience the
baptism unto the Greater Noah, Christ Jesus.
Coming under the protection of the organization
of Christ Jesus, the "other sheep" now find
shelter, and if they continue there to seek righteousness and meekness, rendering themselves
in obedience unto the Lord, they have the promise of deliverance from the wrath of God at
Armageddon. True, the Jonadabs are not counted members of the capital organization, but
their protection and safety is from Jehovah God
by and through his organization of which Christ
Jesus is the Head. As the Red sea brought destruction upon the Devil's representatives, who
were pursuing the Israelites, and there the
Israelites had protection by reason of being
baptized unto Moses; so likewise the deluge of
waters destroyed those who reproached God
and opposed Noah, and the ark furnished protection and safety to them from the disaster
wrought by the flood. That baptism, which provided safety and salvation for some and destruction for others, appears to be referred to by the
words of John to those who came to him for
baptism, to wit: "He [Christ] that cometh after
me is mightier than I, . . . he shall baptize you
with the holy [spirit], and with fire." (Matthew
3:11, 12) The "fire" baptism evidently refers
to the fire of Armageddon, which immersion
will be the destruction of all of the Devil's organization, and protection to those who find
refuge in Jehovah's organization. That "fire"
will be a time of tribulation such as the world

has never known; and never again will it occur, because it will completely destroy the wicked. Baptism is required because it is an act of obedience; and all who please God are required to be obedient.

MEMORIAL

Just preceding his crucifixion Jesus instituted the Memorial of his death. Is it necessary and proper that the Lord's "other sheep", the Jonadabs, partake of the emblems of the Memorial? No, such is not required, and, in fact, it is very improper for those who will compose the great multitude to partake of the emblems of the Memorial, for the following reason: God made a covenant with his beloved Son, Christ Jesus, for the kingdom. Jesus must die as a man, be raised out of death a spirit, ascend into heaven and there receive the authority of the kingdom. It is the will of God that Jesus shall have associated with him in his kingdom 144,000 taken out of the world. Such faithful ones must die as human creatures, be raised out of death, and become members of the royal organization of Jehovah. They must follow in the footsteps of Jesus.

To his faithful disciples Jesus said: "And you are they who have continued with me in my trials. And I covenant for you, even as my Father has covenanted for me, a kingdom, that you may eat and drink at my table in my kingdom, and sit on thrones, judging the twelve tribes of Israel." (Luke 22:28-30, *Diaglott*) Just preceding this declaration of Jesus he took a loaf of bread and broke it, which symbolized

his body; he took a cup of wine, which he said
represented his blood, and invited all his faithful disciples to drink of it. (Matthew 26:26-29)
The broken bread pictured the broken body of
the Lord, and the wine pictured his lifeblood
poured out; and inviting his disciples to drink
of it meant that he invited them to partake of
his death that they might partake with him of
life in the kingdom. Those who hope to share
with Christ Jesus in his kingdom of heaven,
therefore, must celebrate the Memorial, thus
testifying to their agreement to be dead with
Christ, that they may live with him.—2 Timothy
2:11, 12.

At the present time, since the coming of
the Lord Jesus to the temple, those faithful
ones drink the cup of the new wine of joy because the time has come for the vindication of
Jehovah's name; and this fills them with joy.
(Matthew 26:29) As the Israelites were hidden,
shielded and protected by reason of their baptism unto Moses, even so those who are baptized
into the death of Christ are hid with him; as
it is written: "For ye are dead, and your life is
hid with Christ in God. When Christ, who is
our life, shall appear, then shall ye also appear
with him in glory." (Colossians 3:3, 4) The
members of the body of Christ, therefore, must
be "baptized into [Christ's] death", which is entirely separate and distinct from water immersion and has nothing to do with water immersion.—Romans 6:3-5.

Those who form the great multitude will not
die as human creatures and be resurrected as
spirit creatures. They are not called to the

heavenly calling, and therefore are not a part of the kingdom. They find life on the earth under the King and kingdom. They are not baptized into the death of Christ. If the "other sheep", or great multitude, should partake of the Memorial wine, which is a symbol of the blood of Christ, they would in effect say: "We have agreed to be dead with Christ Jesus, and know that we must die with Him." Thus it is seen that it is improper for them to partake of the Memorial emblems.

EVERLASTING COVENANT

The flood had ended, and at the command of God Noah and his family went forth out of the ark. Those eight persons were then the only human creatures left on the earth. God then made known to Noah his covenant concerning the sanctity of life, and which is called "the everlasting covenant". Its terms apply to all living creatures, and it shall stand forever. It is a unilateral or one-sided covenant, because it is the solemn and emphatic declaration of Jehovah God concerning his purpose; and such he will never change, but will perform the terms thereof regardless of what creatures may do. That covenant, disclosing the sanctity of life, is a further vindication of Jehovah's name. God is the "Fountain of life". (Psalm 36: 9) He gives life, and he takes it away. No creature can properly take life except in strict accord with God's law. The everlasting covenant is with and applies to man, beast and fowls. (Genesis 9: 12) That all creatures might have a tangible token of that covenant God set the rainbow in the cloud; and when one looks upon the rainbow he is forcibly reminded of God's everlasting covenant concerning life.

The terms of the everlasting covenant are stated in these words, to wit: "And the fear of you, and the dread of you, shall be upon every beast of the earth, and upon every fowl of the air, upon all that moveth upon the earth, and upon all the fishes of the sea; into your hand are they delivered. Every moving thing that liveth shall be meat for you; even as the green herb have I given you all things. But flesh with the life thereof, which is the blood thereof, shall ye not eat. And surely your blood of your lives will I require; at the hand of every beast will I require it, and at the hand of man; at the hand of every man's brother will I require the life of man. Whoso sheddeth man's blood, by man shall his blood be shed; for in the image of God made he man."—Genesis 9:2-6.

HUMAN LIFE

No man can give life, and therefore no man can take away life except he act strictly in accord with the law of God concerning the same. The command given to individuals by Almighty God is, "Thou shalt not kill." (Exodus 20:13) This command is not a contradiction of Genesis 9:6: "Whoso sheddeth man's blood, by man shall his blood be shed; for in the image of God made he man." If a man commit murder, he shall be punished by the taking of his life, and the executioner of the murderer cannot be self-appointed, but must act as the representative of God. The words of the foregoing text, "for in

the image of God made he man," do not refer to
the creation of Adam, but mean that the executioner of the murderer acts as the representative of God and upon authority delegated by God
and therefore acts in the image of God. Noah
was righteous in the sight of God because of his
faith and obedience, and the commission God
gave to him was that he should execute the willful murderer of another.—Exodus 21:12-24;
Leviticus 24:16-21.

Some examples are here cited. Moses, as the
representative of Jehovah God, delivered God's
law to the Israelites, and to them he said concerning the inhabitants of the land of Canaan:
"And when the Lord thy God shall deliver them
before thee; thou shalt smite them, and utterly
destroy them: thou shalt make no covenant with
them, nor shew mercy unto them: neither shalt
thou make marriages with them; thy daughter
thou shalt not give unto his son, nor his daughter shalt thou take unto thy son. For they will
turn away thy son from following me, that they
may serve other gods; so will the anger of the
Lord be kindled against you, and destroy thee
suddenly." (Deuteronomy 7:2-4) Why should
those people be killed? Because they were
opponents of God and were the servants of the
Devil and engaged in persecuting God's chosen
people. Therefore God appointed Joshua and
others with him as executioners of those enemies
of the Most High. For forty years God led the
people of Israel by the hand of Moses on their
long journey from Egypt to Canaan, the land
of promise. On the way the Amalekites, without
cause or excuse, assaulted the Israelites and be-

gan to destroy them, and tried to prevent the
Israelites from entering the promised land.
(Exodus 17 : 8-14) The Canaanites were in the
land of promise when the Israelites reached that
land, and tried to prevent the Israelites from
entering. The Canaanites were God's enemies,
fighting against his covenant people. The execution of the Canaanites by Joshua and his army
was in harmony with God's command, because
those Canaanites were God's enemies and practitioners of the devil religion. The one exception
amongst those people was the Gibeonites, who
voluntarily sought out Joshua, expressed their
faith in God, and asked Joshua to give them
protection. In this the Gibeonites pictured the
great multitude, who flee to the Greater Joshua,
Christ Jesus, and ask for protection and salvation.

The Canaanites that fought against God's
chosen people pictured those nations and peoples of earth who today practice the devil religion, oppose God, and wickedly persecute his
chosen people now on the earth, and which religious persecutors therefore are God's avowed
enemies. At Armageddon the Lord Jesus Christ,
as Jehovah's Executioner, will punish and
completely destroy all of God's enemies.
(Psalm 21 : 8) Today the representatives of Satan, and particularly the religionists, are in a
conspiracy to destroy those persons on earth
who are devoted to God and to his kingdom.
Their purpose is to prevent God's covenant people from entering into the kingdom and there
having the blessings of Jehovah. In this they
were pictured by the Canaanites. (Psalm 2: 2-9;

Psalm 83: 2-18) The destruction of God's enemies is a vindication of his name. He is the
source of life, and from those who willfully oppose him he takes what little life they have. It
is therefore written in God's Word: 'A time for
every purpose under heaven; a time to kill, and
a time to heal.' (Ecclesiastes 3: 1-3) God deter-
mines the time and occasion to take life, and
therefore it is written: "To me [Jehovah] belongeth vengeance [vindication], and recom-
pence." (Deuteronomy 32: 35) "Dearly beloved,
avenge not yourselves; but rather give place
unto wrath; for it is written, Vengeance is mine,
I will repay, saith the Lord."—Romans 12: 19.

WAR

Two men engage to fight a duel, and in doing
so one of them is killed. In most countries the
law of the land declares that the man who killed
his antagonist in the duel is a murderer. When
two nations declare war against each other, or
begin war without a declaration, and the citizens
of each nation respectively are required to go
on the battlefield and kill, there is in fact no
difference between such and the two men fighting a duel. In both instances the "everlasting
covenant" is violated. When a nation prosecutes
a war of conquest against another people in
order to gain more territory or other things of
material value, such is a violation of the everlasting covenant. If a people are attacked by in-
vaders and those who are attacked defend themselves and their families, during which defense
some are killed, such is not a violation of the
everlasting covenant, because the wrongdoer is

the aggressor. (Exodus 22:2) When a nation goes to war for commercial reasons and men volunteer to go and fight, and do so, and kill, such is a violation of the everlasting covenant, because it is the taking of life without authority from Jehovah. Because a Christian has agreed to do the will of God a Christian properly refuses to kill voluntarily, because the same is a violation of the everlasting covenant. For this reason those wholly devoted to God and his kingdom refuse to go to war against their fellow creatures, because they prefer to obey God and suffer at the hands of men or earthly governments rather than to disobey God and suffer complete destruction. It should be kept in mind that the law of Almighty God is supreme and far above the laws that are made or can be made by any earthly governments.

All the nations of "Christendom", as is well known, have violated the everlasting covenant. A modern instance follows: For the purpose of enlarging national territory and satisfying the ambition of a dictator Italy prosecuted a war against Abyssinia, in which many were killed. In Spain political and ambitious men have made a rebellion against the government, causing many human creatures to be slain. Both as to the slaying in Abyssinia and as to the war in Spain, the leading religious organization on earth, to wit, the Roman Catholic Hierarchy, has not only approved, but aided and abetted, such unrighteous war. The Papal system therefore is guilty of breaking the everlasting covenant with reference to both Abyssinia and Spain. The same rule applies concerning Germany and its assault on Austria and Czechoslovakia. Today the nations of earth are in a condition of wickedness and woe. Concerning all such nations God declares: "The earth also is defiled under the inhabitants thereof, because they have transgressed the laws, changed the ordinance, broken the everlasting covenant." (Isaiah 24:5) Punishment shall come upon such nations for the breaking of the everlasting covenant, as God further says: "Therefore hath the curse devoured the earth, and they that dwell therein are desolate: therefore the inhabitants of the earth are burned, and few men left."— Isaiah 24:6.

Those who compose the great multitude must now learn what is the will of God concerning life and the sanctity thereof, and, learning, must see to it that they do not violate the everlasting covenant. God emphatically declares that he alone is the source of life. No creature can take away life of his own volition, and for the purpose of punishing another, without violating the everlasting covenant. Lucifer was made man's overlord. He rebelled against God and led man into death, and therefore it is emphatically written against him that he is a murderer. (John 8:44) The Devil ultimately shall be completely destroyed, together with all persons who have willfully followed his lead in breaking the everlasting covenant.

BEAST

God created the beast of the field and the fowl of the air and the fish of the sea and gave them life. (Genesis 1:25) The life of such can proper-

ly be taken only as provided by God's law. The
animals and fowls are included in the everlasting covenant. 'I establish my covenant with you,
and with every living creature that is with you,
the fowl, the cattle, and the beast.' (Genesis
9:9, 10) Noah took many animals into the ark
with him that they might be preserved to pro-
duce their species later. When Noah brought
these animals out of the ark and set them at
liberty they would quickly scatter through the
earth and increase rapidly and thus endanger
the life of Noah and his family. For the protection of man and to safeguard the animals
also, God said to Noah: "And the fear of you,
and the dread of you, shall be upon every beast
of the earth, and upon every fowl of the air,
upon all that moveth upon the earth, and upon
all the fishes of the sea; into your hand are they
delivered."—Genesis 9:2.

The fear and dread which the beasts had for
man caused them to keep out of man's way and
not to molest him. In his law God provided that
man could have the animals for food as he might
require, and could kill them for that purpose.
(Genesis 9:3-5) If a man required a beast for
food he was permitted to kill it, but the blood
of that beast he must pour out on the earth, and
not eat it, because the life is in the blood and
eating the blood is a violation of the everlasting
covenant. The law which God gave to the people
through Moses fully supports this conclusion.
God specified in that law what hunters must do,
and such law shows that no one is justified to
hunt animals or fowls for sport, thrills or ad-
venture: "And whatsoever man there be of the

children of Israel, or of the strangers that so-
journ among you, which hunteth and catcheth
any beast or fowl that may be eaten; he shall
even pour out the blood thereof, and cover it
with dust. For it is the life of all flesh; the blood
of it is for the life thereof: therefore I said unto
the children of Israel, Ye shall eat the blood of
no manner of flesh; for the life of all flesh is the
blood thereof; whosoever eateth it shall be cut
off."—Leviticus 17: 13, 14.

It follows to a certainty that the Devil induces
men to violate the everlasting covenant in order
to turn them from God. As Satan is a rebel, so
he attempts to make rebels of men. Noah's son
Ham begot a son and called his name Cush.
Nimrod was a son of Cush. Nimrod became a
rebel and a violator of the everlasting covenant.
Because he is the outstanding one of early times
who violated that covenant mention is made of
him in the Scriptures. (Genesis 10: 6, 8-10) He
was a wanton slayer of beast and fowls.

The first huntsman mentioned in the Bible is
Nimrod. The slaying of animals by Nimrod was
done in defiance of God's law and was done at
the instance of Satan for the purpose of defying
and reproaching Jehovah's name. It is not
Scripturally correct to say, as some critics have
said: "The sin of Nimrod and of the people that
followed him did not include the wanton slaying
of animals, and the Scriptures are silent in the
matter; and Nimrod's sin was solely worshiping the creature instead of the Creator." Concerning him it is written in the Scriptures: "And
Cush begat Nimrod; he began to be a mighty
one in the earth: he was a mighty hunter before

the Lord; wherefore it is said, Even as Nimrod the mighty hunter before the Lord." (Genesis 10: 8, 9) If Nimrod was a mere hunter to obtain necessary food, that certainly would not have caused the people to hail him as a mighty hunter "before the Lord".

The word "before", in the above text, as commonly used today does not convey the proper thought. The correct meaning of that word, however, furnishes a key which discloses the kind of man Nimrod was, and shows that he was a willful and deliberate sinner and that one of his great sins was slaying of animals in violation of the everlasting covenant. Other translations of this scripture, and the definition of the word "before", will clarify this matter; and which follow, to wit: "Before" means "against" (Jehovah) (*Septuagint* [*LXX*]); "in defiance of" (Jehovah) (Fausset's *Encycl.*); "in opposition to, in defiance of" (Jehovah). (*The Companion Bible*) A footnote of the appendix No. 28 of *The Companion Bible* in this matter says:

"Nimrod persuaded mankind not to ascribe their happiness to God, but to think that his own excellency was the source of it. And he soon changed things into a tyranny, thinking there was no other way to wean men from the fear of God, than by making them rely upon his own power.

"The Targum of Jonathan says: 'From the foundation of the world none was ever found like Nimrod, powerful in hunting, and in rebellions against the Lord.'

"The Jerusalem Targum says: 'He was powerful in hunting and in wickedness before the

Lord, for he was a hunter of the sons of men, and he said to them, "Depart from the judgment of the Lord, and adhere to the judgment of Nimrod!" Therefore is it said: "As Nimrod (is) the strong, strong in hunting, and in wickedness before." '

"The Chaldee paraphrase of 1 Chron. 1:10 says: 'Cush begat Nimrod, who began to prevail in wickedness, for he shed innocent blood, and rebelled against Jehovah.'

"Nimrod was the founder of Babylon, which [symbolized Satan's organization and] partook of his character as being the great antagonist of God's Truth and God's People.

"We cannot fail to see, in Nimrod, Satan's first attempt to raise up a human universal ruler of men."

The name Nimrod means "rebellious one" or "him that rules in rebellion". (See book *Prophecy,* pages 127, 129, 130; see also *Riches,* pages 95 [paragraph 1], 100 [par. 1], 168 [par. 2].) 'The preposition translated "before" means "against the Lord". Nimrod was a killer of men and beasts. He trained men to hardship that they might successfully battle against beasts and men. His prowess in hunting must have co-existed with valor in battle. Hunting and heroism were of old specially and naturally associated.'—McClintock & Strong's *Cyclopædia,* Volume VII, page 109.

"The name Nimrod signifies 'the subduer of the leopard'. This name seems to imply that as Nimrod had gained fame by subduing the horse and so making use of it in the chase, so his fame as a huntsman rested mainly on this, that he found out the art of making the leopard aid him in hunting the other wild beasts."—Hislop's *The Two Babylons*, pages 24, 44.

Nimrod was a religionist. He made himself a great name amongst the people by his wanton slaying of wild beasts, and thus he induced the credulous ones to look upon him as a god. He organized religion and practiced it and caused the people to practice formalism or religion, and that he did for the very purpose of turning the people away from Jehovah. Nimrod was the visible instrument of the Devil to carry out the Devil's defiant challenge to Jehovah, that he could turn all men against God. Nimrod killed the beasts of the forest to show his prowess and to impress men with his greatness and in order that he might receive their applause, that he might gain control over the people and draw them to himself and use them for his selfish purposes of carrying on wars of conquest. His wanton slaying of wild beasts could not have been merely for food and in harmony with God's law and the terms of the everlasting covenant, but was in defiance of God and for the purpose of willfully and maliciously breaking the everlasting covenant.

The example set by Nimrod has influenced the men of every nation since that time. The indisputable facts show that a class of men who indulge in hunting wild beasts and fowls merely for the thrill and selfish pleasure derived therefrom are also the men who indulge and delight in military training and the prosecution of wars and who advocate war, and also that they are to a large degree religionists, given over to formalism and to the praise and adulation of men, all of which is done in direct opposition to and in defiance of God's law, and which is therefore sin.

Thus it clearly appears that the sin of Nimrod and his supporters included the wanton slaying of beasts, together with his prosecution of wars of conquest and the killing of men; also the exaltation of men and causing the people to worship men; also his organizing political bodies to rule and to carry on commerce to unjustly reap personal gain. The purpose of all of such was and still is to hold the attention of men upon human creatures of a supposed higher class and to turn the masses away from their service and devotion to Almighty God. The entire scheme is that of the Devil, brought into being and put into operation in furtherance of his wicked challenge to Jehovah that he could cause all men to curse God. In order to exalt himself Nimrod wickedly violated the everlasting covenant by wantonly slaying men and beasts, and by this means the credulous people were deceived and it became a proverb concerning him that he was a great and mighty one; as it is written: "He began to be mighty upon the earth." (1 Chronicles 1:10) "He was a mighty hunter [killer] in defiance of Jehovah." (Genesis 10:8, 9, *Septuagint*) When he had made a name for himself he set up a kingdom; "and the beginning of his kingdom was Babel," that is, Babylon, and that was in defiance of Jehovah. (Vs. 10) Since Nimrod's time all the nations have been made drunk with the wine of Babylon, that is to say, the wicked doctrine of

Satan's organization, and hence have indulged
in wanton slaying of men and beasts and have
cruelly persecuted those who truly serve God
and his kingdom. Concerning such it is written,
"For the violence done to Lebanon shall cover
thee, and the destruction of the beasts, which
made them afraid."—Habakkuk 2:17, *A.R.V.*

Jehovah's people, both the remnant and Jonadabs, are especially concerned now about these
truths, because they disclose to man the manner
and means by which Satan has turned men away
from God. Those who have covenanted to do
the will of God are now, because of increased
light, exceedingly anxious to know how they can
conform themselves to God's will, not only in one
thing, but in all things. They have a keen desire
to honor God's name and to show their love for
him by diligently keeping his commandments.
The Jonadabs especially, being commanded to
seek meekness and righteousness, must now be
diligent to learn what is right. Seeing from the
Scriptures that the chase or pursuit of and the
killing of beasts and fowls merely for sport is
wrong, because in violation of the everlasting
covenant, they will avoid such and refuse to have
anything to do with so-called "sport" of hunting merely for the thrill that men get by shooting birds and beasts. God will punish every nation that has violated his everlasting covenant,
which means all the nations. Those who are consecrated to do God's will are exceedingly anxious to avoid doing anything that has even a
tendency to violate God's expressed will. If the
people need food, and "clean" animals can be
taken for that purpose, it is in harmony with

Deliverance at Armageddon foreshadowed

"Fill the Earth" Page 323

God's will that they may slay and eat the meat of such clean animals and clean fowls; but no one really consecrated to the Lord will permit himself to indulge in the chase or slaying of wild beasts or fowls merely for so-called "sport" or thrill.

The dictator

PROTECTION

God has provided protection for those who love and serve him. Those who left the ark with Noah numbered in the aggregate only eight persons, and they were the only living human creatures. There were numerous animals that Noah brought out of the ark with him, and these

animals would immediately roam about the
earth and multiply. For the protection of man
God put fear or dread in the minds of the animals that they might fear or dread man; as it
is written: "And the fear of you, and the dread
of you, shall be upon every beast of the earth,
and upon every fowl of the air, upon all that
moveth upon the earth, and upon all the fishes
of the sea; into your hand are they delivered."
—Genesis 9:2.

That certainly means that when men would
come near the wild beasts those beasts, having
fear or dread of man, would run away and
escape from man, and this was done for the
protection of the beast, and particularly for the
protection of men. A few men could not protect
themselves against a great number of wild
beasts. Their dread of man was man's protection.

The Devil put it into the mind of his agent
Nimrod to seek the beasts and kill them. When
the beasts attempted to escape from Nimrod he
would chase them and kill them. He trained other men to do the same thing. He killed those
wild beasts merely to demonstrate his prowess
and in defiance of God. In self-defense, and for
their own safety, many of the animals of the
forest became vicious and learned to attack man.
Thus it was that the Devil, acting through wicked men such as Nimrod, caused the wild beasts
of the forest to become vicious. Had God's commandment been obeyed by men, no doubt the
lion, the bear, the tiger, and other like wild
beasts would never have become vicious and
dangerous to men. Since the time of Nimrod

men who call themselves "sportsmen" have hunted the wild beasts, have lain in wait for them, have chased them, and brutally slain them, and thus the beasts of the forests and the wild fowls of the air have become man's mortal enemies because the huntsmen have become their mortal enemies. Men have wrongfully gone into the wilds and trapped the wild beasts and removed them from their natural homes, and placed them in prisons, such as zoos, and thus inflicted upon them cruel punishment, and their excuse has been that such is to satisfy the curiosity and fancy of men. Jehovah God never imprisoned wild beasts in zoos, but, on the contrary, he provided for the saving of their lives during the flood and for their protection after the flood by including them in his everlasting covenant. The violation of the everlasting covenant concerning both man and beast has brought great sorrow and suffering upon men and upon the beasts as well. God provided the forests as the home of the wild beasts, and men have no excuse or justification to remove the beasts from their homes and confine them, nor have they any right to ruthlessly and wantonly slay them.

Nimrod's commercial example was also in violation of God's law. Following that example, men since have willfully slain animals that they might make commerce out of their skins or bones. The great herd of buffalo that once swarmed upon the wilds of America have been wantonly slain for commercial reasons. The elephant, which has inhabited the wilds of the forests of India and other places, has been wantonly slain in order that the ivory of its

tusks might be used for commercial purposes.
These things originated with the Devil, and the
purpose has been and is to turn men away from
God. God has furnished the means by which man
can protect himself and also that the animals
might be protected, but cruel men following the
lead of the Devil have turned men away from
the righteous course.

For the purpose of providing clothing or raiment for Adam and Eve the Lord caused the
skins of animals to be used. (Genesis 3:21) In
the construction of the tabernacle "antelope
skins" were used. (Exodus 26:14, *Strong's*) It
appears also that certain skins were used for
clothing and raiment amongst the Israelites.
(Numbers 31:20) Of course, it would be necessary to slay the animals in order to get their
skins for a covering or raiment. These scriptures, therefore, would seem to fully justify one
in slaying animals and taking their skins for the
purpose of providing necessary clothing or raiment. Wherever such skins are required for this
purpose the taking of the life of the animal to
provide such clothing or raiment is not a violation of the everlasting covenant. Nor would the
taking of life to provide raiment be limited to
the person who used the furs or skins, but such
could be properly furnished to another. In some
places men have their lands enclosed and the
deer feed upon their pastures and other vegeta-
tion, and when these deer are mature and at
certain seasons of the year they are killed for
food and their skins used for other purposes
needful to man. This is not a violation of the

everlasting covenant, because it appears to be clearly within the terms of God's law.

FOR FOOD

Man may lawfully kill and eat the flesh of beasts, fowls and fish, but the blood thereof he must not eat. The Israelites were Jehovah's covenant people, whom he used to make types and shadows of greater things to come. The statutes or laws which he gave to the Israelites applied to them alone, because they were God's covenant people. At the eleventh chapter of Leviticus God's law specifies what beasts were clean for the Israelites to eat. Among the animals mentioned were swine, as follows: "And the swine, though he divide the hoof, and be clovenfooted, yet he cheweth not the cud; he is unclean to you."—Leviticus 11:7.

Mark the emphasis in this scripture on the words "to you". A similar statute governed the eating of the hare. (11:6) It would follow that such animals were not unclean to all human creatures, because of the use of the words "to you". Other peoples generally do eat the flesh of swine and hare. Bacon and ham constitute the food of many people. It is not a violation of the everlasting covenant to eat such food. The everlasting covenant, applying to mankind in general, concerning the eating of flesh says: "Every moving thing that liveth shall be meat for you; even as the green herb have I given you all things."—Genesis 9:3.

That provision of God's law was made prior to the law covenant with Israel, and it stands for ever. God's covenant with Israel was made

for the specific purpose of holding that nation
in line and under protection until the coming of
Christ Jesus. (Galatians 3:19) When Christ
Jesus came, the nation of Israel ended. (Romans
10:4) Christ Jesus fulfilled the law covenant
and brought it to an end: "Blotting out the
handwriting of ordinances. . . . and took it out
of the way, nailing it to his cross [tree]." (Colossians 2:14) It appears, from what follows, that
the eating of swine, for instance, is not a violation of the everlasting covenant so far as Christians and the "great multitude" are concerned:
"Let no man therefore judge you in meat, or in
drink, or in respect of an holy day, or of the new
moon, or of the sabbath days: which are a shadow of things to come; but the body is of Christ."
—Colossians 2:16, 17.

In order that sincere persons might not suffer
from confusion in regard to the things to eat,
the inspired writer of the Scriptures furthermore said: "Now the spirit speaketh expressly,
that in the latter times some shall depart from
the faith, giving heed to seducing spirits, and
doctrines of devils; . . . forbidding to marry,
and commanding to abstain from meats, which
God hath created to be received with thanks-
giving of them which believe and know the truth.
For every creature of God is good, and nothing
to be refused, if it be received with thanksgiv-
ing: for it is sanctified by the word of God and
prayer." (1 Timothy 4:1, 3-5) (See also Ephesians 2:15, 16.) The terms of the Jewish law
covenant forbidding the eating of swine and
rabbits or hares do not apply to Christians or
others of this day. There are certain animals

that no one does care to eat, such as skunks. The everlasting covenant, which applies to all men, specifically forbids the eating of the blood of the beasts; and the reason is given: because the life is in the blood. At Leviticus 22:8 it is written:

"That which dieth of itself, or is torn with beasts, he shall not eat to defile himself therewith: I am the Lord." Manifestly this law would apply to all persons, and to all animals that died, as there stated, for the reason that the blood of the animal is not poured out but remains in the flesh, and it hence could not be lawfully eaten. In this connection, note the advice of the apostles to Christians and others as to what they should and should not eat: "Forasmuch as we have heard, that certain which went out from us have troubled you with words, subverting your souls, saying, Ye must be circumcised and keep the law; to whom we gave no such commandment. For it seemed good to the holy [spirit], and to us, to lay upon you no greater burden than these necessary things: that ye abstain from meats offered to idols, and from blood, and from things strangled, and from fornication: from which if ye keep yourselves, ye shall do well. Fare ye well."—Acts 15:24, 28, 29.

The governing rule in reference to the taking of the life of animals may be summed up in these words: Animals may be slain for food, but the blood must not be eaten. The man who goes about with his gun deliberately killing animals for the mere sport or thrill of shooting them does violate the everlasting covenant. A Christian or a Jonadab, therefore, could not willfully and wantonly engage in the slaying of beasts, animals or fish merely for the sport or thrill of doing so.

SACRIFICE

God commanded the Israelites to sacrifice certain clean animals, and the killing of them for that purpose, of course, was right and proper. (Exodus 12:5-7) Thereby God was foretelling that the sacrificial blood of Christ Jesus would make an atonement for the sins of the people.

But the killing of all such animals could not be done by everyone, and the victim could not be offered by everyone. The sacrifice must be brought and offered in the proper manner as prescribed by the Lord: "And the Lord spake unto Moses, saying, Speak unto Aaron, and unto his sons, and unto all the children of Israel, and say unto them, This is the thing which the Lord hath commanded, saying, What man soever there be of the house of Israel, that killeth an ox, or lamb, or goat, in the camp, or that killeth it out of the camp, and bringeth it not unto the door of the tabernacle of the congregation, to offer an offering unto the Lord, before the tabernacle of the Lord; blood shall be imputed unto that man; he hath shed blood [of a beast to no valid end]; and that man shall be cut off from among his people: to the end that the children of Israel may bring their sacrifices, which they offer in the open field, even that they may bring them unto the Lord, unto the door of the tabernacle of the congregation, unto the priest, and offer them for peace offerings unto the Lord." "For the life of the flesh is in the blood; and I have given it to you upon the altar, to make an

atonement for your souls: for it is the blood that
maketh an atonement for the soul. Therefore I
said unto the children of Israel, No soul of you
shall eat blood, neither shall any stranger that
sojourneth among you eat blood."—Leviticus
17: 1-5, 11, 12.

Time and again God emphasizes this truth,
that life belongs exclusively to him, and therefore no life can properly be taken when such is
done in disregard of God's law. Foretelling his
purpose to redeem the human race by the sacrificial blood of his Firstborn, Jesus Christ, God
commanded that the firstborn of the animals fit
for sacrifice should be sacrificed unto the Lord:
"All the firstling males that come of thy herd
and of thy flock thou shalt sanctify unto the
Lord thy God: . . . Thou shalt eat it before the
Lord thy God year by year, in the place which
the Lord shall choose, thou and thy household."
—Deuteronomy 15: 19, 20.

The firstling of the animals not acceptable for
sacrifice must be redeemed with a lamb, that is,
an animal suitable for sacrifice. If the firstborn
was not redeemed as provided by law, then it
was proper and lawful to kill that unredeemed
firstborn: "Thou shalt set apart unto the Lord
all that openeth the matrix, and every firstling
that cometh of a beast which thou hast; the
males shall be the Lord's. And every firstling
of an ass thou shalt redeem with a lamb; and if
thou wilt not redeem it, then thou shalt break
his neck; and all the firstborn of man among thy
children shalt thou redeem." (Exodus 13: 12, 13)
"All that openeth the matrix is mine; and every
firstling among thy cattle, whether ox or sheep,

that is male. But the firstling of an ass thou
shalt redeem with a lamb: and if thou redeem
him not, then shalt thou break his neck. All the
firstborn of thy sons thou shalt redeem. And
none shall appear before me empty." (Exodus
34:19, 20) This shows that animals must be
treated or used according to God's law and any
treatment thereof contrary to his law is a sin.
Since the sacrifice of Jesus, the antitype, there
is no further occasion to use beasts for sacrifice.

DESTROYERS

Beasts may be killed under other circumstances that are within the terms of the covenant as follows: Beasts that work injury to
others or kill a human creature must be slain
(Exodus 21:28); or, if that beast is destroying
one's property, it would be proper to slay such
beast, and such does not constitute a breaking
of the everlasting covenant. "Take us the foxes,
the little foxes, that spoil the vines; for our
vines have tender grapes." (Canticles 2:15)
Thus the rule is fixed that animals that destroy
man's food and property may be taken, that is,
killed. The beasts or birds that are found destroying crops of the farmer or gardener may
be slain; and this is for man's protection, and
not in violation of the everlasting covenant.

Likewise God placed a value on the life of wild
beasts of the field and of the forest. Their lives
belong to God, and they are not to be hunted
down and ruthlessly and wantonly slaughtered.
Such pursuit of wild beasts and wanton slaughter of them are entirely out of harmony with
God's commandment to man, to wit: 'Have do-

minion over the beast of the field and the fowl of the air.' (Genesis 1:28) That it is in harmony with God's will to hunt beasts and fowls to be used for food is made certain by his law (Leviticus 17:13; Genesis 27:3-5); but only their flesh must be eaten, and not their blood; and this proves that the killing merely for thrills or pleasure of shooting of beasts or birds is wrong.

STUDY

The prayer of every person of good will toward God is this: "Teach me good judgment and knowledge; for I have believed thy commandments." (Psalm 119:66) Men of the world seek money and power that money brings them. The man who is wise takes the course which God has pointed out for him to take: "Receive my instruction, and not silver; and knowledge rather than choice gold." (Proverbs 8:10) The admonition of the faithful apostle is: "Study to show thyself approved unto God." (2 Timothy 2:15) The "bunk" proclaimed by "higher critics", who think to show their own greatness, does not constitute "knowledge", within the meaning of the Scriptures. Religion and the practice thereof have kept the people ignorant concerning God's purpose and therefore void of true knowledge. The end of religion is now at hand, and all who desire righteousness will be diligent to learn the truth, and such will seek the knowledge that God's Word imparts. Persons of good will toward God will quickly abandon religion and seek the knowledge contained in God's Word relative to him, his King and his kingdom. When God commands them to seek righteousness and meekness, that means that they should be anxious to learn and diligent to learn what is right; and that information is found only in the Scriptures. The persons of good will who will constitute the great multitude will be diligent to learn about the kingdom. Like the faithful men of old, all persons of good will now desire a government of righteousness and peace. To all such the Lord says: "Now therefore hearken unto me, O ye children; for blessed are they that keep my ways. Hear instruction, and be wise, and refuse it not. Blessed is the man that heareth me, watching daily at my gates, waiting at the posts of my doors. For whoso findeth me findeth life, and shall obtain favour of the Lord."—Proverbs 8: 32-35.

CHAPTER VI

GOD'S GOVERNMENT

THE GOVERNMENT of Jehovah God is of paramount importance to all who are seeking the way to life. By and through his government or kingdom Jehovah will vindicate his name and establish lasting peace in the universe, and never again shall affliction rise up. (Nahum 1:9) In all periods of time honest men have desired such a government and have had some vague knowledge of its coming. Now God's kingdom or government is here, and every person of good will toward God will be anxious to learn about that government. The government of Jehovah God is a theocracy because under the immediate direction and administration of Almighty God. It is a righteous government, because all of Jehovah's ways are right and righteous. Jehovah is supreme; and all who have a part in his government must be in full accord with him and joyfully obey his commandments.

Following the rebellion the first ray of hope set before man was God's vague promise to establish a righteous government on earth. Abel had faith and hope in that coming government. Likewise Enoch, Noah, Abraham, and a few others desired that government and by faith looked forward to it. (Hebrews 11:1-16) With the descendants of Abraham God set up a typical theocracy. He used the Israelites to make prophetic pictures of his coming real theocratic government. Moses, Aaron, Joshua and Samuel were representatives on the earth of God's theocratic government. When the Jews requested a man for king they displeased God, and concerning this it is written: "And the Lord said unto Samuel, Hearken unto the voice of the people in all that they say unto thee; for they have not rejected thee, but they have rejected me, that I should not reign over them. According to all the works which they have done since the day that I brought them up out of Egypt even unto this day, wherewith they have forsaken me, and served other gods; so do they also unto thee." —1 Samuel 8: 7, 8.

Religion, brought in by the Devil, was the reason for the Jews' rejecting God as King. They wanted to be like other people. Because of Saul's unfaithfulness he was rejected by the Lord. God then made David king over Israel; and David was a type foreshadowing Christ Jesus, the Beloved of Jehovah, and who is the world's real and true King under Jehovah, the "King of Eternity".—Jeremiah 10: 10, *margin*.

The last typical king of Israel was Zedekiah, the unfaithful and wicked one. He was overthrown, and God declared that the kingdom should be "no more, until he come whose right it is; and I will give it [to] him". (Ezekiel 21: 27) Thereafter the Devil continued as the invisible lord of the nation and carried on his wickedness without interruption, God suffering him to do so in order that the Devil might have full opportunity to carry out his boasted challenge.

God's expressed purpose is to have a righteous world, and concerning this he said: "For behold, I create new heavens, and a new earth; and the former shall not be remembered, nor come into mind. But be ye glad and rejoice for ever in that which I create: for, behold, I create Jerusalem a rejoicing, and her people a joy." (Isaiah 65:17, 18) "Jerusalem," as used in this text, refers to his great antitypical government of righteousness, and the prophecy here recorded is about completely fulfilled. All of God's holy prophets prophesied concerning the restoration of all things pertaining to the kingdom, and which prophecies must come true. (Acts 3:20, 21) God's prophet wrote foretelling the birth of the King and of his righteous and glorious reign. "For unto us a child is born, unto us a son is given, and the government shall be upon his shoulder; and his name shall be called Wonderful Counsellor, The mighty God, The everlasting Father, The Prince of Peace. Of the increase of his government and peace there shall be no end, upon the throne of David, and upon his kingdom, to order it, and to establish it with judgment and with justice, from henceforth even for ever. The zeal of the Lord of hosts will perform this." (Isaiah 9:6, 7) That prophecy must be completely fulfilled.

HIS BIRTH

Approximately four thousand years after the rebellion in Eden Jesus was born at Bethlehem. There the prophecy of Isaiah above quoted was beginning to have fulfillment. It was then and there that the messengers of Jehovah declared:

"Glory in the highest unto God! and on earth peace, among men of good-will." (Luke 2:14, *Rotherham*) Clearly now it is seen that the birth of the child Jesus shall in due time be 'glory to Almighty God' to all creatures that live, and that through him and his government peace shall come to stay and shall be a blessing to all men of good will, and to none other. The above-quoted text from *Rotherham* emphasizes the fact that peace on earth is to *men of good will only*. Why should the kingdom of Jehovah God under Christ ever be a blessing and a joy to anyone who is not of good will toward God? All the enemies of God shall perish for ever, and hence to them the kingdom will be nothing. (Psalms 21:8; 37:20) After Armageddon never again shall Satan and his wicked rule be in vogue. Never again will his religious agents and their organization be in existence. Then the memory of those wicked ones shall perish for ever; as it is written: "The memory of the just is blessed; but the name of the wicked shall rot." (Proverbs 10:7; Isaiah 26:14) Today the people on earth that are of good will toward God and his kingdom have reason to rejoice, and should rejoice, because the time of complete deliverance and peace everlasting is near. For that reason God is now making clear his purpose to those who desire his righteous government.

At the time of the baptism of Jesus he was anointed to be King. (Matthew 3:16; John 18:37) His first public proclamation was: "The kingdom of heaven is at hand." He instructed all persons of good will to continue to pray to God: "Thy kingdom come. Thy will be done in earth, as it is in heaven." (Matthew 6:10) Because he was and is the King under the immediate command of the almighty Theocrat, Jehovah, that beloved One, Jesus, was crucified by Satan's religious agents. It was their hope to destroy him, but God defeated his enemies by raising Jesus out of death and exalting him to the highest place in the universe. Christ Jesus is the "heir of all things", and he is the "express image" of his Father, Jehovah; and concerning the beloved Son God commands 'all the angels to worship him'. (Hebrews 1:6) Furthermore Jehovah commands that 'every knee to him [Christ] shall bow, and every tongue shall confess that Jesus Christ is Lord, to the glory of God'.— Philippians 2:10, 11.

WAITING

Although fully clothed with power and authority as King when He ascended into heaven, Jesus the King must wait to begin his reign until Jehovah selected the body members of his royal organization, and when that is finished the enemy shall be put down. Satan continued his wicked course without interruption. Hence it is written: "The Lord said unto my Lord, Sit thou at my right hand, until I make thine enemies thy footstool." (Psalm 110:1) "But this man, after he had offered one sacrifice for sins for ever, sat down on the right hand of God; from henceforth expecting [waiting] till his enemies be made his footstool." (Hebrews 10:12, 13) Those who shall be associated with Christ Jesus in his kingdom must first be selected, and they must prove their integrity under the test. Such

faithful ones are taken into the covenant for
the kingdom. (Luke 22: 28-30) After the return
of Christ Jesus and his kingdom the faithful are
"made kings and priests unto God" to reign
with Christ Jesus. (Revelation 1: 6; 5: 10) As
the typical kingdom was made up of twelve
tribes of Israel, so in the antitype the associates
with Christ Jesus are of twelve clans or tribes,
all of one family and all together constituting
the 144,000. (Revelation 7: 4) That favored body
of creatures composing "the body of Christ", the
anointed ones, must, every one of them, be put
to the test, prove faithful and true, be baptized
into the death of Christ, and experience the
resurrection change from human to spirit, and
be for ever with Christ Jesus in his kingdom.
—Romans 6: 3-5; 1 Corinthians 15: 51-55; Revelation 20: 4.

The period of "waiting", according to God's
good pleasure, has been approximately 1900
years, during which time the members of the
body of Christ have been selected, and the resurrection change of the remnant of the 144,000 soon
shall take place. Those of the elect who died in
Christ have already been resurrected. (1 Thessalonians 4: 15-17; 2 Timothy 4: 1) The period
of waiting ended in A.D. 1914, and the King assumed his high office under the command of Jehovah, the great Theocrat. "The LORD shall send
the rod of thy strength out of Zion [saying]:
rule thou in the midst of thine enemies. Thy
people shall be willing in the day of thy power,
in the beauties of holiness from the womb of the
morning: thou hast the dew of thy youth."
(Psalm 110: 2, 3) "Saying, We give thee thanks,

O Lord God Almighty, which art, and wast, and art to come; because thou hast taken to thee thy great power, and hast reigned. And the nations were angry, and thy wrath is come, and the time of the dead, that they should be judged, and that thou shouldest give reward unto thy servants the prophets, and to the saints, and them that fear thy name, small and great; and shouldest destroy them which destroy the earth."— Rev. 11: 17, 18.

The first work of the enthroned King is to oust the rebel Satan, and therefore the "war in heaven" began in 1914. (Revelation 12: 1-17) The battle of Armageddon will dispose definitely of all those who oppose Christ the King, and that will be the end of Satan's reign.

THE KINGDOM

The kingdom of heaven consists of Christ Jesus, the Head of God's capital organization called Zion, together with 144,000 associates, who are designated as kings and priests unto God and Christ. All of such are spirits in the likeness of Christ Jesus. The number will be no more and no less than 144,000 members. The kingdom is the creation of Jehovah God, and he is over all and above all. He is the great and almighty Theocrat. The King, Christ Jesus, will fully and completely carry out Jehovah's purpose. The kingdom or government of peace is THE Theocracy.

PRINCES

At all times since the challenge was flung into His face by the Devil Jehovah God has had on

earth some faithful and true servants. Among
such are mentioned Abel, Enoch, Noah, Abraham, Jacob, Joseph, Moses, and others. (Hebrews chapter 11) Included therein are all of
God's faithful prophets from Samuel to John
the Baptist. Those men had faith in God and in
his promise to set up a government and peace,
and they fully devoted themselves to God, refusing to compromise in any manner whatsoever with Satan's world or organization. None
of them can ever be members of the heavenly
kingdom or government of Jehovah, for the
manifest reason that they all died before the
ransom sacrifice was provided and paid over.
Those faithful men of old, faithful and true to
God, others have long looked upon and spoken
of as "our fathers". (Psalm 39: 12; 22: 4) Those
true and faithful men told their children of God
and of their own faith in his promises. "We
have heard with our ears, O God, our fathers
have told us, what work thou didst in their days
in the times of old." (Psalm 44: 1) Those men
are held forth in the Scriptures as examples of
faith and true devotion. (Hebrews 12: 1) Being
faithful, they received at God's hand a "good
report". They were witnesses to the name and
majesty of Almighty God, and he approved
them, and concerning them the inspired apostle,
who is a member of the kingdom, wrote: "These
all died in faith, not having received the promises, but having seen them afar off, and were
persuaded of them, and embraced them, and
confessed that they were strangers and pilgrims
on the earth." "And these all, having obtained
a good report through faith, received not the

promise: God having provided some better thing for us, that they without us should not be made perfect." (Hebrews 11:13, 39, 40) The apostle Paul spoke also of himself when he said "us", and he knew that he could not be made perfect until the coming of Christ Jesus, the King of glory (2 Timothy 4:8); and therefore the faithful men of old could not be made perfect until the setting up of the kingdom. It is certain, then, from the Scriptures that these men shall be brought back from death as "perfect" men. What, then, shall be their place in Jehovah's arrangement and under his theocratic government?

The kingdom or government of Jehovah is spiritual; therefore invisible to human eyes. God had his representatives on earth during the tenure of his typical kingdom, and so he will have his representatives on earth during the reign of Christ the King of glory; and those visible representatives, acting with authority, will be made up of the faithful men of old mentioned at Hebrews eleven and who for centuries have been designated in the Scriptures as "our fathers", and concerning whom it is written: "Instead of thy fathers shall be thy children, whom thou mayest make princes in all the earth."—Psalm 45:16.

The King, Christ Jesus, is the ruler, and the earthly representatives of that great Ruler are called the "princes", who shall represent the kingdom on the earth; and concerning which it is written: "Behold, a king shall reign in righteousness, and princes shall rule in judgment." (Isaiah 32:1) Furthermore, says the Scripture:

"For out of Zion [God's capital organization, of which Christ Jesus is Head] shall go forth the law, and the word of the Lord from Jerusalem." (Isaiah 2:3) As Samuel the prophet, under the typical kingdom, went about among the people delivering to them the commands of Jehovah, so under the reign of Christ the faithful men of old, the princes in the earth, shall go among the people directing them according to the commands of the Lord. That is the theocratic government in operation.

COMING SOON

The abundance of Scriptural evidence, together with the physical facts that have come to pass showing the fulfillment of prophecy, conclusively proves that the time for the battle of the great day of God Almighty is very near and that in that battle all of God's enemies shall be destroyed and the earth cleared of wickedness, preparatory to the complete establishment of righteousness. The affairs of the earth then will be under the complete control of Christ Jesus; and the faithful men of old above mentioned, resurrected as perfect creatures, will act as the representatives on earth of the theocratic government. The evidence also abundantly shows that those faithful men will be back on the earth at the beginning of Armageddon. From the Scriptures it appears to be absolutely certain that some of the remnant will be on the earth when those faithful men appear, and certainly those who compose the great multitude will also be on the earth, and all of these will meet and greet earth's princes.

BETH-SARIM

At San Diego, California, there is a small piece of land, on which, in the year 1929, there was built a house, which is called and known as Beth-Sarim. The Hebrew words *Beth Sarim* mean "House of the Princes"; and the purpose of acquiring that property and building the house was that there might be some tangible proof that there are those on earth today who fully believe God and Christ Jesus and in His kingdom, and who believe that the faithful men of old will soon be resurrected by the Lord, be back on earth, and take charge of the visible affairs of earth. The title to Beth-Sarim is vested in the WATCH TOWER BIBLE & TRACT SOCIETY in trust, to be used by the president of the Society and his assistants for the present, and thereafter to be for ever at the disposal of the aforementioned princes on the earth. To be sure, everything then on the earth will belong to the Lord, and neither the Lord nor the princes need others to build houses for them; but it was thought well and pleasing to God that the aforementioned house be built as a testimony to the name of Jehovah and showing faith in his announced purposes. The house has served as a testimony to many persons throughout the earth, and while the unbelievers have mocked concerning it and spoken contemptuously of it, yet it stands there as a testimony to Jehovah's name; and if and when the princes do return and some of them occupy the property, such will be a confirmation of the faith and hope that induced the building of Beth-Sarim.

BETH-SARIM

GREAT MULTITUDE

The theocratic government, that is to say, the heavenly kingdom, the royal house, is composed exclusively of Christ Jesus and 144,000 members with him; and over all is Jehovah God. Jehovah predetermined the number of the royal house, but he did not fix the number that shall constitute the Lord's "other sheep". Hence the number collectively is called the "great multitude, which no man could number" (Revelation 7:9); or, otherwise stated, the great multitude without specific number. The great multitude will not be a part of the theocratic government or kingdom of heaven, but will live forever on the earth and operate under the immediate direction of the Lord. The members of the great multitude must and will maintain their integrity toward Jehovah God and will thus have a part in the vindication of his name. The Lord has graciously revealed in his Word what will be at least some of the functions of the great multitude, and this is now causing many to rejoice.

vealed in his Word what will be at least some of
the functions of the new creation shall do, and this is
now causing many to rejoice.

CHAPTER VII

PRIVILEGES

JEHOVAH having expressed his purpose to
do a thing, he will certainly perform that
purpose. "I have spoken it, I will also bring
it to pass; I have purposed it, I will also do it."
(Isaiah 46:11) "So shall my word be that goeth
forth out of my mouth; it shall not return unto
me void; but it shall accomplish that which I
please, and it shall prosper in the thing whereto
I sent it." (Isaiah 55:11) Jehovah's purpose in
creating the earth is stated in these words: "I
have made the earth, and created man upon it;
I, even my hands, have stretched out the heavens, and all their host have I commanded." "For
thus saith the Lord that created the heavens;
God himself that formed the earth and made it;
he hath established it, he created it not in vain,
he formed it to be inhabited; I am the Lord, and
there is none else." (Isaiah 45:12, 18) God
created the earth. (Genesis 1:1) The foregoing
text proves that he created it to be inhabited by
man for ever. This conclusion is further supported by the command which Jehovah gave to
Adam and Eve, to wit: "And God blessed them,
and God said unto them, Be fruitful, and multiply, and replenish [fill] the earth, and subdue
it; and have dominion over the fish of the sea,
and over the fowl of the air, and over every living thing that moveth upon the earth." (Genesis

1:28) The command of Jehovah, "Be fruitful, and multiply, and replenish [(*Rotherham*) fill] the earth," is herein referred to as "the divine mandate".

Adam joined the Devil in rebellion, and for that reason he became a sinner, and he and Eve could not and did not carry out the divine mandate. God's purpose, however, cannot fail because of man's wrongdoing. Adam was righteous when the divine mandate was given to him, but he became unrighteous by reason of his sin; and no unrighteous man could carry out the divine mandate. All of Adam's children were born sinners, and for that reason none of them can carry out the divine mandate unless first made righteous. (Romans 5:12; Psalm 51:5) Today the earth is filled with unrighteousness and wicked persons. The kingdom class cannot carry out that divine mandate of populating the earth, for the reason that the kingdom company is made up exclusively of spirit creatures. If the millions that have lived and died should be raised out of death and 'restored to human perfection', that would not fulfill the divine mandate, for the reason that the mandate must be carried out by righteous men under the direct command of the Lord. If 'restitution of man' were God's purpose, which it is not, that could be accomplished only by the Lord Jesus Christ, and hence would not constitute a fulfillment of the divine mandate. As the command of God was given, so must it be carried out; but how and by whom? An abstract answer is given, and the proof in support thereof follows:

The "great multitude" will be granted the privilege of carrying out the divine mandate to multiply and fill the earth. The great multitude is formed by the "other sheep" of the Lord, which he brings into his fold and to whom he grants life everlasting on the earth. Those who compose the great multitude are the persons of good will who are now being gathered to the Lord. These are made righteous by the Lord by reason of their faith and obedience; and life everlasting on the earth will be theirs, and they shall be under the immediate command and control of the theocratic government.

FOR INSTRUCTION

The scriptures set out in the Bible were given by inspiration of God and caused to be recorded by his faithful servants, the prophets and the apostles, for the instruction of men of good will in the way of righteousness, to the end that such men of good will may be thoroughly furnished unto all good works. This includes the anointed remnant and their "companions", the great multitude. (2 Timothy 3:16, 17) Recorded in the Bible are many prophetic pictures produced by the command of Jehovah God and couched in language that could not be understood by men until the end of Satan's world, where we now are. (1 Corinthians 10:11) The time has now come when God makes known and understandable those prophetic pictures for the aid, comfort and hope of the persons who are devoted to him and to his kingdom. (Romans 15:4) Among those prophetic pictures is the one pertaining to the flood, or great deluge, the facts leading up to that flood, and the connection of Noah and his family therewith; and which directly concerns the carrying out of the divine mandate to fill the earth.

Many of the angels associated with Lucifer joined him in the rebellion, and they, together with the Devil, have since indulged in great wickedness. The Devil knew that God had commanded Adam to multiply and fill the earth, and he set about to defeat God's purpose. Prior to Noah's day and during his time angels materialized in human form. Some angels that had not joined in Satan's rebellion but that yielded to his seductive influence were overreached and induced to marry or take wives of the daughters of men, which resulted in a race of giants being born on the earth. Evidently it was the purpose of Satan and his wicked associates to mock God and to fill the earth with a race superior to ordinary men and all of whom should be against God. The result was that in Noah's time the Devil and those wicked angels debauched "the sons [angelic ones, materialized] of God", who married the daughters of men and raised a race of people on earth known as Gibborim, all of which were extremely wicked; and therefore it is written that "the earth was filled with violence". (Genesis 6: 11) "And God saw that the wickedness of man was great in the earth, and that every imagination of the thoughts of his heart was only evil continually." "And the Lord said, I will destroy man, whom I have created, from the face of the earth; both man, and beast, and the creeping thing, and the fowls of the air; for it repenteth me that I have made them. But

Noah found grace in the eyes of the Lord." "And God said unto Noah, The end of all flesh is come before me; for the earth is filled with violence through them: and, behold, I will destroy them with the earth. Make thee an ark of gopher wood: rooms shalt thou make in the ark, and shalt pitch it within and without with pitch." —Genesis 6:5, 7, 8, 13, 14.

THE PROPHETIC PICTURE

Jehovah God, having purposed to destroy the earth, commanded Noah to build an ark, into which he was to take his family and certain animals. The ark was a type of God's organization under Christ Jesus. The name of Noah's father was "Lamech", which means "powerful"; and Lamech played the part representing or picturing Jehovah God, while Noah represented Christ Jesus, the beloved Son of God. When Lamech witnessed the birth of his son, "he called his name Noah, saying, This [son] shall comfort us concerning our work and toil of our hands." (Genesis 5:28, 29) The name of Noah means "Rest; comfort". The record concerning Noah is that following the deluge he offered a sacrifice unto God: "And the Lord smelled a sweet savour [savour of rest], and the Lord said in his heart, I will not again curse the ground any more for man's sake." (Genesis 8:21) The prophecy uttered by Lamech was nearly 600 years before the flood. "All the days of Lamech were seven hundred seventy and seven [777] years." (Genesis 5:30, 31) The number *seven* is symbolic of fullness of the things heavenly, or completeness in heaven; and three sevens appearing point to the fact of the everlasting years of Jehovah. "From everlasting to everlasting, thou art God."—Psalm 90: 2.

Because of this faith and obedience unto God Noah was counted a righteous man. He warned the people then on the earth of the impending disaster of the flood. He was "a preacher of righteousness" and continuously bore testimony to the name of Jehovah God. (2 Peter 2: 5; Hebrews 11: 7) After Noah was 500 years old his three sons were born. (Genesis 5: 32; 6: 9, 10) In the prophetic drama relating to the flood those three sons played the part picturing the Lord's "other sheep", who compose the great multitude; whereas Noah pictured Christ Jesus, who is "the Everlasting Father", who ministers life to all who get life. (Isaiah 9: 6) Noah's sons were born a short time before the flood; and likewise the "other sheep" of the Lord that form the great multitude are brought forth a short time before Armageddon, which is the antitype of the flood. Noah's sons were born a short time before the end of the wicked "world that then was", and now the "other sheep" are brought forth at the end of the present wicked world. As Noah was old when his sons were born, even so a long time elapsed from the birth of the man-child Jesus until he brings forth his "other sheep". The facts that have come to pass now clearly disclose that the flood and everything in connection therewith constituted or pictured what God's purpose is concerning the wicked world that now is, and which he will destroy at Armageddon.

In obedience to God's commandment Noah builded the ark, which was God's provision for the protection and salvation of Noah and his family from the devastation of the flood: "And, behold, I, even I, do bring a flood of waters upon the earth, to destroy all flesh, wherein is the breath of life, from under heaven; and every thing that is in the earth shall die. But with thee will I establish my covenant; and thou shalt come into the ark; thou, and thy sons, and thy wife, and thy sons' wives, with thee. And of every living thing of all flesh, two of every sort shalt thou bring into the ark, to keep them alive with thee; they shall be male and female." "Thus did Noah; according to all that God commanded him, so did he. And the Lord said unto Noah, Come thou and all thy house into the ark; for thee have I seen righteous before me in this generation."—Genesis 6: 17-19, 22; 7: 1.

The scheme of Satan was to corrupt all creation on the earth and thereby bring about the destruction of all men, and this he tried in his effort to carry out his wicked challenge. The Devil failed! The flood resulted in the destruction of all flesh on the earth, save Noah and his family, the salvation of whom was a defeat of Satan's scheme and was in vindication of Jehovah's name. It therefore clearly appears that the primary purpose of the flood was to vindicate the name of Jehovah and his word. Furthermore, the purpose was to clear the earth of the wicked and to preserve only the righteous ones, to wit, Noah and his family, whom God counted righteous by reason of their faith and obedience. That was a picture of the result of Armageddon, which great battle shall clear away from the earth all the wicked and preserve alive only the righteous ones, whom God counts righteous by reason of their faith and obedience, and which righteous ones will also be a vindication of Jehovah's name.

God declares that his purpose in providing the ark was to keep alive the righteous ones. (Genesis 6: 18; 7: 3) Noah and the members of his family were counted righteous in God's sight because of their faith and obedience. The flood having ended, the occupants of the ark went out. "And God spake unto Noah, saying, Go forth of the ark, thou, and thy wife, and thy sons, and thy sons' wives with thee. And Noah went forth, and his sons, and his wife, and his sons' wives with him. And Noah builded an altar unto the Lord; and took of every clean beast, and of every clean fowl, and offered burnt offerings on the altar. And the Lord smelled a sweet savour." —Genesis 8: 15, 16, 18, 20, 21.

At that time Noah and his sons and their wives, eight persons in all, were the only human creatures alive, and all of them were counted righteous in the sight of Jehovah. It is certain that God would commission no creatures to fill the earth who are not counted righteous by him. Immediately following the flood God restated the commandment to righteous Noah and his family to "be fruitful and multiply and replenish [fill] the earth". At this point Noah pictured Christ Jesus, "the Everlasting Father," who ministers life according to the will of Almighty God (Isaiah 9: 6; Romans 6: 23), and also the members of the body of Christ, who will be associated with Christ Jesus in the work of regeneration. (Luke 22: 28-30; Matthew 19: 28) While the filling of the earth must be done under the direction of Christ Jesus, it is certain that human creatures must be employed to bring forth human children, and therefore the sons of Noah and their wives pictured the Lord's "other sheep", that form the great multitude. Immediately upon leaving the ark Noah and his sons received from Jehovah this commandment: "And God blessed Noah and his sons, and said unto them, Be fruitful, and multiply, and replenish the earth." (Genesis 9: 1) This is conclusive proof that the sons of Noah pictured the earthly creatures that shall have the privilege of fulfilling the divine mandate to multiply and fill the earth. That the flood and attending circumstances and Noah and his family were typical, constituting a prophetic picture, is further made sure by the words of Jesus, to wit: "And as it was in the days of No′e, so shall it be also in the days of the Son of man. They did eat, they drank, they married wives, they were given in marriage, until the day that No′e entered into the ark, and the flood came, and destroyed them all. Even thus shall it be in the day when the Son of man is revealed."—Luke 17: 26, 27, 30.

The Lord Jesus will be revealed to all flesh on the earth in and by the expression of Jehovah's wrath at Armageddon, which is very near and concerning which it is written: "And to you who are troubled, rest with us; when the Lord Jesus shall be revealed from heaven with his mighty angels, in flaming fire taking vengeance on them that know not God, and that obey not the gospel of our Lord Jesus Christ: who shall be punished with everlasting destruction from the presence of the Lord, and from the glory of his power."—2 Thessalonians 1: 7-9.

As the end of the flood did not show the end of the picture or prophetic drama, so likewise the end of Armageddon does not complete the fulfillment of that prophetic picture, but things as shown in the prophecy are to be fulfilled following Armageddon. As the divine mandate was given immediately following the flood, this is proof that the beginning of the fulfillment of the divine mandate will immediately follow the battle of Armageddon. The divine mandate was first given to Adam and thereafter restated to Noah and his sons, and at no other place in the Scriptures is the same stated; and in both instances, when stated, it was given to men righteous in the sight of God. After the battle of Armageddon has ended those of the great multitude will be the only human creatures on the earth, aside from some of the remnant of Christ's body and the "princes" of the earth. Will the remnant, that is, the members of the body of Christ, bring forth children in fulfillment of the divine mandate? What Noah did may enable us to arrive at the proper conclusion, as Noah represented The Christ; and what his sons did is also proper for consideration in ascertaining the correct answer to this question.

Noah lived 349 years after coming out of the ark. The record does not show that Noah brought forth or begot children after the flood. Had he raised sons following the flood, that would mean that the human race would have more than three primary branches, to wit, Shemitic, Japhetic and Hamitic. The Bible record shows only these three branches of the human race. (Genesis 10:1-32) Concerning all the patriarchs from Adam to Noah's father, Lamech, the Bible record is that, after each had begotten the next in line of descent, 'he begot sons and daughters.' (Genesis 5:3-30) The Bible record concerning Noah and his sons is: "And Noah was five hundred years old; and Noah begat Shem, Ham, and Japheth." (Genesis 5:32) There is no Bible record that Noah had other sons than those three sons above named, either before or after the flood and after the giving of the divine mandate to "fill the earth". As to Noah's three sons, the names of their children and grandchildren, born after the flood and after the restating the divine mandate, are set forth in the record to the number of seventy persons. (Genesis 10:1-32) There is a complete absence of anything in the record of any children's being born to these three sons before the flood, and a complete absence in the record that Noah had any children after the flood. For this reason it appears that the divine mandate to "multiply and fill the earth" does not apply to the spirit-begotten ones, that is, to the remnant, but that such as were pictured by Noah, the faithful ones who inherit the kingdom with Christ Jesus, are included in and associated with Christ Jesus, "the Everlasting Father," who administers life to all who receive life after Armageddon, including those who shall be raised from the dead.

Seeing that the divine mandate was given only to righteous men or those counted righteous by

the Lord, and that the great multitude who survive the battle of Armageddon will be the only
ones of the human race to abide on the earth, and
that those of the great multitude will be counted
righteous by the Lord by reason of their faith
and obedience, is it not reasonable and Scriptural to conclude that the members of the great
multitude will carry out the divine mandate
according to the will of Jehovah God under the
immediate command and direction of Christ?
The question then arises, Since the Lord is now
gathering his "other sheep", who will form the
great multitude, should those begin now to
marry and bring forth children in fulfillment of
the divine mandate? No, is the answer; which
the Scriptures fully support. The sons of Noah
and their wives had no children during the flood.
There is no evidence that any children were
taken into the ark. Only eight persons came
forth from the ark, and that is conclusive proof
that no children were born to Noah's sons either
before the flood or during the flood. (Genesis
7:13; 8:16) In the prophetic picture it is shown
that no children were born to Noah's sons and
their wives until after the flood, and the first one
mentioned was born two years after the flood.
(Genesis 11:10) The apostle Peter, under inspiration of the holy spirit, corroborates this
when he says: "The ark . . . wherein few, that
is, eight souls were saved by water." The conclusion, therefore, seems inevitable that the beginning of the fulfillment of the divine mandate
is after Armageddon. In support of this conclusion the words of Jesus relating to Armageddon
are here set forth, to wit: "And woe unto them

that are with child, and to them that give suck
in those days!" (Matthew 24: 19) Jesus warned
those who would be saved from the destructive
results of Armageddon to flee to the kingdom
now, because it will be too late to flee after Armageddon begins; and he also warns that they
should not be burdened unnecessarily when so
fleeing.—Matthew 24: 16-21.

The Lord Jesus Christ is the great Executive
Officer of Jehovah God, and whatsoever is done
in the kingdom must be done by him or under his
immediate direction. The reasons therefor are
set forth fully in the Scriptures. The perfect
man Adam lost everything. Jesus became the
owner of every thing that Adam lost. Christ
Jesus is the "heir of all things". (Hebrews 1: 2;
Romans 8: 17) He is "the author of eternal salvation" and the minister of life. (Hebrews 5: 9;
Romans 6: 23) The carrying out of the divine
mandate must be done under the immediate direction of Christ Jesus. His "other sheep", the
great multitude, are to be used according to the
will of his Father. The divine mandate must be
carried out on earth by human agents who are
in full harmony with Christ Jesus. The great
multitude will be the only ones on earth at the
conclusion of Armageddon who could do this.
That Christ Jesus will do the regenerating of
mankind by and through his earthly agents is
made certain by his words: "And Jesus said unto them, Verily I say unto you, That ye which
have followed me, in the *regeneration,* when the
Son of man shall sit in the throne of his glory,
ye also shall sit upon twelve thrones, judging
the twelve tribes of Israel."—Matthew 19: 28.

The great multitude, as shown by the Scriptures, serve "before the throne of God" (Revelation 9:15); which means they serve under the direct command of the Lord Jesus Christ. The prophetic picture clearly shows that Noah's family, his sons and their wives, refer to the great multitude; and since the command was given to those in the type to multiply and fill the earth, it follows that the great multitude, under the direction of Christ, will be used for that purpose. The members of the body of Christ are the agents of Jehovah to carry out the purpose of Jehovah as he delegates to them certain things to do. The great multitude are the "companions" of the body of Christ and agents of The Christ to carry out the work assigned to them. The prophetic picture, supported by other Scriptures, shows that the great multitude will be used by the Lord to carry into operation the divine mandate to multiply and fill the earth. Such will be the great privilege which the Lord extends to those who are of his "other sheep".

NEW EARTH

Since the rebellion in Eden the earth has been under the curse. (Genesis 3:17) Satan has ruled the earth in wickedness, and unrighteous men have been his active agents in that rule. But it will not for ever be so, for the reason that God has given his Word that the wicked shall be wiped out, that to be followed by the "new earth". God gave his emphatic word of promise to create new heavens and a new earth: "For behold me! creating new heavens and a new earth, and the former shall not be mentioned, neither shall they come up on the heart." (Isaiah 65:17, *Rotherham*) The apostle Peter believed and faithfully served God and Christ. He was the inspired witness of the Lord, and under inspiration of the spirit of God and with positive authority he wrote: "Nevertheless we, according to his promise, look for new heavens and a new earth, wherein dwelleth righteousness."—2 Peter 3:13.

The "heavens" mean the ruling power invisible to human eyes. Satan has long been the invisible ruler of this world. (2 Corinthians 4:4) The new heavens consist of The Christ, Head and body, served by the holy angels of heaven. The wicked earth has been ruled by unrighteous men. The "new earth" will consist of righteous men who, in the years past, proved their integrity to God and who shall be resurrected as perfect men and made princes in the earth and rule in righteousness. (Psalm 45:16; Isaiah 32:1) Associated with those princes will be the great multitude. Every creature that gets everlasting life on the earth must become righteous, and the righteous will never die. (Matthew 25:46) The new heavens and new earth together constitute the righteous world, which the inspired writer of the Scripture says is "the world to come", the "world without end". (Hebrews 2:5; 6:5; Ephesians 3:21) In fulfillment of his promise God has created a new heavens consisting of Christ, as aforesaid, and has enthroned Christ to rule; and the Scriptures show that following the battle of Armageddon Christ will proceed to put in operation the new earth. It is then that the great multitude will begin to fulfill the prophetic divine mandate and to multiply and fill the earth with righteous children. God will fill the earth only with righteous creatures, and hence he will use righteous agencies. Aside from the great multitude there appears to be no other human agencies for that purpose. Manifestly the "other sheep" of the Lord, which form the great multitude, are brought into existence for the use of the Lord. All the Scriptural evidence and extraneous facts point to the great multitude as the earthly agency to carry out the divine mandate to fill the earth.

As the flood, which was typical, cleared the earth of the wicked and left surviving only eight persons, so the battle of the great day of God Almighty will clear the earth of the wicked and there will be comparatively few who survive. "And the slain of the Lord shall be at that day from one end of the earth even unto the other end of the earth; they shall not be lamented, neither gathered, nor buried; they shall be dung upon the ground." (Jeremiah 25:33) Armageddon will clear the earth of unrighteousness, and thereafter those who live must be on the side of God and Christ his King. The Scriptures appear to clearly show that the survivors of Armageddon will be those Jonadabs who henceforth 'seek righteousness and meekness' and who form the great multitude. (Revelation 7:9-15) Together with the faithful prophets and servants of God, who maintained their integrity toward God before the first coming of Christ Jesus, these shall live for ever on the earth. The entire number will doubtless be but a few millions, a small number compared to the mass of humanity now on earth. But there is no need to be appalled by the great world-wide destruction of Armageddon. It is certain that the day of Jehovah's wrath will conclude with the victorious war of Christ against Satan and then there will be found on earth a far greater number of persons than those who survived the deluge of Noah's day. But the fact that a great multitude of persons do maintain their integrity toward God and are carried over Armageddon conclusively disproves and nullifies Satan's wicked challenge and will be a vindication of Jehovah's name and his word. The power of God is unlimited, and there is nothing that can hinder him in carrying out his mandate to "fill the earth". When stripped of wickedness, the earth will be in a condition for the execution of that divine mandate in harmony with the will of Almighty God. Only eight persons survived the flood; and now, after centuries, brief indeed so far as God is concerned, the earth is filled with creatures the most of whom have turned to violence and wickedness. If a few millions survive Armageddon and are wholly devoted to God and his King, Christ Jesus, what may those few millions do under the direction of Christ Jesus toward 'filling the earth' within a few short centuries? As to how long will be required to fill the earth, it is not revealed, but it seems certain that the entire thousand years will not be required to carry out the divine mandate.

CONCEIVED IN RIGHTEOUSNESS

After Armageddon all degenerate and wicked ones will be dead, and neither they nor the Devil

can debauch or influence the children born to
those of the great multitude. The kingdom of the
Lord, then in operation, will mean everlasting
life to all obedient ones. Hence the children of
the great multitude will be conceived in righteousness and unto life. Christ Jesus will accomplish what Lucifer failed to do, and righteous
men and women will perform the functions
which sinful man could not perform, and in
righteousness God's commandment to multiply
and fill the earth will be accomplished. That will
be a vindication of Jehovah's word and name.
It was God's will that perfect Adam and Eve
should multiply, and therefore it must be in harmony with the will of God that those men and
women whom the Lord counts righteous and
who will form the great multitude shall marry
and bring forth children. The counsel as set
forth at 1 Corinthians 7 did not apply to perfect
Adam, and will not apply to those of the great
multitude, who will fulfill the mandate which
Adam did not fulfill, by reason of his disobedience. Neither would the counsel of 1 Timothy
5 : 11, 14 apply to the great multitude.

BABES WILL NOT DIE

The regeneration of the human race will be a
time of delight and joy. It will be a time of complete peace and great rejoicing. It will be a real
joy to the parents to rear their children and to
teach them righteousness under righteous conditions. Parents are anxious to have their children to live. The babes born to those of the great
multitude will not die as babes. If they should
die as babes there would be no purpose in their

birth, because it is God's time to fill the earth
with righteous, living creatures. Because the
father of the human race (that is, Adam) sinned,
all babes have been born in sin, inheriting the
imperfection and condemnation, and therefore
many have died because of the iniquity of Adam.
(Romans 5:12) Jesus has bought the human
race; and those of the great multitude having
received the full benefit of the ransom sacrifice
and being commissioned by the Lord to fill the
earth, their children will not inherit the death
resulting to the human race by reason of Adam's
sin. The children of the great multitude will be
conceived in righteousness and born to live, if
they obey the Lord. Those who die thereafter
will die because of their own individual wrongdoing; as it is written: "Every one shall die for
his own iniquity," and not because of inherited
sin. (Jeremiah 31:29, 30; Ezekiel 18:17) It follows that the infants, not being sufficiently responsible until they grow up, would not die as
infants, but that the Lord will give each one an
intelligent, full and fair opportunity to prove
his or her devotion to God and righteousness.

Concerning the great multitude it is written:
"For the Lamb [Christ Jesus], which is in the
midst of the throne, shall feed them, and shall
lead them unto living fountains of waters; and
God shall wipe away all tears from their eyes."
(Revelation 7:17) If the babies of the great
multitude should die as babes in arms, surely
their parents would shed tears of bitterness.
But there will be no tears of bitterness shed.
The kingdom of heaven is symbolically called
"the holy city, [the] new Jerusalem", which

rules the world in righteousness and which is the dwellingplace of God by and through which he ministers blessings to the people, and concerning which it is written: "And God shall wipe away all tears from their eyes; and there shall be no more death, neither sorrow, nor crying, neither shall there be any more pain: for the former things are passed away." (Revelation 21:4) The reason why sorrow, crying and suffering will cease plainly appears from the scriptures that follow.

"Jerusalem" is the name applied to Jehovah's universal organization, while "Zion" is the name of the capital organization exercising the will of God over all. "Jerusalem," therefore, includes the Lord's "other sheep" when they are all gathered into the fold of the Lord. (John 10:16) Already the "new heavens" are in operation. Note now the prophetic words of Jehovah: "For behold me! creating new heavens and a new earth, and the former shall not be mentioned, neither shall they come up on the heart. But joy ye and exult perpetually in what I am about to create, for, behold me! creating Jerusalem an exultation, and her people a joy; therefore will I exult in Jerusalem and joy in my people, and there shall be heard in her no more the sound of weeping or the sound of a cry: there shall be thenceforward no more a suckling of a few days or an elder who filleth not up his days, but a youth a hundred years old may die, yea a sinner a hundred years old shall be accursed." (Isaiah 65:17-20, *Rotherham*) This shows that the great multitude begin to multiply and their babes are a joy to them. The parents will know how to properly feed and care for their babes and how to instruct them in the way of righteousness that they may grow up to maturity without sickness, suffering or death; and therefore it is written:

"There shall be henceforward no more a suckling of a few days or an elder who filleth not up his days"; which clearly means that the babes will grow up to maturity and full individual responsibility. What, then, is meant by the words of the text, "But a youth a hundred years old may die, yea a sinner a hundred years old shall be accursed"? The number ten is symbolic of completeness of things pertaining to the earth. The multiple of ten times ten, or one hundred, would therefore refer to the full and complete opportunity of each one of the children of the great multitude to prove his integrity to the Lord. The 'one hundred years' would not therefore mean that literally every person must have a one hundred years' trial, but does mean that each one must have a full and complete opportunity to prove his integrity to the Lord. Those proving their integrity and therefore being made righteous shall live forever; and those who fail to prove their integrity and who become willful sinners die as accursed ones. Whether one hundred years or five hundred years are required would make no difference, but during that length of time the person would be a youth as compared to those who never die. Hence "a youth" having full opportunity and becoming a willful violator of God's law would perish, and would perish for his own iniquity and therefore would be accursed. No one would mourn because of the death of the willful sinner. Not even the parents would mourn, because to mourn for such would mean that the mourner is not in full heart harmony with God and his purposes and his kingdom. God has commanded that those who are fully devoted to him shall not mourn because of the death of the willfully wicked. (See Ezekiel 24:16, 17.) Therefore, in God's organization, "there shall be heard in her [Jerusalem] no more the sound of weeping or the sound of a cry."

The children born to the great multitude are the seed of those who are blessed by the Lord, and which obedient children shall be blessed. "They shall not labour in vain, nor have children for terror, for the seed of the blessed ones of [Jehovah] shall they be, and their offspring with them." (Isaiah 65:23, *Rotherham*) The kingdom in full operation will bring blessings to all obedient ones, and nothing therein shall be permitted to offend or bring sorrow upon those devoted to the Lord.—Isaiah 65:25.

Judas Iscariot, who betrayed the Lord Jesus, was a willful sinner, and no one mourned because of his death; and this illustrates and emphasizes the truth that no one will sorrow because of the death of one who has had a full opportunity to know and to obey the Lord and who then deliberately opposes God and his kingdom. The kingdom of God is a great joy to all who love the kingdom and who render themselves in obedience to its laws. It is the kingdom that vindicates Jehovah's name, and therefore all in God's organization or under it shall rejoice. During all the time that Satan has operated as the god of this wicked world sorrow and suffering and death have afflicted the people. Under the reign of Christ Jesus weeping shall cease, joy will take the place thereof, and in due time even death itself shall be destroyed. (1 Corinthians 15:26) By faith the anointed remnant now see and appreciate what God's kingdom means to them and to all who obey; and they seeing that the Lord Jesus is enthroned and has taken his power and has begun his reign, they greatly rejoice. (Revelation 12:12) The Lord's "other sheep", now being gathered to him, by faith see the kingdom and the blessings it will bring to them and their offspring, and they hail Jehovah and the Lord Jesus with great joy. (Revelation 7:9, 10) When those of the great multitude perform their functions and privileges under the kingdom their joy will be full. To now see and appreciate the great truth that they will be permitted to bring forth children that will live forever on the earth, to the glory of God, brings them much joy.

PERSONAL OBLIGATIONS

The time designated in the Scriptures as "the last days" is now here. It is the time of great emergency and impending disaster. The great mass of the people on earth are wicked, and that includes most of the children. The "other sheep" of the Lord now being gathered to him have resting upon them weighty responsibilities to which they must give careful attention. There are Jonadabs now who are fully devoted to God and his kingdom and many of whom now have children. What must be expected for them? The obligation is upon the parents to teach their children the truth of and concerning Jehovah and his kingdom under Christ and thus to lead them that they may 'seek righteousness and meekness', and, they so doing, the divine promise will apply to such children, to wit: "Seek righteousness, seek meekness; it may be ye shall be hid in the day of the Lord's anger." (Zephaniah 2:3) Children born before Armageddon are brought into the world while Satan's wicked, oppressive organization affects the lives of all on the earth, and there is but one way of finding protection and safety for such children, as well as others, and that is, to devote themselves to God and his kingdom and find refuge in the organization of Jehovah under Christ. They must seek to learn the truth and conform themselves to God's expressed will. Therefore the Jonadabs should see to it that their children are properly taught and afforded an opportunity to place themselves fully under the protection of the kingdom of God. It would therefore appear that there is no reasonable or Scriptural injunction to bring children into the world immediately before Armageddon, where we now are. If children are born, then the parents should see to it that such children are properly instructed concerning the Lord and his kingdom until the child reaches the age when it must freely exercise intelligently its own will and bear its own responsibility. While it is not the obligation of the consecrated to seek out children not their own and to give them instruction, yet all children who accompany their parents or foster parents or those friendly to them and who desire

to attend and do attend meetings with the
grownups and there seek righteousness and
meekness should be given aid and encouragement. Such aid and encouragement can be given
by having the children sit quietly at such study
meetings and listen to the instructions that are
given.

At the "feast of weeks" those other than
Israelites were permitted to attend, concerning
which God there gave the commandment, to wit:
"And thou shalt rejoice before the Lord thy
God, thou, and thy son, and thy daughter, and
thy manservant, and thy maidservant, and the
Levite that is within thy gates, and the stranger,
and the fatherless, and the widow, that are
among you, in the place which the Lord thy God
hath chosen to place his name there." (Deuteronomy 16:11) At the "feast of tabernacles",
when his people assembled at the temple, God
commanded thus: "Gather the people together,
men, and women, and children, and thy stranger
that is within thy gates, that they may hear, and
that they may learn, and fear the Lord your
God, and observe to do all the words of this
law."—Deuteronomy 31:12.

Separate meetings called "Sunday schools",
which are used for the juveniles, are not Scriptural, but the children should accompany their
parents to the place of study of God's Word,
the place of worship; and when other children
come with them that they too might learn, such
should be required to sit quietly in the meeting
and learn.

Some of the anointed remnant now on the
earth have children; and suppose children are

born to some of these now since the coming of the Lord Jesus to the temple? What is the status of such children? and what will be their relationship to the divine mandate concerning the filling of the earth? While it clearly appears from the Scriptures that the divine mandate to "fill the earth" does not apply to the remnant of the anointed, yet in the natural course of events some of these do now multiply and bring children into the world. The solemn duty devolves upon the parents of such children to see to it that their children are properly instructed concerning Jehovah God and his kingdom under Christ Jesus. Even the laws of the world compel the parents to see to the education of their offspring. The law of God has placed a greater responsibility upon the parents. From the time the child is old enough to have some understanding and be taught, from that time forward the consecrated parents should see to it that each day the child has some instruction concerning God and his kingdom. This is an obligation laid upon them by the Lord. Children thus properly instructed until they reach the age of personal responsibility will be equipped to choose to serve God and his kingdom, and, if they do so, and if they continue to seek righteousness and meekness, they will doubtless be of the "great multitude" class, the "other sheep", that will be protected, and may be safely carried through Armageddon, even as Noah's sons were carried over the flood by being under the protection of the ark.

Many children, because of the evil day and the power exercised by the evil one and his dupes, grow up in wickedness, refuse instruction in righteousness, and continue in wickedness. What is the status of such children, and what protection will they have during Armageddon? and what, if anything, will be their relationship to the divine mandate relative to the filling of the earth? There is but one means of salvation, and that is by faith in the shed blood of Christ Jesus and by obedience to the commandments of the Lord. "He that believeth not the Son shall not see life; but the wrath of God abideth on him." (John 3:36) Faith in God and in Christ Jesus is an individual matter; and those who intelligently refuse to believe and serve God and Christ Jesus are not relieved of the wrath of God, which is against all the offspring of Adam. Jehovah God's commandment to his executioner, which commandment applies at Armageddon, is, to wit: "Slay utterly old and young, both maids, and little children, and women; but come not near any man [the word *man* here manifestly applies to both sexes] upon whom is the mark." (Ezekiel 9:6) The flood being a type of Armageddon, it appears that in the antitype, that is, Armageddon, God makes no exception: no favor to those who refuse to believe on him and obey his commandments.

Will the offspring born to the Jonadabs come under the redemptive provision made through the sacrifice of Christ Jesus? Yes; the children born to the Jonadabs before Armageddon, just as all those raised out of death, would necessarily come under the divine provision of redemption. The earthly parents being imperfect, that imperfection is transmitted to the offspring. Also all children born of Jonadabs after Armageddon must belong to Christ by reason of the redemptive price paid, and all who get life must receive it from that great Life-giver, "the Everlasting Father," Christ Jesus, who administers such gift. (Isaiah 9:6; Romans 6:23) The ransom sacrifice, of necessity, then, must apply to all who get life everlasting.

Would the carrying out or fulfillment of the divine mandate to "fill the earth" as accomplished by the great multitude do away with the resurrection of the dead? No, not at all. Undoubtedly many of Adam's offspring before and after the flood died in ignorance of God's redemptive provision through Jesus Christ's sacrifice, and the Scriptural testimony conclusively proves that such must be brought forth from the grave in God's appointed time that they may have an opportunity to take advantage of the ransom sacrifice and the kingdom. This would not mean, however, that such would have anything to do with 'multiplying and filling the earth'.

RESURRECTION

The resurrection of the faithful dead began at the coming of the Lord Jesus to the temple and the building up of Zion. (Psalm 102:16; 2 Timothy 4:1, 7, 8; 1 Thessalonians 4:14-17) Those who have part in "the first resurrection" are members of the body of Christ. (Revelation 20:6) The faithful men of old, who shall be made princes on earth, have a "better resurrection" than those of the general resurrection and are next in order to the body of Christ. (Hebrews

11:15-39) The Scriptures do not state the specific time of the general resurrection of those who have died without an opportunity to know the Lord. The reasonable conclusion is that the divine mandate to "fill the earth" will have well progressed before the awakening of those dead ones begins. Before anyone would be counted righteous he must exercise faith in God and His kingdom and prove his integrity. Those awakened out of death are not such as have shown faith in God and maintained their integrity toward God, and hence they would not have anything to do with carrying out the divine mandate.

Will not all the dead be awakened to the resurrection? and is not that made sure by the words of Jesus (John 5:28, 29), to wit: "Marvel not at this; for the hour is coming, in the which all that are in the graves shall hear his voice, and shall come forth; they that have done good, unto the resurrection of life; and they that have done evil, unto the resurrection [by judgment (*A.R.V.*)]"? The Scriptures do not support that conclusion. There appears no reason or Scriptural proof that God would resurrect the willfully wicked.

THE WICKED

Judas Iscariot, the Pharisees and scribes, and other wicked ones died and doubtless were buried, but are those men included among the ones that Jesus mentioned as those "that are in the graves"? The word here rendered "graves" is *mnemeion*, and means "monument in remembrance of the dead". (*Strong's Conc.*) Those included within the meaning of that word are held in the memory of God. Does God hold in memory those wicked ones, that is, those who have deliberately joined the Devil and fought against righteousness and who have betrayed, opposed and persecuted the servants of God because such servants have been faithfully doing the will of God? The answer to that question is found in this text, to wit: "The memory of the just is blessed: but the name of the wicked shall rot." (Proverbs 10:7) Certainly God would not hold in memory those creatures, those religionists who not only have refused to hear and obey God's Word but who have opposed him and his servants. They must be included within the class whose name and memory shall rot. Who, then, shall hear the voice of the Lord and come forth? Only those who are in "the graves", that is, in the memory of God. Jewish religionists blasphemed the name of God, and their counterparts continue to do so at the present day. Pretending to represent the Lord, they have blasphemed against the light; assuming to be equal to God, yet they are devoted wholly to the Devil, and Jesus says they shall not be forgiven.—Matthew 12:24-32; Mark 3:29, 30.

At Acts 17:31, according to the Authorized Version, it is written: "Because he hath appointed a day, in the which he will judge the world in righteousness, by that man whom he hath ordained; whereof he hath given assurance [*marginal reading*) hath offered faith] unto all men, in that he hath raised him from the dead." According to *Rotherham* this text reads: "Offering faith unto all by raising him [Jesus] from among the dead." The "offering faith" does not mean that all will accept that offer. Certainly such men as Judas Iscariot, the scribes and the Pharisees, who opposed and brought about the death of Jesus, and the higher critics of the present time and other religionists who today deliberately refuse to exercise faith in Christ Jesus and Jehovah God, do not and will not receive the 'offering of faith'. If after God had raised Jesus from the dead the religious leaders had no faith, but wickedly opposed the truth by bribing the guards to lie about the matter, certainly, then, they would not accept the offering of faith if brought back from the dead. Jesus spoke a parable concerning those who refused to have faith, in which he used these words: "If they hear not Moses and the prophets, neither will they be persuaded though one rose from the dead." (Luke 16:30, 31) Therefore the conclusion must be that Acts 17:31 does not include those who are wicked and beyond recovery and who died in that condition. Since 1918 we are in the judgment day, when the Lord is upon his judgment seat, dividing the people, separating the "sheep" from the "goats"; and if the "goats" now refuse to hear the Word of God and to take their stand on the side of the Lord Jesus Christ, and refuse to have any faith therein and in his kingdom, and the facts show they are doing that very thing, what more could be done for them if the Lord would bring them out of death and give them a "second chance"?

The Lord Jesus says that these goats go away into everlasting "cutting-off", or destruction (Matthew 25:46, *Diaglott*), and his words are

conclusive proof that those in such class receive
the execution of final judgment and will not be
awakened out of death. The Lord designates the
modern-day wicked as "goats", and the argument hereinbefore made is that such "goats"
will not be brought back from the dead. Is that
conclusion contradicted by the following statement of Jesus: "The men of Nineveh shall rise
in judgment with this generation, and shall condemn it; because they repented at the preaching
of Jonas; and, behold, a greater than Jonas is
here"? (Matthew 12:41) The clear meaning
thereof shows that these words of Jesus do not
contradict the foregoing conclusion concerning
the "goats". The context thereof shows that
Jesus referred specifically to the scribes and
Pharisees (vs. 38), which class, ignoring the
commandment of God, practiced religion and
were chiefly the ones responsible for that generation being "evil and adulterous", that is, those
who had wrongfully mixed with the Devil's religious organization. On another occasion Jesus
said to those same scribes and Pharisees: "Ye
serpents, ye generation of vipers! how can ye
escape the damnation of hell [*Gehenna,* destruc-
tion]?" (Matthew 23:33) It is not probable that
such generation of "serpents" would be amongst
the generation that shall rise with the Ninevites
during the thousand-year judgment period, any
more than that the "goats" of the present time
will be awakened out of death. Mark these words
of Jesus: "The men of Nineveh [those who
heard God's word at the mouth of Jonah the
prophet and who repented] shall rise in judgment with *this generation.*" These words of

Jesus do not necessarily include the scribes and Pharisees, who not only ignored the Word of God but had deliberately sinned against the light thereof. They not only had rejected God's Word, but had been the instruments used to keep the others of that generation in ignorance. Concerning the same reprobate class of scribes and Pharisees Jesus said: "But he that shall blaspheme against the holy [spirit] hath never forgiveness, but is in danger of eternal damnation." —Mark 3:29.

Those religionists had the words of God's prophet foretelling the coming of Christ, and the obligation was upon them to read it and make it known to others, particularly concerning the coming of the Messiah. Now Christ Jesus, the Messiah, had come and they had seen and heard him speak, and they had deliberately rejected him and charged Jesus with having a devil. Those religionists had every opportunity and refused the provision God had made for humankind, and they rejected God's favor and went even farther, in preventing others from receiving the message of salvation. Why should they be brought back again to life? The present-day religious leaders are in exactly the same class and in the same condition. They have professed to be the servants of God, they have his Word in their possession, they claim to teach it, and yet they reject God's provision for salvation and they do everything within their power to prevent the people from hearing and understanding the Word of God and learning of his kingdom under Christ Jesus, which is the only means of salvation. For such "goats" it appears from the Scriptures that there is no future life.

The following saying of Jesus should also be considered here: "And whosoever shall not receive you, nor hear your words, when ye depart out of that house or city, shake off the dust of your feet. Verily I say unto you, It shall be more tolerable for the land of Sodom and Gomorrah in the day of judgment, than for that city." (Matthew 10: 14, 15) Also the words of Jesus concerning the population of certain Jewish cities, to wit: "Woe unto thee, Chorazin! woe unto thee, Bethsaida! for if the mighty works which were done in you had been done in Tyre and Sidon, they would have repented long ago in sackcloth and ashes. But I say unto you, It shall be more tolerable for Tyre and Sidon at the day of judgment, than for you." (Matthew 11: 21, 22) Jesus was not here speaking of individuals, but of the entire population of the cities of Jews, which had received a better opportunity to know the Lord and to do his will than the heathen cities had received, and which Jewish population had rejected or failed to hear that message. For that reason, therefore, it would be less tolerable for the population or people of the Jewish cities than for those of the heathen cities. The Jewish clergy had proclaimed false doctrines to the people of the Jews' cities, and those people had followed the clergymen in obeying the traditions and teachings of men, whereas those of the heathen cities had received no such opportunity of hearing and believing the truth. Certainly such individuals as Judas Iscariot would not have a resurrection, whereas the population of the city where Judas resided would have an awakening out of death. Judas and the clergy were guilty of wicked deeds against the light, and the Lord had entered the final judgment against them. Those Jews who had yielded to the influence of the clergy would find it much harder in the time of judgment than the people of the heathen cities, whereas the willful wrongdoers sinning against light would have no more opportunity. The apostle appears to refer to a similar class when he wrote these words to Timothy. "Some men's sins are openly evident, leading on into judgment, with some, however, they even follow after; in the same way the noble works also are openly evident, and they that are otherwise cannot be hid." (1 Timothy 5: 24, 25, *Roth.*) Otherwise stated, the final decision did not need to wait until the judgment day, but the sins of such are open and deliberate, and final judgment was entered beforehand against the deliberate wrongdoers. By way of comparison it is written: "The good works of some are manifest beforehand" (*Authorized Version*); and hence the destiny of such is fixed before the day of judgment. Thus it is seen that the final judgment may be entered concerning the wicked and the good before the day of judgment. For this reason Paul, with propriety, says of himself: "I have fought a good fight, I have finished my course, I have kept the faith; henceforth there is laid up for me a crown of righteousness, which the Lord, the righteous judge, shall give me at that day; and not to me only, but unto all them also that love his appearing." (2 Timothy 4:7,8) To the same effect is 2 Thessalonians 1:4,5. If the final and adverse judgment against the willfully wicked is entered against them before death, there would be no reason to awaken them out of death; and the weight of the Scriptural evidence is that such will not be awakened out of death.

It may be said that the words of Peter contradict this conclusion, to wit: "The Lord knoweth how to deliver the godly out of temptations, and to reserve the unjust unto the day of judgment to be punished." (2 Peter 2:9) This need not, however, be understood to mean that all the "unjust" are to be brought forth at the end of the thousand years. In verses four and five he specifically names the wicked "angels" which are "reserved unto judgment"; in verses six to eight he tells of the wicked of Sodom and Gomorrah 'turned into ashes', that is, destroyed, and which were 'ensamples unto those that afterwards should live ungodly'; and shows how they shall be destroyed. In verses 10-22 he describes a class to be utterly destroyed in the day of judgment, that is, from 1918 onward, which includes a spirit-begotten class that become wicked, and also those who have learned of and then despise God's kingdom, and all of which are unjust and are to be punished at the time the godly "remnant" and "other sheep" escape. That willfully wicked class still exists and includes the "goats" to be punished in this day of judgment with everlasting "cutting-off". (Matthew 25:46, *Diaglott*) The "unjust" mentioned at Acts 24:15 are those unjust by virtue of inherited sin and are not included within the class mentioned by Peter.

Concerning the resurrection it is written (Luke 20:37, 38): "Now that the dead are raised, even Moses shewed at the bush, when he [that is, God's angel, acting as the representative of Jehovah] calleth the Lord the God of Abraham, and the God of Isaac, and the God of Jacob. For he is not a God of the dead, but of the living; for all live unto him." This supports the conclusion that final judgment is entered by the Lord as to some before or at the time of death; and as to those who have maintained their integrity toward God, the judgment is that they shall live, and thus God speaks of such things as are to come to pass as though they were already come to pass, and of such as are dead as though they were alive.—Romans 4:17.

That Abraham, Isaac and Jacob did maintain their integrity toward God and did receive his approval, and that they shall be made perfect and live, is made certain by the plain declaration of the Lord's Word, set out at Hebrews eleven. That same scripture says of others, that they endured great affliction that they might have "a better resurrection" (11:35), and they "obtained a good report through faith" (11:39); and for that reason it is properly said of them beforehand that 'they lived unto God'. God put them to the test and approved them and counted them worthy to have a resurrection from the dead. They are in his memory, and he purposes to raise them up and give them life; hence, as stated in Romans 4:17, he speaks of that fact as though it had already come to pass, and consequently he is the God of Abraham, Isaac and Jacob. Therefore the words of the text at Luke 20:38, that "all live unto him", refer only to those who have received God's approval while alive on the earth. That text has no reference whatsoever to the willfully wicked, such as Judas, the Pharisees, and the modern-day religious leaders who fight against God and his kingdom. The argument of Jesus there recorded was to prove and did prove that there will be a resurrection of those men who had proved faithful unto God and maintained their integrity toward him. The Sadducees did not believe in the resurrection. Jesus proved that the resurrection is true.

Another text deserving consideration in this connection is: "The wicked shall be turned into hell, and all the nations that forget God." (Psalm 9:17) It has been contended by some that this text of the Psalm means that the lawless shall be brought forth from the grave during the thousand-year reign of Christ, finally judged, and then returned or turned back again into hell. (See *Studies in the Scriptures*, Volume 5, page 361.) But the context does not support that conclusion; neither does the text mean anything of the kind. The Hebrew word *shuwb* is here translated "turned". Strong's *Hebrew Dictionary*, concerning this word, says it is "a primitive root" meaning "to *turn* back (hence to turn away); transitive or intransitive, literally or figuratively". The word, therefore, means 'turned away from God and his favor and blessings', in the same way or manner that the "goats" are turned away from God and sent away into destruction. This is further proved

by the context of Psalm 9:17. Verse three of
that Psalm refers to Armageddon, and says:
"When mine enemies are turned back [(Hebrew) *shuwb*], they shall fall and perish at thy
presence." At Armageddon Jehovah's "presence" is made manifest through his faithful
Field Marshal, Christ Jesus; and there the enemies of God, engaging the Lord in battle, will
be "turned back" in defeat and shall "perish".
Further considering this Psalm, note that verse
four says: "For thou hast maintained [upheld]
my right and my cause; thou satest in the throne
judging right." The words here used (verse 4),
"my right and my cause," mean the right and
cause of Christ Jesus, the world's rightful King.
When the fight is on at Armageddon, the Lord
will completely defeat the enemy and Jehovah
will maintain his right and cause in accomplishing that fact. Then verse five says: "Thou hast
rebuked the heathen, thou hast destroyed the
wicked, thou hast put out their name for ever
and ever." This shows that such is the end of
those who are wicked and that their memorial
is perished with them, because it is written, in
verse six: "O thou enemy! destructions are come
to a perpetual end; and thou hast destroyed
cities; their memorial is perished with them."
The next verse shows that the Lord endures for
ever and that before his judgment of the world
in righteousness he cleans out these wicked ones
for ever, and this he does at Armageddon. "But
the Lord shall endure for ever; he hath prepared
his throne for judgment: and he shall judge the
world in righteousness, he shall minister judg-

ment to the people in uprightness."—Psalm 9:7, 8.

Not all will find refuge in that trouble, but only the oppressed who seek meekness and righteousness. Verses nine and ten are further proof. That the oppressors find their end when turned back at Armageddon, note the following: "The heathen [nations] are sunk down in the pit that they made; in the net which they hid is their own foot taken." (Verse 15) They set a net for God's people, and they get into it and are destroyed at Armageddon: "The Lord is known by the judgment which he executeth; the wicked is snared in the work of his own hands." (Verse 16) Then immediately follows the text: "The wicked [that is, those who oppose God's 'strange work' and who are destroyed by his 'strange act'] shall be turned into hell, and all the nations that forget God." (Verse 17) They perish in the battle of the great day of God Almighty after they have assaulted God's faithful people. In their plans to rule the world, such as set forth now by the Roman Catholic Hierarchy in combine with Fascism, they leave God out of their consideration altogether, and thus they constitute "all the nations that forget God".

Today the political, commercial and religious elements boastfully proclaim the greatness of man and applaud the deeds of men and point with great pride to what man has attained unto, and with the worst kind of presumption they say: "We can bring about a condition in the earth that will be satisfactory to all." The totalitarian rule or dictatorial power is now arising with a great flare of trumpets. It has succeeded in grabbing many countries and is moving forward to rule the whole world. Such a movement is backed by the mighty religious organization, the Roman Catholic Hierarchy and supporters. Now the needy and poor population are regimented and their rights are taken away and they are forgotten; and in connection with the turning of these wicked oppressors into hell God, by the mouth of the psalmist, says: "For the needy shall not alway be forgotten; the expectation of the poor shall not perish for ever." (Verse 18) Therefore the prophet David, representing God's people, prays: "Arise, O Lord; let not man prevail; let the heathen be judged in thy sight. Put them in fear, O Lord; that the nations may know themselves to be but men. Selah."—Verses 19 and 20.

During the time of the resurrection there will be no "nations" to be "turned" or returned into hell, because those nations will be destroyed at Armageddon. Thus it is seen that the 'turning of the wicked into hell' is by destroying them at the battle of Armageddon, and does not mean the turning of them back into the grave from which they are supposed to come during the thousand-year reign of Christ. Manifestly the conclusion set forth in the *Studies in the Scriptures,* Volume 5, page 361, concerning the return of the wicked into hell is wrong.

ORDER OF RESURRECTION

From the Scriptures it appears that the order of resurrection of the dead is this: The faithful apostles and others like them who have died in faith waiting for the coming of the Lord, "at his appearing and his kingdom" (2 Timothy 4:1, 8; 1 Thessalonians 4:16); those who shall be "changed, in a moment, in the twinkling of an eye", at the second coming of the Lord (1 Corinthians 15:51, 52); the faithful men of old who have a "better resurrection" (Hebrews 11:35), and which may include the faithful Jonadabs who die immediately preceding or during Armageddon (Jonathan, who was slain at the battle of Gilboa, pictured such). Then the general resurrection, meaning all who have died without an opportunity to prove their integrity and who shall be awakened and given such opportunity during the reign of Christ. These, however, would appear to have nothing to do with filling the earth according to the divine mandate, because they must first be made righteous.

The thief that was crucified at the time of the crucifixion of Jesus will undoubtedly be awakened out of death and given an opportunity to prove his integrity. In response to the thief's request Jesus said: "Shalt thou be with me in paradise?" (Luke 23:43) These words of Jesus suggest that paradise on earth will be in existence before the thief is awakened out of death, who will then have opportunity to prove whether he is on the side of Christ Jesus, the King, or not. God planted the garden of Eden, making it a paradise, and then created man and put him in Eden. (Genesis 2:8, 15) That appears to fix the order of action concerning men and paradise. That being so, it seems probable that the filling of the earth will have progressed and paradise will have been established in the earth before the general resurrection.

It is written: "There shall be a resurrection of the dead, both of the just and [the] unjust." (Acts 24:15) "The unjust" here mentioned surely does not apply to the earthly wicked, but to those who have had no opportunity to be justified by faith and obedience. All must prove their integrity before they get life. Being brought forth from the tomb during the reign of Christ would afford them such an opportunity.

At Revelation 20:5 it is written: "But the rest of the dead lived not again until the thousand years were finished." While the authenticity of this text has been questioned, the weight of authority is that it is authentic. The "rest of the dead" here mentioned, therefore, would include all those who do not get life until they stand the test at the end of the thousand-year reign. At that time, it would appear from the Scriptures, the divine mandate would have been completely fulfilled and paradise fully established in the earth. Since righteous men must perform the functions required by the divine mandate, it would necessarily follow that those who participate in the general resurrection would have no part in the fulfillment of that divine mandate. Such as participate in the general resurrection, and who maintain their integrity, would be the ones counted worthy to obtain the "world to come" and "without end".

RESURRECTION AND MARRIAGE

Will those awakened out of death during the general resurrection marry and have part in the

fulfillment of the divine mandate? The Scriptures clearly show that they will not, because
that mandate is given only to those who are
righteous at the time the fulfillment begins. The
Sadducees denied the resurrection of the dead
and sought by subtle questions to entrap Jesus,
and hence they propounded a question which relates to levirate marriage, which they did not
understand. (An explanation of levirate marriage appears in the book *Jehovah,* pages 296-
299.) The Sadducees stated a hypothetical case
of a woman that married a man, which man had
brothers, and her first husband died, and then
in regular order she married six others, so that
she had seven brothers for husband. Their question to Jesus was: 'In the resurrection whose
wife will she be of the seven? because all seven
had her.' (Luke 20: 27-33) They did not succeed
in entrapping Jesus: "And Jesus answering
said unto them, The children of this world
marry, and are given in marriage; but they
which shall be accounted worthy to obtain that
world, and the resurrection from the dead,
neither marry, nor are given in marriage;
neither can they die any more; for they are equal
unto the angels; and are the children of God,
being the children of the resurrection."—Luke
20: 34-36.

The Sadducees were without faith in Jesus as
the Messiah. They did not understand the Scriptures because they did not believe them. The
presumption must be that their question related
to those who had died during the time of the
operation of the law covenant and who were
ignorant of God's purpose; and hence, as Jesus

told those Sadducees, they did not understand the power of God. (Matthew 22:25-30) The answer of Jesus would have no reference whatsoever to the great multitude that survive Armageddon, and who shall have the privilege of carrying out the divine mandate. They are not "children of the resurrection", because they prove their fidelity and integrity while on the earth and before Armageddon.

Due consideration must be given to all the words of Jesus contained in his answer. Amongst other things, he said concerning those who are resurrected under the circumstances mentioned: "They which shall be accounted worthy to obtain that world, and the resurrection from the dead." What world? The Scriptural answer is, "the world to come," "wherein dwelleth righteousness" (2 Peter 3:13); the "world without end" (Ephesians 3:21); the "world without end" (Isaiah 45:17); the earth made "glorious" during the reign of Christ (Isaiah 60:13), the "footstool" of Jehovah (Isaiah 66:1), the earth brought up to a condition of paradise during the thousand-year reign of Christ Jesus. Those who are counted worthy to obtain that world "neither marry, nor are given in marriage". The divine mandate will at that time have been completely fulfilled. No more will occasion for marriage exist. Those who receive favorable judgment and approval of the Lord will not die, as Jesus stated. How could they be "equal unto the angels"? In this: that they cannot be put to death without the approval of God, but must for ever enjoy the provisions of life because they have proved their faithfulness and integrity. Each one of them brought forth will be an individual and will be dealt with individually. They are brought forth to life, and their course of action will determine their faithfulness, and, if continuing faithful, they shall live forever, even as the angels do although not immortal. They are brought forth from the grave and receive life from God by and through Christ. They are individuals, and, like the angels, do not have any ties of wedlock. Whatever marriage ties they may have had when living on the earth are dissolved by death. The divine mandate to "fill the earth" having been fully performed, there will then be no occasion for anyone to marry. Together with all others, they must be tested.

FINAL TEST

Jehovah's Word makes known that there shall be a final test applied to earthly creatures. "And when the thousand years are expired, Satan shall be loosed out of his prison, and shall go out to deceive the nations which are in the four quarters of the earth, Gog and Magog, to gather them together to battle; the number of whom is as the sand of the sea. And they went up on the breadth of the earth, and compassed the camp of the saints about, and the beloved city; and fire came down from God out of heaven, and devoured them."—Revelation 20:7-9.

It appears that such test will be applied to every creature on earth and will make manifest who are the faithful and true ones, that is, "the saints," and who shall live for ever; and also make manifest those who will be deceived by the

Devil and go into destruction. The Devil at that time will see 'the earth filled' with righteous human creatures in obedience to the divine mandate, and which then will be proof that the Devil himself is a liar; and he will know it. "The saints," that is, those who maintain their integrity toward God and who are granted life everlasting, will be a vindication of Jehovah's word and name. Surely the offspring of the "great multitude" must be put to this test, even as the spirit-begotten ones are now put to a like test, and to which latter class these words are addressed: "Beware lest any man spoil you through philosophy and vain deceit, after the tradition of men, after the rudiments of the world, and not after Christ." (Colossians 2:8) Will some of the offspring of the righteous great multitude fall under that test? Such is entirely probable. The babes and those others who have died in ignorance of God's gracious provision and who are awakened out of death and are judged must surely be subjected to that test before they are "accounted worthy to obtain that world" "without end", and it is certain that many of them will be deceived; and concerning such as turn to the Devil it is written: "Fire came down from God out of heaven, and devoured them [meaning many; which of necessity must include all the deceived ones who join the Devil]." (Revelation 20:9) The inhabiters of "Gog and Magog" (20:8), and the Devil himself, shall be destroyed, and the memory of such wicked shall cease for ever.—20:10, 14.

DESTINY

What was the fate of that train and its load of passengers rushing upon the burning bridge? Were any of them saved? Impossible for them to escape! Those who left the train at the next preceding station stop did escape and were saved. Likewise today, all the nations and peoples of earth are face to face with the greatest emergency. They are being warned as God commands, that the disaster of Armageddon is just ahead. But only a small number, comparatively speaking, give heed to that warning, and those who do give heed thereto are leaving the organization of the world, controlled by Satan, and are seeking refuge under God's kingdom. Such persons as continue faithful henceforth will escape Armageddon, find protection from it, and be saved.

Armageddon having ended, the righteous rule shall prevail everywhere in the earth, and gradually the earth will be brought to a condition of Edenic paradise, because such is the promise of Almighty God, who made the earth to be inhabited by righteous men. Gradually the earth will be filled with righteous people who will be a vindication of the name and the word of Jehovah, the Most High.

Having been warned, each one thus warned must now choose the course he will take, whether the way to eternal destruction, or the way to everlasting salvation provided for obedient men by Jehovah, the Almighty God, through Jesus Christ, the beloved Son of

the "KING OF ETERNITY".

INDEX

NOTE: Numbers refer to pages; Roman numerals, to paragraphs.

A

Abel, exercised faith, 50, II
  must wait to receive ransom
    benefit, 178, I
Abomination of Desolation,
  defined, 13, I
  evidence of world's end, 20, I
  political dictators and Hier-
    archy form, 118, III
  stands where it ought
    not, 20, I
Abominations in Christendom,
  141, I; 142, I
Abraham, pleaded for righteous in Sodom, 72, I
  proved worthy of resurrec-
    tion, 350, I, II
Adam, and Eve did not fulfill
  divine mandate, 17, I
  created as perfect man, 42, I
  informed, not deceived, will-
    ful sinner, 42, I; 43, I
  involved in Lucifer's
    rebellion, 15, II; 43, I
  Jehovah's judgment just
    against, 180, I
  no redemption, second
    chance, for, 43, I
  ransom not for, 176, I-178, I
  sentenced to death, 17, I;
    43, I
Adam's Offspring, Jesus
  ransomed, 176, I-178, I
  ransom benefits the worthy
    ones of, 177, I; 178, I
Agorazo, meaning, 180, II
  Scripture usage of, 180, II-
    185, IV
Allegiance to Jehovah, 157, I
Angels, commanded to worship
  Jesus, 304, I
  equal unto the, 356, III; 358, I
  induced to marry women,
    317, I
  more than ransom required,
    170, I
  spirits; higher than man,
    40, I
  warned Lot, 72, I
Animals: see Beasts
  suitable for food, 293, I-
    295, II
  when death-dealing, killed,
    214, I; 298, I
Anointed Christians, bond
  slaves of Christ, 182, I-

184, II
  bought by Christ's blood,
    182, I-184, II
  redeemed from Satan's or-
    ganization, 204, I
  should instruct children,
    338, III
Anointing of Jesus, 304, I
Anti, as meaning "in behalf
  of", 191, II; 192, I
Antilytron, meaning and use
  of, 175, I; 176, I
Antitypes, realities, 63, II
Approval, by pleasing God,
  32, II
  for salvation to life, 33, I
  obtained by faithfulness,
    50, II; 51, I
  upon holy ones, 241, I
    270, II; 271, I
Ark, baptism unto Noah in,
    270, II; 271, I
  God commanded Noah to
    build, 317, I; 318, I
  hid Noah and family, 26, I
  pictured God's organization,
    71, I; 318, I
  purpose of, 320, I; 321, I
Armageddon, baptism of fire,
    271, I
  battle of Gibeon pictured,
    92, II; 95, I-96, I
  clears earth of wicked, 329, I
  complete deliverance at,
    204, I
  destruction world-wide at,
    25, I; 79, I; 329, I
  divine mandate follows,
    323, I; 328, I
  enemies turned back at,
    351, I-354, I
  flee before, 28, I; 76, I, II;
    92, II
  fought between whom? 25, II
  God's wrath expressed at,
    23, I
  Kingdom in control after,
    233, I
  last affliction, 25, I
  Lord Jesus revealed at, 322, I
  no unransomed cases beyond,
    217, I; 218, I
  protection from, 237, I
  retribution by Redeemer at,
    211, I-213, I
  Satan's organization de-
    stroyed at, 204, I; 220, I;
    227, I; 278, I

tion of, 213, I
cases of violating, 279, I;
280, I
destruction to violators of,
281, I
eating unclean animals does
not violate, 293, II-295, II
established, 275, I
killing in self-defense not
violative of, 279, I
nations have all broken,
78, II; 79, I; 280, I; 287, I
Nimrod violated, 283, I-287, I
one-sided, 275, I
sport hunting violates, 282, I-
286, II; 288, I; 295, II
terms of, 276, I, II
Everlasting Father, Christ
Jesus, 105, I, II; 178, I
Evil Servant, Ephraim pictured, 205, II; 206, I
Executioner, for Jehovah,
67, II; 82, II
of God's enemies, 277, I;
278, I
of murderer, 276, II

F

Faith, defined, 33, I
good report obtained
through, 50, II
in Christ's shed blood, 89, I
needed to please God, 32, II;
33, I; 48, II; 234, I
not on religious organizations, 33, II
of Noah, 32, II
offered, refused, 343, I
Rahab showed importance
of, 83, I; 86, I-91, I
the rule unto life, 47, I
Faithful Men of Old, back
soon, at Armageddon's
beginning, 310, I
Beth-Sarim to be at disposal
of, 311, I
called "fathers", 307, III;
309, I
devoted; guided by spirit,
241, I
dwell forever on earth,
158, II
faith and sufferings of, 50, II
have better resurrection,
341, II; 350, I, II
judgment of; unto life,
350, I, II
made perfect after elect,
52, I; 307, III
made princes in earth,
309, I, II
many sit down in kingdom
with, 158, II; 159, I
new earth consists of, 328, I

not members of heavenly
kingdom, 307, III
not perfected until kingdom,
307, III
visible representatives of
kingdom, 309, I
Faithfulness unto death required, 197, II
Famine in Egypt and world,
symbolic, 98, II; 99, I; 109, I
Fathers, children instead of,
309, I
faithful men called, 307, III
Fear, causes politicians to con-
sult pope, 253, I
flag salute and, 267, I
induced League of Nations,
252, II
of God rather than men,
261, I; 265, I; 267, I
of man ensnares into re-
ligion, 250, II; 251, I
of man put on beasts, 281, II;
282, I; 289, I; 290, I
Fear of God, defined, 47, I;
252, I
Gibeonites showed, 92, I;
93, I
not of men or devils, 58, I
protects against Devil's
snares, 252, I, II
Feast of Tabernacles (Ingathering), dwelling in
booths during, 157, I
fulfillment of, 156, I
great multitude join in,
133, I; 156, I
Jesus associated himself
with, 156, I
See Palms
Feet of Him, remnant of
Christ's body, 154, II;
155, I; 156, II
Fire, baptism with, 271, I
destroys Satan and deceived
ones, 359, I, II
Flag, compulsory salute to;
against freedom, 263, III
meaning of Christian's
salute to, 259, III-261, II
state without power to compel salute to, 263, IV
symbol; held sacred, 260, I;
262, I-263, III
Flee, before Armageddon
begins, 92, II
on seeing abomination of
desolation, 13, I; 20, I
to mountains, 28, II
too late at Armageddon, 28, I
without delay before Armageddon, 76, I, II
Flood, an emergency, 10, II
baptism of destruction, 271, I

was made flesh, 171, I

Lord's Goat, blood of; sprinkled, 197, I, II

Lot, heeded warning before destruction, 76, II
pictured people of good will, 74, I
rescued from Sodom's destruction, 72, I; 74, I
wife of; looked back, 75, II; 76, I

Love, defined, 246, II
for other sheep, Jonathan class, 123, I
God is, 38, I; 45, I; 247, I
involved in redemption, 225, I, II
mutual, 122, I; 123, I; 126, I
of God for Jonathan and David, 123, I
of Jonathan for David, 120, I; 121, I; 126, I
of mercy required, 245, I; 246, II; 247, I

Lucifer, coveted what was God's, 15, II
God changed name of, 15, II; 259, III
rebelled, 15, II
spirit, overlord of world, 15, II; 259, III

M

Man, in linen, with inkhorn at side, 141, I; 142, I
lower than angels, 40, I; 170, I, II

Mandate: see Divine Mandate

Mankind, born sinners, 44, I; 45, I
bought, owned by Jesus, 39, II-41, I; 177, I; 178, I

Man of Sin, no ransom for, 221, I
Saul pictured, 117, I

Marriage, and the great multitude, 324, I; 330, I
no more occasion for, 358, I
not by those in general resurrection, 356, II-358, I
of angels with women, 317, I

Mediator, for all entering into covenant, 192, II
one, between God and men, 176, I, II; 180, I

Meek, described, 29, I; 30, I; 62, III
must seek righteousness, meekness, 28, II-30, I

Meetings, parents should bring children to, 336, I-338, III

Memorial of Christ's Death, great multitude do not partake of, 273, I; 274, II

those in Kingdom covenant celebrate, 273, I, II

Memory, wicked not held in God's, 342, II

Men that sigh and cry for abominations, 141, I; 142, I

Men of Good Will, peace on earth to, 160, I, II; 303, I
See People of Good Will

Mercy, defined, 45, I; 225, I
extended to sinners, 45, I; 193, I; 227, II
not due to all, 225, I, II
not to willful opposers, 45, II-46, II; 230, II
of God to man, 247, I
requirement to love, 245, I; 246, II; 247, I
rule for receiving, 47, I
to faithful and obedient, 46, I, II

Message of Hope, 133, I, II

Minister of God, for good and wrath, 255, I-256, I

Mordecai, refused obeisance to Haman, 147, I
supporters of; people of good will, 148, I

Moses, announced cities of refuge, 76, III
baptism unto, 270, III; 271, I
type of Christ Jesus, 45, I; 76, III; 270, III; 271, I

Mountain, of the Lord's house, 151, I
symbol of kingdom, 151, I

Mountains, flee to, 28, I

Murderer, execution provided for, 78, II
executioner of, 276, II
no atonement for willful, 218, I
pays with life to redeemer, 211, I-213, II

N

Name of Jehovah, to be declared throughout earth, 15, II; 24, I; 59, I
See People; Vindication

Nations, fortifying against emergency, 10, I
have broken everlasting covenant, 78, II; 280, I; 287, I
in distress at world's end, 21, I, II
separated as sheep and goats, 160, III-163, I
that forget God, destroyed at Armageddon, 351, I-354, I

Nethinim pictured great multitude, 134, I

Q

Queen of Sheba pictured great multitude, 134, II; 136, I
Question, of supremacy raised by Satan, 15, II
  raised as to man's integrity, 48, I

R

Rahab, acknowledged Jehovah, 87, I
  aided spies' escape, 88, I
  assembled household in home, 89, I
  delivered by faith, 91, I
  displayed scarlet thread, 89, I-91, I
  foreshadowed great multitude, 83, I-91, II
  made covenant with spies, 88, I
  shielded spies, 86, I
  shows how reputedly mean seek Jehovah, 83, I; 85, I
  two spies visited, 84, II
Ransom(ed), applications of word, 214, I-224, I
  from power of the grave, 205, II; 206, I
Ransom (Price), benefits worthy ones, 177, I-179, I
  Christians have no part in, 182, I
  cover charge, not corresponding price, 214, I-216, I; 223, I
  defined, 175, I; 194, III; 200, II
  did not buy kingdom of heaven, 181, I
  faithful have found, 216, II, III
  "for all" that accept, 176, I, II; 180, I; 192, II
  Greek words translated, 175, I; 176, I; 191, II; 192, I
  Hebrew words translated, 201, II; 205, II; 214, I-224, I
  higher critics disbelieve, 199, I
  Jesus' lifeblood, 41, I; 175, I
  Jesus turned perfection, life right, into, 177, I
  like requirements for, 170, I, II
  ("lytron") in behalf of many, 191, II; 192, I
  no bribe gifts for, 218, I; 219, I, II
  not always corresponding exactly, 222, II; 223, I
  not automatically benefiting all, 180, I
  not for conspiring religion-

ists, 221, I
  not for "man of sin", 221, II
  not for willful sinners, 222, I; 223, II; 230, II
  not for willful slayers, 217, I; 218, I
  not forced on unwilling, 224, II-227, I
  of Jesus corresponded to what was lost, 228, I
  wealthy excluded from, 218, II
  wicked become r. for righteous, 220, I
Ransoming, Jesus alone performed act of, 195, I
  of church before gathering other sheep, 200, I
Rebellion, as witchcraft, 116, I
  of Lucifer, 15, II
Rechabites, descendants of Jonadab, 66, II
  God promised perpetuation of, 66, II
  kept agreements, 66, II; 242, I
  pattern of people of good will, 67, I
Redeem(ed), "agorazo" translated, 180, II
  applications of word; defined, 201, III-213, II
  "exagorazo" translated, 186, I
  from curse of law; disobedient Jews not, 186, I-187, I
  from death when justified, 205, II
  from men and earth; 144,000 are, 185, III, IV
  from Satan's organization, 203, II-207, I; 209, I
  Hebrew words translated, 201, II-213, II
  justice not involved in, 225, I-227, I
  ("lytro'o") elect are, 187, II
  mature Christians are, 185, I, II
  none automatically, 185, II
  with a purchase price, 209, I; 210, I
  without purchase price, 204, I; 205, I-206, I; 209, I
Redeemer, kinsman served as, 210, I
  of faithful, not wicked ones, 208, I
  revenger of blood, 211, I-213, II
Redemption, ("apolytrosis") of remnant, believers, 188, II
  applies to children of Jona-

seekers must, 30, I; 168, I
Substitute, Jesus not Adam's,
177, I; 178, I; 228, I
Suckling, no more of few days,
333, I-335, I
Sufferings, for obedience to
God, 265, I
not part of ransom, 181, I
of Christ and followers for
test, 53, I
of faithful men, 50, II
precedent to reigning, 197, II
Sunday Schools, 338, II
Supremacy, Devil raised question of, 15, II
established at Armageddon,
227, I
God emphasizes issue of,
17, I
Survivors of Armageddon,
96, I; 104, I
a vindication of God's Word
and name, 329, I
fulfill divine mandate, 329, I

T

Tabernacle in Wilderness, a
pattern, 64, I; 159, II
atonement day sacrifices at,
172, II; 173, I; 195, II-197, II
Tears, God wipes away all,
332, I-334, I
Temple, began building, 132, I
Christ Jesus appears at,
160, III
completed in eighth month,
133, II
dedication of, 132, I-133, I
strangers used in building,
131, I-132, I
Zion's children gathered to,
205, II; 206, I
Temple Servants, Nethinim,
134, I
Ten, symbolic, 154, II; 334, I
Ten Half Brothers, Joseph
made himself known to,
104, I-105, I
Joseph tested, 100, I; 101, I
pictured great multitude,
96, II, III
pictured religious persons at
first, 96, III
showed change of heart,
101, I; 102, I
sold Joseph into Egypt, 97, I
Ten Men take hold of Jew's
skirt, 154, I-155, I
Test, necessity of, 54, I
put on Christ and Church,
53, I
Satan allowed to put on men,
48, II; 359, I, II
the final, 359, I, II

upon Joseph's brethren and
Jonadabs, 100, I-103, I
Testimony of Jesus Christ,
59, I
Theocracy, Jehovah's government, 301, I; 307, II
made up of Christ and
144,000, 312, I
typical, set up, 301, II
visible, earthly representatives of, 307, III-310, I
Thief in paradise, 355, I
Thousand Years, destruction
of Satan at end of, 356, I, II
final test at end of, 359, I, II
judgment day of a, 344, I;
356, II
reign of Christ a, 197, II;
358, I
rest of dead lived not till
end of, 356, II
Time, for everlasting life on
earth, 233, I
Totalitarian Ruling Powers,
described, 257, II
destroyed at Armageddon,
353, I-354, I
Goliath pictured, 118, II
grown out of League of
Nations, 253, I
Hierarchy forms part of,
118, III
Traditions of Men, basis of religion, 35, I
lead to destruction, 34, I
Tribulation (Great), battle of
Armageddon, 22, II
follows Kingdom gospel,
21, III
Truth sanctifies, 243, I
Type, defined, 63, II
Types, God used men to make,
63, I, II
now understood, 63, II

U

Universal Redemption (Salvation) prevents learning
means of salvation, 38, I
Unjust, reserved to judgment
day for punishment, 349, I
resurrection of just and,
356, I

V

Vengeance is God's, 278, I
Vindication of Jehovah's name,
by maintaining integrity,
17, I
chief Bible doctrine, 55, I
chief purpose of flood, 320, II
destruction of enemies a,

278, I
divine mandate fulfilled a,
330, I
everlasting covenant a, 275, I
imperfect men by maintaining integrity are, 169, II
survivors of Armageddon a,
329, I
Virgin, defined, 150, II
Virgins, companions of king's
daughter, 150, I-III

W

Waiting, before beginning
reign, 305, I; 306, I
of Jesus has ended,
22, II, III; 306, I
War, approved, supported by
religionists, 78, II; 79, I;
280, I
Christian refuses to go to,
279, I
in heaven began, 206, I; 307, I
of conquest, 279, I; 280, I
Warning, Armageddon escaped
by those heeding, 361, I
choice of course after,
361, III
given amid opposition, 25, II
God acts after, 23, II
witnesses sent to give, 23, II
Water of Life, invitation to,
107, II; 167, I, II
Way of God, how learned,
248, I
Weeping will cease, 332, I-
334, I
Wicked (Willfully), become
ransom for righteous, 220, I
destroyed after final test,
359, I, II
final judgment entered before death against, 347, I
no mourning for death of,
334, I; 335, II
no resurrection for, 342, I-
354, I
not bought or saved, 184, II
not brought back from death,
223, II
not held in God's memory,
342, II
not redeemed, 208, I
ransom does not benefit,
179, I; 213, II
turned into hell, 213, II;
351, I-354, I
unjust ones such as are not,
356, I
Wickedness on earth before
flood, 317, I
Will of God, concerning great
multitude, 235, I

consecration to do, 235, I
his expressed law, 237, I
remnant and Jonadabs conform to, 288, I
sanctification to do, 242, I
Wine, as Memorial emblem,
273, II
cup of; new, 274, I
Winter, too late to flee in, 28, I
Wisdom, gaining of, 47, I
Wise, course of, 34, I
Witness, elect class must bear,
54, I
the faithful and true, 54, I
Witnesses: see Jehovah's witnesses
sent to warn, 23, II
Woes, responsibility for
world's, 20, I
Word, Jesus' prehuman name,
17, II
was made flesh, 17, II
Work, required, if to live, 114, I
World, accounted worthy to
obtain that, 356, II-358, I;
359, II
God's purpose to have righteous, 302, II
Satan the god of this, 243, II;
259, III
See End; New World
to come, without end, 328, I;
358, I
World War, began, 22, III
evidence of world's end, 20, I
Jesus foretold, 12, I
Wrath of God, abides on unbelieving, 194, I, II
completed at Armageddon,
23, I
halted expression in 1918,
23, I
has come, 22, III

Y

Youth a hundred years old
dies, 333, I; 334, I

Z

Zeal, for Jehovah, 68, I
Jesus suffered for his, 70, I
Jonadabs must show, 68, I
Zion, birth of other children of,
205, II
God's capital organization,
52, I; 333, I
Jehovah, husband and redeemer of, 208, II, III
redeemed (ransomed) come
to, 201, II; 207, I; 208, III
redeemed without purchase
price, 204, I; 206, I

Chief Office and Official Address of

WATCHTOWER BIBLE & TRACT SOCIETY
Incorporated

INTERNATIONAL BIBLE STUDENTS ASSOCIATION

is

124 Columbia Heights, Brooklyn, N. Y.

————◦•◦————

Address of factories and publishers:

America,	117 Adams St.,	Brooklyn, N.Y.
Argentina,	Calle Cramer 4555,	Buenos Aires
Australia,	7 Beresford Rd.,	Strathfield, N.S.W.
Belgium,	66 Rue de l'Intendant,	Brussels
Brazil,	Rua Eca de Queiroz 141,	Sao Paulo
British Guiana,	5 Croal St., Georgetown,	Demerara
Canada,	40 Irwin Ave.,	Toronto 5, Ont.
Chile,	Avda. Buenos Aires 80 (Blanqueado),	Santiago
China,	Box 1903,	Shanghai
Denmark,	Sondre Fasanvej 54,	Copenhagen-Valby
England,	34 Craven Terrace,	London, W. 2
Estonia,	Suur Tartu - Maantee 72-3,	Tallinn
Finland,	Vainamoisenkatu 27,	Helsinki
France,	129 Faubourg Poissonniere,	Paris IX
Greece,	Lombardou 44,	Athens
Hawaii,	1228 Pensacola St.,	Honolulu
Hungary,	Zsigmond U. 68,	Budapest III
India,	Jiji House, Ravelin Street,	Bombay 1
Jamaica, B.W.I.,	151 King St.,	Kingston
Japan,	58 Ogikubo, 4-Chome, Suginamiku,	Tokyo
Java,	Post Box 59,	Batavia Centrum
Latvia,	Cesu Iela 11 Dz. 25,	Riga
Lithuania,	Aukštaičių g-ve 8. b. 1,	Kaunas
Luxemburg,	37 Cote d'Eich,	Luxemburg
Mexico,	Calzada Melchor Ocampo 71,	Mexico, D.F.
Netherlands,	Camplaan 28,	Heemstede
New Zealand,	G.P.O. Box 30,	Wellington
Norway,	Inkognitogaten 28, b.,	Oslo
Philippine Islands,	1132 Rizal Ave.,	Manila
Poland,	Rzgowska ul. 24,	Lodz 7
Rumania,	Str. V. Ghergel. 38,	Bucuresti 2
South Africa,	Boston House,	Cape Town
Straits Settlements,	Post Box 566,	Singapore
Sweden,	Luntmakaregatan 94,	Stockholm
Switzerland,	Allmendstrasse 39,	Berne
Trinidad, B.W.I.,	Box 194,	Port of Spain
West Africa	71 Broad St., Box 695,	Lagos, Nigeria
Yugoslavia,	Dalmatinska ul. 59,	Beograd

All communications for literature should be addressed
Watchtower Bible & Tract Society, Inc., at the above
addresses respectively.